Striking Features

Striking Features is a fascinating and timely application of analytic theories to the question of racial passing. Through subtle, empathetic, and insightful close readings, Donavan Ramon suggests new ways of thinking about both Freudian theory and contemporary debates on race: his book is an important contribution to both fields.

—Rubén Gallo, author of *Freud's Mexico: Into the Wilds of Psychoanalysis*

Striking Features is a thoughtful, nuanced, and eminently readable analysis of racial passing, cogently arguing that a psychoanalytic lens offers us a new and dynamic way of reading a narrative that is part and parcel of American cultural history.

—Baz Dreisinger, author of *Near Black: White-to-Black Passing in American Culture*

Striking Features deploys Freudian psychoanalysis in innovative and provocative ways to frame its discussion of racial passing in American literature. Privileging thematic continuities (race learning, the death drive) over texts' historical proximity and foregrounding works of fiction and nonfiction by both white and African American writers, *Striking Features* significantly expands both the "canon" of passing literature and existing scholarly treatments of the subject. It is essential reading for anyone interested in the ongoing ramifications of racial passing in American literature and life.

—Sinéad Moynihan, author of *Passing into the Present: Contemporary American Fiction of Racial and Gender Passing*

Donavan Ramon's probing study of light-skinned African American's motivations to pass for white connects to psychological principles of Freud, Fanon, and others. Their themes of figurative death (of identity and family), sexual deviation (miscegenation), and racial gratification (white privilege) adds an important perspective on both the literary imagination and the lived experience.

—E. Dolores Johnson, author of *Say I'm Dead: A Family Memoir of Race, Secrets, and Love*

VOICES OF THE AFRICAN DIASPORA

This series presents the development of the intellectual tradition of the African diaspora. The series will bring together a variety of disciplines, including literary and social/cultural criticism, anthropology, sociology, religion/philosophy, education, political science, psychology, and history—by publishing original critical studies and reprints of classic texts. The reprints will include both nineteenth- and twentieth-century works. The goal is to make important texts accessible and readily available both to the general reader and to the academic.

CHESTER J. FONTENOT, JR.

SERIES EDITOR

Striking Features

Psychoanalysis and
Racial Passing Narratives

◌℞

DONAVAN L. RAMON

MERCER UNIVERSITY PRESS
Macon, Georgia

MUP/ P696

© 2024 by Mercer University Press
Published by Mercer University Press
1501 Mercer University Drive
Macon, Georgia 31207
All rights reserved.
This book may not be reproduced in whole or in part, including illustrations, in any form (beyond that copying permitted by Sections 107 and 108 of the U.S. Copyright Law and except by reviewers for the public press), without written permission from the publisher.

28 27 26 25 24   5 4 3 2 1

Books published by Mercer University Press are printed on acid-free paper that meets the requirements of the American National Standard for Information Sciences—Permanence of Paper for Printed Library Materials.

Printed and bound in the United States.

This book is set in Adobe Garamond.

Cover/jacket design by Burt&Burt.

ISBN   978-0-88146-930-1

Cataloging-in-Publication Data is available from the Library of Congress

CONTENTS

Acknowledgments	vii
"Bold Hypotheses": An Introduction to Psychoanalysis and Race	1
Chapter 1: Race-Learning and the Trauma of Passing	23
Chapter 2: Passing and Freud's Death Drive	73
Chapter 3: Passing and Life Writing	135
Chapter 4: He "Colored Himself Just as He Chose": A Case Study of Coleman Silk	191
Conclusion: The Passing Hustle and the Failed Language of Race	221
Works Cited	235
Index	249

This book is dedicated to
Mrs. Ofelia Austin (1968–2007) and
Dr. Cheryl Wall (1948–2020).

ACKNOWLEDGMENTS

The first time I heard about passing in an academic context was in a Black Women Writers course in my junior year at Hunter College. One of the early texts we encountered in Dr. Candice Jenkins' class was Nella Larsen's novella *Passing*, which piqued my interest. I read it as a racial detective novel and challenged myself to find out who deceived whom, especially since Irene and Clare passed in different ways. The class—and especially this book—intrigued me because I did not realize there existed an entire literary genre centered on light-skinned African-Americans pretending to be White. Larsen's most famous text raised several questions for me, as revealed by the marginalia in my well-worn copy of the text: What are the moral implications for jumping the color line? How can you turn your back on your family for societal gain? How can folks pass for so long and thwart discovery? Do passers feel fear, guilt, or remorse at their deception?

Perhaps I could have looked to my own family for answers to these questions. A few years before I encountered Larsen's *Passing*, one of the other teenagers at my first summer job asked me if my family is "Garifuna," when we discovered that our mothers are both Honduran. I had never heard this term before, but I could not wait to return home and query my mother about its definition and whether we were Garifuna too? She was, after all, born and raised in the Bay Islands off the coast of Honduras in the Caribbean Sea. My mother had a strong answer for me, but not one I expected: she made it explicitly clear that we are absolutely *not* Garifuna, and it was insulting to even inquire about it. I knew she was annoyed based on her tone and facial expression, so I just dropped the subject…until it came up again in my early adulthood. This time, I was a first-year graduate student still trying to figure out my identity and role within academia, introducing myself as "a Honduran-Jamaican from NYC" to my colleagues. One of them, trying to pinpoint my ethnicity, exclaimed "oh you must be a Garifuna!" When I told her otherwise, she did not know what else to say and quickly turned back to her books, as though she could not talk to me without attempting to fit me in her limited conception of my identity.

Just as she retreated into her books, I dived into mine, but with a different purpose: I wanted to learn more about the Garifuna people and any potential influence they could have had on my family. According to Caribbean oral legend, the Garifuna descended from Nigerians who escaped shipwrecked Spanish slave ships near St. Vincent in the seventeenth century. The ones who survived assimilated with the Carib-Arawak population in St. Vincent. The British viewed the Garifuna as a threat to colonialism in the eighteenth century, thus killing hundreds of them while forcing the rest to abandon the island.

When they left, they dispersed throughout Central America, including the coasts of Belize and Honduras, where they have remained and flourished for hundreds of years in places like Roatán (one of the Bay Islands off the northern coast of Honduras). I trace my matriline to Belize and Roatán, noting that I still have distant relatives in both areas. The Garifuna people have resided in these places long before my maternal great-grandparents' late nineteenth-century births. As a result, I suspect that if either or both of them were Garifuna, my family has remained silent about it for generations in order to hide our African roots. This would explain my mother's annoyance with the questions about our possible Garifuna heritage: I was tapping into a history of passing that was more real to me than any fictional novel could have articulated.

These ideas are all speculation at this point, based on the disbursement of Garifuna descendants, the time periods of my mother's grandparents' births, and the physical features of some of my relatives. I must travel to Central America to conduct comprehensive research on my family to draw more concrete conclusions. For now, I cannot help but observe parallels between my family's silence about our potential Garifuna (read *African*) roots, and the silence that racial passers in America have towards their own Blackness. I set aside my study of the Garifuna to focus on the research that yielded this book project: exploring racial passing narratives through the lens of psychoanalysis. I returned to my interest in Larsen's *Passing* after re-encountering it as a graduate student and writing a seminar paper on the ways in which Irene Redfield passes psychologically. That essay helped me to understand that there is some internal force in the psyche of those who want to shed their identities to fashion new ones, whether it is the Blacks in America who pretend to be White or my relatives who may have purposely obscured any relationship to the Garifuna. Finally, I wondered how my own family's passing (as native-born Central Americans sans an African ancestry) was imbedded in my psyche and drew me towards a deeper understanding of passing narratives. In pondering these issues, I discovered that racial passing in an American context is a psychoanalytical endeavor, as this book will make clear.

There are many people whom I must credit with assisting me in the realization that passing and psychoanalysis are intricately tethered. I must first thank Michelle Stephens, who taught Race and Psychoanalysis in fall 2011;

thankfully, I saved all the texts and notes from that provocative graduate seminar at Rutgers University. I am also indebted to Carter Mathes, Sterling Bland, and Evie Shockley, my professors who made me write with more clarity and nuance while at Rutgers. It is there that I also forged some of my closest friendships, with colleagues who support me and always push me to my academic limit, particularly Kaia Shivers and Rafael Vizcaíno, who consistently encourage me to think critically. Kaia invited me to speak about Afro-Latinidad at NYU in 2019, which motivated me to study my family's potential passing experience and meditate on the parallels to my research. Rafael recommended I read Rubén Gallo's *Freud's Mexico*, as well as J. Lorand Matory's *The Fetish Revisited: Marx, Freud, and the Gods Black People Make*, which were both instrumental in deepening my understanding of the global influence and international reach of Freudian psychoanalysis. Additionally, I have countless friends, mentors, and colleagues who provided years of support in ways they might not have realized. Special thanks to Alicia Bralove-Ramirez, Howard Rambsy, Tara Green, Marcia Cantarella, Anthony Browne, Tamara Mose, and Candice Jenkins, among many others. Thank you, too, to the anonymous readers who provided excellent feedback and whipped my work into better shape.

This book would have been impossible without the support of the Woodrow Wilson Career Enhancement Fellowship, which provided me with much needed time to restructure my ideas to make the most logical sense. Additionally, thanks to the South Atlantic Modern Language Association, the Northeast Modern Language Association, and the College Language Association, for allowing me to present and publish my theories about passing at their conferences. I had countless conversations with scholars at these conferences, who contributed ideas, citations, and words of encouragement for this monograph.

Special thanks to my late sister Ofelia, who continues to guide my hand so I can reach the potential she always saw in me. Ofelia started researching information about our family and shared tidbits with us, which inspired me to complete the family history she set out to tell. She was also one of the first people who predicted my success in life, which motivated me to study hard and pursue graduate study. In my home office, her picture sits near my favorite picture from my doctoral graduation, where I am flanked by two of the women who have had the most influence over my life: my no-nonsense mother, Ms. Francis Ramon, who encouraged me to think critically, work diligently, and never settle for mediocrity, and Cheryl Wall, who fostered my keen interest in racial passing narratives, even though it was already a deeply studied topic. Cheryl did not get a chance to see this book make it to print, but her influence is all over it. In our very last conversation, she observed that today's literary scholarship has gotten away from deep, close readings. It came at a time when I was grappling with the direction of this book, but I ultimately decided to advance deep, close readings to buoy my assertions on racial passing narratives. She encouraged me to write with precision, nuance, clarity, and depth; I would not be the scholar I am today without her guidance and support. I owe her tremendous gratitude for allowing me to rehearse these ideas when I was her doctoral student.

Lastly, I would be remiss if I did not acknowledge *all* of my ancestors—Garifuna, Honduran, Jamaican, Central American, and everyone in between—who sacrificed in ways I could never fully comprehend. Without them, I would not be here, presenting such speculative ideas about a wildly speculative intersection: racial passing and psychoanalysis.

MERCER UNIVERSITY PRESS

Endowed by

TOM WATSON BROWN
and
THE WATSON-BROWN FOUNDATION, INC.

"BOLD HYPOTHESES":
AN INTRODUCTION TO
PSYCHOANALYSIS AND RACE

> Freud himself taught us that interpretation is an art that must encompass unconscious as well as conscious material, and that the analyst—including the cultural analyst—must not be afraid to propose bold hypotheses, strong arguments, and speculative constructions.
> —Rubén Gallo, *Freud's Mexico: Into the Wilds of Psychoanalysis* (2015)

From the inception of psychoanalysis in the United States, many scholars who study African-Americans have vacillated in employing it to fully understand Blackness. Charles Gibson's 1931 essay for *The Psychoanalytic Review*, for example, situates racial passing as a conflict between the conscious and subconscious mind: "But, being unable to leave his subconscious behind, he cannot avoid the conflicts, soon to follow, between it and the conscious. Unmindful of this, the pale individual sets out with bright prospects, crosses the color line and 'passes.'"[1] Richard Wright disagreed with this specific use of psychoanalysis, arguing in 1946 that its primary flaw was its failure to understand the ways in which racism and poverty complicate the lives of African-Americans. He viewed the social order as the most important reason African-

---

[1] Gibson, "Concerning Color," 422. *The Psychoanalytic Review* is the premier peer reviewed journal for psychoanalysis. It has been published continuously since 1913 and included the works of early Black psychoanalysts. For instance, the journal published "Imitation of Life," a complex article about Fannie Hurst's novel of the same name. Though it was edited by Dr. Ben Karpman, the chair of psychiatry at Howard University College of Medicine, he collaborated with his students at Howard University. His contemporaries included Charles Prudhomme, who published "The Problem of Suicide in the American Negro" in 1938, which highlights the lower suicide rates of African-Americans. Prudhomme alludes to passing, when he notes "that this drive toward the goal of complete amalgamation with the majority race is a large factor in lowering the suicide rate, [specifically that] the desire to reach the 'white' goal" will lead to a long life for Black Americans (389). Although his argument is compelling, his sample size is limited (eight), and he extrapolates from such few cases. As such, it is difficult to understand *all* the reasons African-Americans commit suicide, considering they are not always reported.

Americans suffered, yet psychology could not account for this because the field pathologized Blacks.[2]

Since the 1960s, Black feminists have sustained the most powerful criticisms of psychoanalysis. They question its efficacy due to the focus on "anatomical differences, thereby reducing women to emotional and static subjects," while Black Power writers dismissed it as an extension of European hegemony that could not properly service marginalized voices.[3] Barbara Christian renders it unusable because it "mystifies rather than clarifies [the African-American] condition,"[4] while Hortense Spillers argues that "little or nothing in the intellectual history of African-Americans within the social and political context of the United States would suggest the effectiveness of a psychoanalytic discourse, revised or classical, in illuminating the problematic of 'race' on an intersubjective field of play."[5] To support this point, one need look no further than "the Jeffersonian notion that Blacks lacked psychic interiority," which Ahad believes epitomizes the failure of psychoanalysis "to approach the matter of Black subjectivity."[6] Similarly, Gwen Bergner notes that psychoanalysis "ignored race as a constitutive factor of identity, perpetuated colonialist ideologies of the savage primitive," and saw its paradigms, which explicitly derived from European culture, as universal for everyone.[7] As these critical responses make clear, scholars of race and literature remain skeptical about applying psychoanalysis to understanding African-Americans.

Indeed, African-Americans have had a fraught history with psychoanalysis. This is best summed up by Claudia Tate, whose scholarship broke new ground in employing psychoanalysis to understand race. In recounting the criticism she received for studying "black textuality and psychoanalysis," Tate concedes that psychoanalysis "has carried a lot of irritating baggage that has made it virtually an anathema in the Black intellectual community."[8] She uses psychoanalysis to analyze noncanonical texts by Black writers, to uncover "marginalized desire as a critical category of black textuality" while also

---

[2] Wright, "Psychiatry Comes to Harlem," *Free World*, 47.
[3] Ahad, *Freud Upside Down*, 111.
[4] Christian, "The Race for Theory," 15.
[5] Spillers, "All the Things You Could Be by Now," 376.
[6] Ahad, *Freud Upside Down*, 6.
[7] Bergner, *Taboo Subjects*, xix.
[8] Tate, *Psychoanalysis and Black Novels*, 16.

illuminating the "latent content in their corresponding noncanonical works."⁹ Her monograph is most interested in noncanonical works because racial politics is not "their centermost concern," thus making them ripe for psychoanalytical analysis.¹⁰ Tate makes it clear that, despite long-standing criticism of applying psychoanalysis to matters of race (and specifically African-American literature), the novels in her analysis comprise "unconscious discourses" that resemble dreams. This is the basis of psychoanalysis, and it would be strange not to read these texts through a Freudian lens. Thanks to Tate's astute scholarship, psychoanalysis has gained traction as a viable theoretical perspective for people of color in recent years.¹¹ Critics invoke it to create new theories for Black subjectivity while situating the historical criticism of the racelessness, pathologizing, and implicit racism imbedded in classic psychoanalysis. These critics have not, however, fully explored the significant role that race played in the creation of classic psychoanalysis, nor are they carefully attuned to a particular aspect of Black subjectivity—racial passing—that psychoanalysis is most useful for interpreting.

My book intervenes in this critical lacuna by exploring racial passing through a psychoanalytical perspective. It explores a range of racial passing narratives by Black and White authors, to uncover the internal trauma and psychological consequences of jumping the color line for real and fictional racial passers. The main premise of this book is that psychoanalysis utilizes race in subtle ways that are not exclusively racist, which opens up this book's exploration of its effects on mixed-race subjectivity and racial passing. The close readings advanced therein explore psychoanalytic impulses displayed throughout twentieth-century racial passing narratives, since these narratives

---

⁹ Tate, 5.
¹⁰ Tate, 12.
¹¹ For more on race and psychoanalysis, see Altman, *The Analyst in the Inner City* (2009); Abel, Christian, and Moglen, eds., *Female Subjects in Black and White* (1997); Bergner, *Taboo Subjects*; Cheng, *The Melancholy of Race* (2001); Cheng, *Second Skin* (2011); Crawford, *Dilution Anxiety and the Black Phallus* (2008); Gilman and Thomas, *Are Racists Crazy?* (2016); Khanna, *Dark Continents* (2003); Lane, *The Psychoanalysis of Race* (1998); Mohamed, *The Death-Bound Subject* (2005); Scott, *Extravagant Abjection* (2010); Seshadri-Crooks, *Desiring Whiteness* (2000); Stoler, *Race and the Education of Desire* (1995); Tate, *Psychoanalysis & Black Novels*; Tuhkanenn, *The American Optic*, (2009); Viego, *Dead Subjects* (2007); and Walton, *Fair Sex, Savage Dreams* (2001).

respond to the distinctly American formulation of race and racism. My goal is not to psychoanalyze the writers, or to privilege one specific psychoanalytical theory over another, but to fully understand internal motivations and psychological consequences of a feigned racial identity. Psychoanalysis provides very useful answers to the broad question "why do people pass?" Social and economic gain provide one set of answers, as does the avoidance of explicit racism. Yet psychoanalysis suggests a wider range of reasons that influence racial passers, which have hitherto gone unnoticed. For instance, if an individual's environment yields problems as an adult, it makes logical sense that a racialized environment (such as school, which was a racially contested space for African-Americans throughout the twentieth century) would emerge as a primary area of study to explore why some Black students pass as White.

Since I am not invested in therapizing writers or characters, I am able to use many strands of Freudian psychoanalysis throughout this monograph. Not relying on a specific psychoanalyst opens up the myriad ways in which several different elements of psychoanalysis undergird the passing narrative tradition. This is particularly important given Farhad Dalal's observation that the theoretical field consists of "a number of different theories each with distinct world views."[12] In fact, writers of both real and fictional passing narratives selectively draw upon psychoanalysis, which is unsurprising given all the ways psychoanalysis elucidates the inherent dilemmas of jumping the color line. As a result, Freud and Lacan share space with Frantz Fanon, Otto Rank, and Erik Erikson in this monograph. Writers invoke different aspects of classical psychoanalysis in depicting their passing protagonists, further proving that psychoanalysis is a viable area of study for Black Americans.

This book might generate pushback regarding my use of psychoanalysis and the range of writers explored, yet I invoke Freudian psychoanalysis for many reasons. For one, Sigmund Freud was deeply concerned with his own race and sexuality, thus he created psychoanalysis as a way to comprehend both. As explained later in this introduction, Freud's life paralleled those of racial passers, in that he fashioned an identity for himself lest he get revealed. Embedded in this identity was a drive to hide his racial origins and hidden sexual proclivities, which he tried to diagnose by developing psychoanalysis. Tate reminds us that psychoanalysis "centers the individual's primary

---

[12] Dalal, *Race, Colour and the Processes of Racialization*, 32.

nurturing environment," which is precisely what Freud sought to understand regarding the identities he created for himself.[13] As a result, it is a deeply racialized area of study, evident by his own relationship with race and the diction of race that his disciples infused when developing their own theories of psychoanalysis.[14] Moreover, due to the prevalence of Freud's ideas in the first half of the twentieth century, psychoanalysis influenced many writers, including several in this book. I highlight the investments the writers in this book maintained in psychoanalysis, and the different ways in which the theory made its way into their writings. This monograph attempts to recoup psychoanalysis as a critical area of study for African-Americans since it began as

---

[13] Tate, *Psychoanalysis and Black Novels*, 16.

[14] For instance, Otto Rank, one of Freud's most prominent students, published his own psychoanalytic theory as *The Trauma of Birth*, which first appeared in English in 1929. It argues that birth is the original trauma from which all humans try to recover. He believes that religion, art, philosophy, and myth, comprise our attempts to return to an idyllic life in the womb. Most germane to this monograph is his observation on displacement:

> One can observe clearly how the fear of animals originally referring to the mother changes into fear of the father, resting on sexual repression. Then it can become perfectly rationalized through displacement to robbers, criminals, *Black men*, etc., according to the phobia mechanism. Here, the so-called real fear arising from danger comes into existence as a connecting link and as an outlet for the displaced primal anxiety (19, emphasis mine).

In noting that fear moves from animals, to parents, and then to "robbers, criminals, [and] Black men," Rank taps into the long history of irrational fear of Black men, which was prevalent from the nineteenth century and still continues today. In the mid-1920s, these anxieties about Black men contributed to lynchings in the United States and helped to fuel the eugenics movement in Europe and America. Today, these anxieties persist in myriad ways, from cell phone footage of Black men being harassed for doing pedestrian activities to police killings of unarmed African-Americans. Freud initially welcomed *The Trauma of Birth* when he read its initial draft, but he later took great umbrage to the book's subtle critique of the Oedipus Complex. One must wonder whether Rank's subtle reference to Black men played any role in Freud's later dismissal of the book. Whereas Freud mentioned race in a general way via his invocation of mixed-race status, his protégé specifically locates a fear of Black men—a racialized other like Freud—that the latter only alludes to. In other words, by publishing his theory of psychoanalysis, Rank named what Freud was only able to theorize about at a distance.

a meditation on Freud's race before it developed into a major influence for twentieth-century writers.

There is not only a breadth of psychoanalytic scholarship in this monograph, but also a breadth of primary texts assessed. Race is a very complex and messy subject, and the range of writers invoked in this book helps me to contextualize the complexities. I envision a wide readership for this project; specifically, students, faculty, and lay readers alike who are interested in race, psychoanalysis, and/or African-American literature would take interest in this monograph. I invoke noncanonical narratives, such as Alice Dunbar-Nelson's short story "The Stones of the Village" and Vera Caspary's novel *The White Girl* because so few scholars have written on these specific texts, yet they clearly belong in the passing narrative tradition. This is the same logic that inspired the inclusion of the real-life passing stories of Anita Reynolds and Anatole Broyard. They were both interested in Freud's theory and structured their lives like the passing narratives they read; their feigned identities were as fictional as the lives created by their respective contemporaries, Nella Larsen and Philip Roth. I situate them as passing subjects whose lives were inspired by narratives of racial passing and psychoanalysis. Reynolds and Broyard followed the familiar passing narrative script, which included leaving home, experiencing difficult situations in racialized education systems, living anonymously as White in big cities, and having intimate romantic relationships with people who were non-Black in hopes it would obscure their race. Yet what sets Reynolds and Broyard apart is the collection of writings they left behind. Analyzing their fiction alongside their life stories suggests that real-life passers want to live as White, although their creative writing leaves clues of their Blackness. Another intervention for my book then, is a redefinition of racial passing literature to include narratives that are canonical, noncanonical, and true, using psychoanalysis as a theoretical apparatus to understand why and how the color line is transgressed.

Du Bois's Double Consciousness and Freud's Inner Africa

To better clarify my rationale for using psychoanalysis, we must first explore Freud's logic for theorizing psychoanalysis in the first place. Understanding the theorist helps us contextualize his theory and its relationship with African-Americans. Freud's most prominent Black contemporary was W. E. B. Du

Bois, who theorizes the "double consciousness" in *The Souls of Black Folk* (1903). In it, he defines it as the

> Sense of always looking at one's self through the eyes of others, of measuring one's soul by the tape of a world that looks on in amused contempt and pity. One ever feels his twoness, —an American, a Negro; two souls, two thoughts, two unreconciled strivings; two warring ideals in one dark body, whose dogged strength alone keeps it from being torn asunder.[15]

For Du Bois, African-Americans are afflicted with an inherent duality by living in a country circumscribed by and suffused with race, as they are forced to be divided between being Black and being American. His theory of double consciousness is pivotal in understanding life on the color line for African-Americans. The African-Americans who are most aware of this are racial passers; they straddle the color line by navigating their Black ancestry while living as White in America. Racial passers are acutely aware that they consist of "two souls, two thoughts, two unreconciled strivings" through their lives on the color line.[16]

Du Bois's terminology developed as a result of his own relationship with race, as a light-skinned African-American intellectual who witnessed racial segregation firsthand throughout his travels. While studying abroad in Berlin, Du Bois also observed the treatment of Jews up close. For instance, he reported being "several times mistaken for a Jew," such as when a taxi driver in Slovenia misidentified him as Jewish and brought him to "a little Jewish inn."[17] In 1893, he meditated on anti-Semitism he observed in Germany: "It may surprise one at first to see a recrudescence of anti-Jewish feeling in a civilized state at this late day. One must learn however that the basis of the neo-anti-Semitism is economic and its end socialism....[The progress Jews have made makes them] a menace to the newly nationalized country."[18] He reiterates this anti-Semitism a decade later in *The Souls of Black Folk*, which is peppered with exaggerations about southern Jews. These reflections

---

[15] Du Bois, *The Souls of Black Folk*, 215.
[16] Du Bois, 215.
[17] Du Bois, *Autobiography*, 122.
[18] Du Bois, "The Present Condition of German Politics," 175.

support Daniel Boyarin's conclusion that "Jewishness functioned racially in Austro-Germany as 'Blackness' does in the United States."[19]

Double consciousness was also used to describe "the state of the German Jewish psyche as understood and described at the turn of the century"—a time that also saw the beginning of Sigmund Freud's career.[20] Matory describes Freud as having "very dark eyes and hair," prompting Freud's mother to render him her "little blackamoor."[21] This label came at a time when "European minorities were called 'the negroes of Europe'" in the late nineteenth and early twentieth century.[22] As a result of the anti-Semitism Freud was subjected to, as well as widespread anti-Blackness, Freud tried to pass as an assimilated Jew and created psychoanalysis to comprehend both his personal and the global neuroses of race.

In creating his pivotal theory, Freud defined his own version of double consciousness in response to the anti-Semitism to which he was subjected. Through justifying his version of the unconscious in 1915, he notes:

> We shall also be right in rejecting the term 'subconsciousness' as incorrect and misleading. The well-known cases of 'double conscience' (splitting of consciousness) prove nothing against our view. We may most aptly describe them as cases of a splitting of the mental activities into two groups, and say that the same consciousness turns to one or the other of these groups alternatively.[23]

In this definition, he literalizes the double consciousness as a mental division that afflicts everyone, wherein consciousness is divided into two groups that alternate from one to the other. The specifics of each theory differ but the points of convergence are clear: Du Bois and Freud maintain the similar position that all humans inhabit dualities, whether through race or through mental states, that comprise our subjectivity. Within these dualities is the notion of passing, which broadly refers to creating new identities for ourselves. If we all maintain dualities, then it eases the process of identity creation, as the process of racial passing exemplifies. According to Coviello, "knowledge of the preoccupations and emphases of one allows us to see those of the other

---

[19] Boyarin, "What Does a Jew Want?," 220.
[20] Gilman and Thomas, *Are Racists Crazy*, 56.
[21] Matory, *The Fetish Revisited*, 119.
[22] Matory, 120.
[23] Freud, *The Unconscious*, 170–71.

in new, revelatory ways."[24] In short, understanding Freud's theory is a generative way of comprehending Du Bois's, while understanding Du Bois helps us to interpret Freud.

This book is not asserting that one specifically influenced the other, since double consciousness has its beginnings in the nineteenth century, before either theorist published his pivotal work. Instead, the two theorists developed the term in response to the specific racial classifications that defined their home countries. As Dickson Bruce Jr. notes, the transcendentalist meaning of double consciousness derived from Emerson's 1843 essay "The Transcendentalist," but as early as 1817, medical journals used the term to reference cases of double personality disorders. Pragmatist philosopher and psychologist William James first defined the theoretical implications of these cases in 1890 while mentoring Du Bois at Harvard University.[25] Though Du Bois was the first to use double consciousness to theorize Black subjectivity exclusively, he was hardly the first to use the term, as evidenced by its psychological and transcendentalist implications. Yet Du Bois was the first to apply the term to African-Americans and not anyone with a specific medical disorder, noting that African-Americans experiencing a double consciousness also experienced a psychic break. These multiple meanings all add to its historical importance as "yet another aspect of the concept's doubleness."[26]

The history of the theorization of double consciousness complicates a direct line of influence between Du Bois and Freud, which each man's publication dates makes clear. Du Bois and Freud each contextualized the term to fit his specific theoretical and racial need: whereas the former theorized double consciousness in 1903, the latter expressed a more literal variation of this concept in his second book, *The Interpretation of Dreams*, in 1900. Without using the phrase explicitly, Freud argues that childhood experiences form the bases of dreams. He justifies this argument by highlighting his desire to travel to Rome:

> Moreover, when I finally came to realize the consequences of belonging to an *alien race*, and was forced by the anti-Semitic feeling among my classmates to take a definite stand, the figure of the Semitic commander assumed still greater proportions in my imagination.

---

[24] Coviello, "Intimacy and Affliction," 22.
[25] Bruce, "W. E. B. Du Bois and the Idea of Double Consciousness," 300.
[26] Bergner, *Taboo Subjects*, xvi.

Hannibal and Rome symbolized, in my youthful eyes, the struggle between the tenacity of the *Jews* and the organization of *the Catholic Church*. The significance for our emotional life which the anti-Semitic movement has since assumed helped to fix the thoughts and impressions of those earlier days. Thus the desire to go to Rome has in my dream-life become the mask and symbol for a number of warmly cherished wishes.[27]

Freud depicts the historical opposition between Jews and Catholics using diction that parallels Du Bois's. Whereas the former describes the dichotomy of these two groups, Du Bois observes the division between African-Americans and Whites. In fact, in the italicized text above, "Jews" and "the Catholic Church" could be replaced by an observation about "Blacks" being dominated by "Whites" in Du Bois's theorization. While Du Bois sees his Blackness as a "problem" and "handicap," Freud recognizes that his Jewishness places him in an "alien race." Beverly Stoute reiterates this in an essay for the American Psychoanalytic Association: "Jews were thought of as 'the Negroes of Vienna,' psychoanalysis was a 'Black thing,' and Freud was labeled as a 'Black Jew.'"[28] In short, the two primary thinkers at the beginning of the twentieth century keenly recognized racial differences vis-à-vis duality and their relationships with dominant groups.

These two theorists share more than a critical eye to dualities in their pivotal works: they both first discovered their racial differences while in primary school. Freud understood his affinity for Hannibal only after encountering the anti-Semitism of his classmates, while Du Bois discovered his racial difference after a classmate refused to accept his card. This incident profoundly affected Du Bois—it precipitated his prescient theory and inspired him to pursue racial equality throughout his entire life. In the first chapter of this book, I explore the classroom as an important site for racial development; as Freud and Du Bois demonstrate, realizing race through being surrounded by their peers at an early age in school is powerful enough to provide the collective impetus for their racial affinities and important theorizations. Moreover, both thinkers employ similar images to advance their assertions. Freud's trip to Rome became "the mask and symbol for a number of warmly

---

[27] Freud, *The Interpretation of Dreams*, 228, emphases mine.
[28] Stoute, *Race and Racism*, 13.

cherished wishes."²⁹ One of the premises undergirding his theories is that our unconscious desires are typically masked, yet they manifest themselves in several ways—such as through dreams and linguistic slips. The psychological mask we all wear is penetrable, according to Freud's analytic tools. For Du Bois though, the mask image is reprised as the veil that African-Americans are born with, which evolves into a double consciousness. Unlike Freud's "mask," Du Bois's "veil" has a more crippling effect, as Black Americans can only see themselves through the eyes of others. By employing splitting in the verbiage of identity formation, understanding race through interactions in school, and using comparable images of masking/veiling in their respective works, Du Bois and Freud highlight the importance of delineating types of consciousness in the early twentieth century for different racial groups.

Both theorists were deeply attentive to these matters and comprehended them similarly. In fact, Du Bois and Freud "share in illuminating ways a number of premises and concerns."³⁰ One such anxiety was about people of mixed-race heritage, which Freud made explicitly clear in *The Unconscious* and is particularly apt for studying matters of race and racial passing:

> Their mixed and split origin is what decides their fate. We may compare them with individuals of mixed race who, taken all around, resemble white men, but who betray their coloured descent by some striking feature or other and on that account are excluded from society and enjoy none of the privileges of white people.³¹

This quote continues his logic from *The Interpretation of Dreams*, where he simultaneously notes both his classmates' anti-Semitism and his growing understanding of his position in an "alien race." In this section of *The Unconscious*, he draws a vivid comparison between racial passing and the ambivalence of the unconscious, yet a closer look at this metaphor also reveals Freud's own racial anxiety. His use of "mixed race" is a provocative formulation since he was a Jew during a time when many assumed that Jews were either Black or at least of mixed-race. This might explain why he "was famously ambivalent about his origins as an Eastern Jew. Bearing witness to the subjugation of Eastern Jews, Freud constructed his own self-image as an

---

²⁹ Freud, *The Interpretation of Dreams*, 228.
³⁰ Coviello, "Intimacy and Affliction," 22.
³¹ Freud, "The Unconscious," 191.

acculturated Jew."[32] He did this by attempting to hide his Jewish identity, yet in analyzing photographs of Freud and other Jewish intellectuals holding cigars, André Aciman observes that he was unable to completely pass because he assimilated within mainstream Europe, after becoming successful enough to create a "pan-European culture."[33] Boyarin agrees, asserting that Freud aspired to be a "bourgeois European" but could not fully pass because of his Jewishness.[34]

In the process of trying to create a new identity to escape anti-Semitism, he dropped clues of his racial anxiety within his early writings—similar to some of the passers analyzed in this book—thus further underscoring the parallel stereotypes and discrimination that Jews (like him) and Blacks endured. Since Jews were seen as having African ancestry, the illusion of "one-drop" circulated for both groups in the racial imagination at the turn of the twentieth century. Freud's theorization imagined the implications of racial passing by developing psychoanalysis, and scholars are beginning to tease out this connection between Freud's background and his psychoanalytic theories. For instance, Bénédicte Boisseron believes that Freud "addressed the question of racial passing" in his work, using "the image of racial passing to pinpoint the location of fantasy, between the preconscious and the unconscious,"[35] while Boyarin makes it clear that his "position between white and Black greatly contributed to his psychological and ethnological theories."[36] Ahad asserts that "Blackness figures as a defining category that essentially determined Freud's formation of the white or off-white Jewish subject."[37] Instead of qualifying the influence of Jewishness on Freud's writing, I strongly believe that Freud's preoccupation with race—especially mixed race, which to him entailed Europeans having African ancestry—unequivocally led him to create psychoanalysis. It helps to explain why the rhetoric of double consciousness and race pepper his writings. His own racial position "between White and Black" applies to racial passers as well, who are equally caught between these conflicting racial forces. Being Jewish exposed him to anti-Semitism, just as

---

[32] Ahad, *Freud Upside Down*, 18.
[33] Aciman, "Reflections of an Uncertain Jew."
[34] Boyarin, "What Does a Jew Want?," 219.
[35] Boisseron, *Creole Renegades*, 50.
[36] Boyarin, "What Does a Jew Want?," 220.
[37] Ahad, *Freud Upside Down*, 19.

being African-American exposed one to racism; members of both groups created new identities for themselves to prevent discriminatory backlash in the early twentieth century. While Du Bois responded by theorizing the double consciousness, Freud reacted by conceiving and promoting psychoanalysis, which also provided him with the opportunity to pass in several ways.

Racial passing was just one way in which Freud obscured his identity; sexuality was another. Although Freud notes some "striking feature" in analogizing the unconscious and racial passing, this ambiguous term can also refer to him, for he did not want any "feature" to reveal him as Jewish given his desire to suppress his heritage, nor did he want his relationship with Wilhelm Fliess to reveal his sexuality. Fliess, a Jewish doctor, helped Freud theorize that people are born bisexual and are motivated primarily by sexual impulses.[38] Freud himself rendered the relationship "homosexual cathexis,"[39] leaving Matory to surmise that their "homosexual affair seems to have been critical to the development of psychoanalysis."[40] Much like the founder of psychoanalysis, passers fear the exposure of their racial duplicity and taboo sexualities. In chapter two, I argue that transgressing one boundary often implies transgressing other seemingly rigid boundaries, such as sexuality. Based on this contextualization and intersections of Freud's race and sexuality, I develop a theory of death and taboo sexualities, guided by close readings of passing narratives from the early twentieth century. In addition to race and sexuality, Freud's anxieties were also "shaped by the nineteenth century rise of capitalism, overseas imperialism, pseudoscientific racism, and Jim Crow," as well as "class insecurity."[41] He tried to distance himself from the alleged Blackness of Jews by repudiating Judaism, particularly in his quest to be remembered as a Western scholar.[42] His image of this scholar was of a

---

[38] Matory, *The Fetish Revisited*, 139.
[39] Jones, *The Life and Work of Sigmund Freud*, 281.
[40] Matory, *The Fetish Revisited*, 139.
[41] Matory, 37.
[42] For example, in 1911, Freud joined the International Society for the Protection of Mothers and Sexual Reform, "which advised its members to breed selectively" (Ahad, *Freud Upside Down*, 19). Actions like this support Matory's observation that Freud "resisted a number of contemporaneous intellectual trends that recognized the equality of whites and nonwhites" (137). Like a textbook case of a racial passer, he was preoccupied with racial purity at a time when eugenics emerged as a "scientific" way to further separate the races. Medical sciences in Central Europe helped to

heterosexual man without any features that would indicate even the possibility of Black heritage.

Despite Freud's best efforts to obscure any confusion about his race, his language in *The Interpretation of Dreams* (1900) and *The Unconscious* (1915) reveals a reckoning with a potential mixed-race status. He buried commentary about mixed race in a section of *The Unconscious* entitled "Communication Between the Two Systems," a provocative yet ambiguous subtitle for his comparison that denotes dual meanings: the "two systems" explicitly refer to the preconscious and the unconscious that he theorized, while implicitly alluding to the systems of race under which Freud chafed. Moreover, Freud viewed the id as an "inner Africa" and sometimes referred to his patients as his "negroes."[43] I assert that he founded the field of psychoanalysis to understand the messiness of race and to theorize it, especially as a Jewish man considered to have "African" ancestry. This preempts Anatole Broyard and Anita Reynolds, real-life racial passers addressed in chapter three who also left clues of their racial background in their works, complicating their best efforts to hide it. Despite the colonialist implications that many scholars have noted in early psychoanalysis, its rhetoric of race reveals Freud's subtle methods of comprehending racist logic.

Not only can we explore the language of Blackness that seeped into his formulations, but also that of his disciples who also influenced many writers in this monograph. For instance, Jacques Lacan's "The Function and Field of Speech and Language in Psychoanalysis" (1953), explains aggression by citing "the aggressiveness of the slave who responds to being frustrated in his labor with a death wish" and the anxiety of knowing that a "patient's freedom may depend on that of his own intervention."[44] In "The Instance of the Letter

---

disseminate anti-Semitism, which "further demonize[d] Jews by aligning them with an even more reviled race, the African" (Ahad, *Freud Upside Down*, 18) especially since Jews were thought to have "interbred with Africans during the period of the Alexandrian exile…making them a 'mongrel' race" (Gilman, *Freud, Race, and Gender*, 21). As a result, Freud wanted to prevent future generations from assuming the Africanness of the Jew. To have "good genes" required selective breeding, as Freud himself believed, and African-Americans were not considered desirable for this elitist and racist endeavor.

[43] Matory, *The Fetish Revisited*, 44, 162.

[44] Lacan, *The Function and Field of Speech and Language in Psychoanalysis*, 208, emphases mine.

in the Unconscious" (1957), he also notes that while the subject of his study "may appear to be the slave of language, [he] is still more the slave of a discourse in the universal movement of which his place is already inscribed at birth, if only in the form of his proper name."[45] In the first text, Lacan explicitly refers to enslavement by highlighting a slave's wish for death over a life in bondage, while in the second text, he uses the language of slavery to show the fallacy of believing that language simply entails speech. These examples are just some of the ways in which Lacan employs references to Blackness throughout his works to expound on his ideas.[46] His invocations of Blackness help us to better understand him and his theoretical predecessors, drawing our attention to psychoanalysts' long-standing need to evoke race, beginning with its founder.

Using psychoanalysis as a pivotal springboard, this monograph explores the following questions: if Freud used the language and imagery of mixed race to create psychoanalysis (as a way to understand race), how can we then understand psychoanalysis as a way to explore one representation of mixed-race subjectivity: racial passing? How has racial passing—both real and fictional—emerged as a deeply psychoanalytic endeavor? How does childhood

---

[45] Lacan, "The Instance of the Letter in the Unconscious," 414.

[46] Slavery and Blackness are also imbedded within Lacan's diction in *Position of the Unconscious* (1960), wherein he argues that the unconscious is situated "in the un-Black." He clarifies this by stating, "The unconscious before Freud has no more consistency than this un-Black—namely, the set of what could be classified according to the various meanings of the word 'Black,' by dint of its refusal of the attribute (or virtue) of Blackness (whether physical or moral)" (704). He is notoriously opaque, yet this quote clearly defines the unconscious, before Freud's theory, against a lack as represented by the "un-Black" (704). He offers some clues a few paragraphs after this one, by highlighting Hegel and stating that "ideals are society's slaves" (705). This might be the closest we come to understanding Lacan's peculiar and at times random references to Blackness and enslavement in his oeuvre: he was influenced by Hegel's master-slave dialectic, which theorizes the ways in which self-consciousness is formed through meeting the other. When developing and articulating this idea in *The Phenomenology of Spirit* (1807), Hegel himself was influenced by the Haitian Revolution. In short, Lacan's use of enslavement derived from Hegel's own response to slavery by theorizing the events of the Haitian Revolution. If history is any guide, his slave diction was also influenced by international events of the 1950s and 1960s, such as African and Caribbean nations fighting for independence and the Civil Rights movement in the United States.

trauma impact racial passing? How is the process of writing complicated by passing? How is Blackness implicated when racial passers die? How are death and passing related to each other? How can we redefine and expand notions of "passing" in the twenty-first century? Perhaps the most prevalent question undergirding the meditations in this book is why *not* use psychoanalysis to comprehend racial passing, given the clear influence that racial anxiety wielded over Freud himself and the passing he pursued?

To answer these questions with nuance, clarity, and efficiency, I cite psychoanalysis when appropriate throughout this monograph to explicate the ways in which it intersects with passing. Each chapter advances a detailed argument using psychoanalysis to fully understand the internal reasoning and psychological consequences of jumping the color line. Using Erikson's *Stages of Psychosocial Development*, coupled with Frantz Fanon's ideas on racialized subject formation in *Black Skin, White Masks*, I argue in chapter one that racial passing begins much earlier than we previously assumed. Closely reading the passing protagonists in Charles Chesnutt's *The House Behind the Cedars* (1900), James Weldon Johnson's *The Autobiography of An Ex-Colored Man* (1912), Jessie Fauset's *Plum Bun* (1929), and Danzy Senna's *Caucasia* (1999) suggests that racial passing begins as a response to classroom trauma and is a youthful endeavor. This contradicts what scholars previously thought, in that racial passing starts in childhood and not in adulthood as the result of physical racial trauma (such as lynching). For male passers, such as the Ex-Colored Man and John Walden, racial passing begins in school, since the interracial classroom space emerges as the first site of trauma for Black students. Their female counterparts, however, are motivated to pass as a result of both school and their mothers' racial passing, which Angela Murray and Birdie Lee make clear. Psychoanalysis is rooted in childhood, as demonstrated by analysts who study youthful actions to predict future behaviors. Chapter one thus explores the ways in which racial passing is a childhood endeavor, because light-skinned children who can pass as White discover their race for the first time at school. With their Blackness made hypervisible during childhood, those children grow up to be adults who transgress the color line. They do not have to witness a lynching or another type of racialized violence to understand the utility of jumping the color line.

In chapter two, I explore the intricate tethering of passing and death. Semantically, the word "passing" has several connotations; the ones most pertinent for this monograph are passing as White and the euphemism "passing away," since characters who pass also engage in multiple types of death. Indeed, in order to pass, they must metaphorically kill off their families to kill off their Blackness. This emerges as a futile endeavor, for they all die with either blackened skin or blackened lips at the end. Moreover, those who jump the color line also transgress other seemingly rigid boundaries, such as sexuality. Being unable to endure the possibility of both their race and their sexuality revealed, racial passers hasten their own deaths. I assert this claim in chapter two by reading Freud's theory of the "death drive" as well as concepts from his *Three Contributions to the Theory of Sex* (1905) through images of death, passing, and sexuality across three passing narratives: Alice Dunbar-Nelson's short story "The Stones of the Village,"[47] Vera Caspary's novel *The White Girl* (1929), and Nella Larsen's novella *Passing* (1929). The primary goal of this chapter is to complicate the notion that racial passers are mere tragic mulattos who succumb to their fate; rather, they are active contributors in hastening their own deaths.

Whereas fictional passers align with the death drive, real-life racial passers sought relief from it by wanting to live in perpetuity. Anita Reynolds and Anatole Broyard—both twentieth-century passers—wanted to immortalize themselves in their creative writing in accordance with Sigmund Freud and Otto Rank. Rank's theory of the "trauma of birth" is particularly relevant in explaining Reynolds's and Broyard's struggle to write their memoirs. However, they could not, lest they revealed their Blackness through their writing. They faced the difficult question of whether to publish their life stories or reveal their race. I explore their writing issues and false personas in chapter three by closely reading Anita Reynolds's autobiography, *American Cocktail: A Colored Girl in the World* (2014), and Bliss Broyard's *One Drop* (2003), a biography of her father Anatole Broyard. The critical scholarship on these two writers is scant, and I begin the scholarly conversation by placing these two real-life racial passers in tandem with each other. Lastly, I contend that Philip Roth's *The Human Stain* (2000) employs psychoanalysis to remix canonical passing narratives that were authored by African-Americans. In chapter four, I use Roth's novel as a case study to not only explore psychoanalytic elements of passing narratives, but to also demonstrate the theories developed in the previous chapters at work. Coleman Silk, the protagonist, has a race-

---

[47] This story was first written between 1900 and 1910, but it was not published until 1988, decades after Dunbar-Nelson's death.

learning, accelerates his own death, and seeks out his neighbor Nathan Zuckerman to help immortalize him through the written word. Silk fits all three paradigms, thus demonstrating the ways in which psychoanalysis resonates with passing narratives by both Black and non-Black authors: Roth is Jewish, and his character, Coleman Silk, passes as Jewish. While each chapter invokes psychoanalysis, the fourth chapter offers a clear and sustained case study exploring the full impact of psychoanalysis on a contemporary passing narrative.

In the concluding chapter, I argue for the use of more accurate terminology to describe race and racism, since popular twenty-first-century neologisms often decontextualize and diminish the importance of race today. This monograph slowly and purposely builds a case for reading racial passing novels through a psychoanalytic scope, which highlights the importance of Freud's theory while employing it to understand its impact on racial passing. For example, contemporary critics have addressed the ways in which Blackness and race made their way into the field's rhetoric. Ahad notes that despite its "glaring absence…Blackness figures as a defining category" in psychoanalysis, while Bergner maintains that race was not "absent from early psychoanalysis, but rather that it is put to stealthy use without being considered a legitimate subject of analysis."[49] I, too, put psychoanalysis to "stealthy use" by framing my close readings and concluding with compelling observations about the intersections of African-American literature, racial passing, and psychoanalysis. Christopher Lane would agree with such a reading: "psychoanalysis challenges conventional understandings of history and temporality, insisting that events are understood retroactively through 'deferred action'; we project onto the past to sustain our perspectives on the present."[50] With this perspective in mind, we can thus understand each racial passer's past and explore how he or she obscured elements of Blackness in favor of a completely new White identity.

Racial passing is a popular topic among writers and theorists alike, and while psychoanalysis has been applied to Black subjects for decades, critics are only now seeing the import of studying the specific intersections of

---

[49] Ahad, *Freud Upside Down*, 19; Bergner, *Taboo Subjects*, xx.
[50] Lane, "The Psychoanalysis of Race," 20.

psychoanalysis and racial passing.[51] Continuing in the vein of Claudia Tate, Gwen Bergner, and Badia Ahad, I do not simply apply psychoanalysis to passing narratives; instead, I read psychoanalysis as providing the answers to why and how some light-skinned African-Americans navigate the color line. I invoke it to frame my arguments and analyze the texts. At times throughout this book, I defer psychoanalysis to the close readings themselves in order to focus more readily on the actions of racial passers, which are far more compelling for my overall literary analysis. This method allows me to quote liberally from the texts under consideration, particularly since a few of them are obscure and thus unfamiliar to readers, whereas most readers already know the basic tenets of psychoanalysis. Moreover, not being beholden to individual psychoanalysts leaves room for me to posit my own theories about racial passing, which are indebted to the works of Freud, Jung, Fanon, Klein, and Lacan, among others. I am equally grateful to the work of sociologists and literary critics who have helped me to further situate my ideas within contemporary conversations on race. For example, according to Ahad, African-American writers have been interested in psychoanalysis from the early twentieth century, beginning with "Pauline Hopkins's appropriation of William

---

[51] Several critical pieces on racial passing have been published over the past several years that underscore its continued relevance in literature. Recent examples include Sinead Moynihan's *Passing into the Present: Contemporary American Fiction of Racial and Gender Passing* (2010), which examines the connection between the trope of passing and textuality because literary passing is now expansive enough to encompass questions of authorship. Moreover, Michele Elam's *The Souls of Mixed Folk* (2011) engages with cultural renderings of the mixed-raced subject in contemporary literature, art, and television, to argue for a poetics of social justice during the "mulatto millennium." Historians revisit the topic of racial passing frequently, by documenting the lives of real-life passing subjects to understand the history of the color line in America. In 2009, Martha Sandweiss published *Passing Strange: A Gilded Age Tale of Love and Deception Across the Color Line*, which details the life of Clarence King, a White nineteenth-century geologist who passed as Black to marry a Black woman. Vanderbilt University law professor Daniel Sharfstein published *The Invisible Line* (2011), which is a sweeping history of three families who have been jumping the color line from the eighteenth century until now: the Gibsons, the Walls, and the Spencers. Allyson Hobbs, a historian at Stanford University, published *A Chosen Exile: A History of Racial Passing in American Life* (2014), which focuses on the lives of those who passed as White from the 1800s through the 1950s. She highlights the points of convergence and divergence across the decades, but the theme that unites the passing subjects in her study is that of loss.

James's notion of the unconscious or the 'hidden self' in her novel *Of One Blood: The Hidden Self* (1902–3)."⁵² White authors also explore race and passing in their works, as evidenced by the fiction of Vera Caspary and Philip Roth. Black and White authors referring to psychoanalysis for much of the past century—especially when it came to meditations on the color line—further compels readers to understand racial passing as a distinctly American phenomenon. This book explores the ways in which those meditations are played out in the literary imagination of racial passing narratives.

The ideas put forth in this monograph are speculative, particularly the correlations between psychoanalysis and racial passing. Yet Freud himself advocated for unique interpretations. He believed that individuals should pursue bold hypotheses, which he modeled himself as a psychoanalyst to his patients. The epigraph to this introduction comes from Rubén Gallo's groundbreaking book *Freud's Mexico: Into the Wilds of Psychoanalysis* (2015), which advances several new premises about Freud's relationship with Mexico—a country he never visited but clearly influenced. This highly imaginative and nuanced reading of Freud underscores the transatlantic reach of his theories and demonstrates the influence that Mexico had on Freud. I am most fascinated by using antiquities to comprehend Freud, since they became his "instruments for writing, thinking, and even analyzing patients."⁵³ Freud placed several of them on or near his desk and often talked to them, treating them all as "universal products of the psyche," which Gallo supports by noting "that Chinese and Egyptians, Greeks and Africans, shared the same complexes and phantasies as his Viennese contemporaries."⁵⁴ These artifacts shared space on Freud's desk and symbolized the humans with whom he interacted, since they shared the same internal issues he was tasked with diagnosing and treating. Though he watched his contemporaries become classified by race, complexion, and ethnicity, his work environment purposely created an egalitarian space for objects that came from the areas he studied. His most cherished possessions were artifacts which represented people from around the world. Just as Freud looked at these timeless and diverse artifacts on his desk for solace and inspiration, I look to his field to better comprehend racial passing, since the analytic tools he created were largely informed by

---

⁵² Ahad, *Freud Upside Down*, 3.
⁵³ Gallo, *Freud's Mexico*, 237.
⁵⁴ Gallo, 267.

race. My primary "speculative construction," to use Gallo's striking term, is that jumping the color line is a deeply psychoanalytical endeavor, and psychoanalysis is a deeply racialized endeavor. The rest of this monograph elucidates this connection.

CHAPTER 1

RACE-LEARNING AND THE TRAUMA OF PASSING

Classroom Trauma and Racial Passing

Brando Skyhorse and Lisa Page's *We Wear the Mask: 15 True Stories of Passing in America* (2017) is an edited essay collection comprised of fifteen personal essays by individuals who pass in different ways. The contributors reflect on transcending categories of race, class, educational status, sexuality, and religion, among other seemingly rigid boundaries. Though they come from divergent backgrounds, the one thing that unites these writers is school, as they observe the ways in which education and passing intersect. For instance, Brando Skyhorse's opening essay, "College Application Essay #2," begins with his recollection of applying to college "as an American Indian named Brando Skyhorse" despite being the son of two Mexicans.[1] His mother passed as American Indian and told him to as well, but he took her directive seriously only after realizing that rendering himself an American Indian would help his application "rise to the top of the affirmative action pool."[2]

While Brando Skyhorse passed in order to get into school, other writers admitted that school contributed to their racial passing. For example, Teresa Wiltz invokes Du Bois in sharing her memory of elementary school classmates distributing birthday party invitations to everyone except her, causing her to find solace in literature instead of her classmates. She learned how to read books by "Dr. Seuss and Grimm's fairy tales, [and] comic books about Martin Luther King Jr.," but when in school with "all those ruby-lipped white kids, I couldn't remember the alphabet."[3] She does not correct her peers when they mistake her for Puerto Rican. For Trey Ellis, "passing as a real prof" is his way of hiding the fact that he is a professor of arts at Columbia University, but has a "lowly and decades-old BA."[4] Though hearing the unfamiliar word "indexicality" at a lecture opens his ruminations about passing

---

[1] Skyhorse and Page, *We Wear the Mask*, 1.
[2] Skyhorse and Page, 2.
[3] Skyhorse and Page, 69.
[4] Skyhorse and Page, 77–78.

as a professor, he acknowledges a "lifetime of various passings" long before sitting at this conference table.[5] He did not see the need to pass racially when he enrolled as a high school student at Phillips Academy years before, but he admits to being "determined to reinvent myself as the mysterious new kid."[6] As these writers make clear, a major theme unifying this essay collection is that school and passing are intricately tethered.

Given the importance of education in subject formation, it should come as no surprise that school appears prominently in an edited collection on passing, as well as in theoretical constructions. According to Louis Althusser's theory of subject formation, the subject develops within two social structures, the Repressive State Apparatus, which includes heads of state, government, police, courts, and the military, designed to intervene in favor of the ruling class by using all types of violence to repress the ruled class, and the Ideological State Apparatus, which refers to "distinct and specialized institutions" that are mostly private and function predominantly via ideology.[7] A prime example of this is school, especially since children endure "a capitalist education system" designed specifically to teach "the rules of good behaviour" that will directly lead to employment.[8] He summarizes the utility of school in capitalist society as the place that teaches "subjection to the ruling ideology" to ensure a productive labor force.[9] Absent from his formulation, however, is a discussion of race.[10] His focus on a capitalist argument overlooks the intersection of class and race, yet the two have a direct effect on each other.

---

[5] Skyhorse and Page, 85.
[6] Skyhorse and Page, 86.
[7] Althusser, "Ideology and Ideological State Apparatuses," 143.
[8] Althusser, 132.
[9] Althusser, 133, emphasis in original.
[10] Race is secondary to Althusser's theory because of his Marxist focus on class. Stuart Hall's "Race, Articulation and Societies Structured in Dominance" is an important intervention on the connections between Althusserian theory and race. More specifically, Hall argues that there are two major trajectories that arise from the study of race, economic and sociological, and neither one can explain race exclusively. Instead, he uses a Structuralist Marxist perspective to examine the confluence of these categories. Also building upon Althusser is *Race, Nation, Class: Ambiguous Identities*, by Etienne Balibar and Immanuel Wallerstein. This essay collection argues that, as a result of contemporary iterations of capitalism, racism is inherently essential in discussions of nationalist ideologies. By implication, racism will not end as long as capitalist systems continue.

Moreover, education provides a litmus test for understanding the history of American racism. Before the Civil War, slave literacy was illegal, as evidenced when Mr. Auld forbids Mrs. Auld from teaching literacy to a young Frederick Douglass.[11] Beginning in Reconstruction, Jim Crow laws kept African-Americans in a social and economic chokehold after the *Plessy v. Ferguson* Supreme Court decision (1896). The "separate but equal" doctrine of legalized segregation meant that African-Americans were systematically denied access to basic privileges that White Americans took for granted, especially the ability to receive a standard education and attend integrated schools.

Once the twentieth century began, school became one of the most contested spaces for racial progress, as Booker T. Washington and W. E. B. Du Bois articulated. The former believed that schools should teach African-Americans vocational skills, while the latter challenged educators to offer liberal arts curricula to cultivate the Black elite. Du Bois also noted that African-Americans needed a liberal arts education to combat the impediments of racism; he felt the proudest of himself—or as he euphemizes, "the sky was bluest"—when his intellect surpassed that of his peers.[12] Washington and Du Bois agreed that the education system did not serve Black students adequately because of its highly racialized nature. After the *Brown v. Board of Education* ruling ended school segregation (1954), students were still forced into separate spaces while stereotypes against Black students remained. Seventy years after this landmark case, African-American students still face an education system that treats them poorly compared to their White counterparts. Given this brief gloss over the racialized history of America's educational system, it is no wonder that Black students who are light enough to pass as anything but Black have done so through their interactions in school. This chapter takes the conjoining of school and race as a point of departure to assert that racial passing begins long before Black students reach adulthood: learning about race through school is the primary impetus for jumping the color line.

School is the initial place where children from different backgrounds are thrown into forced interactions with each other, thereby complicating rigid racial boundaries. As a result, it emerges as a site of trauma for Black students who encounter White students and teachers for the very first time. Many critics agree that school is a traumatic space that hastens subject formation.

---

[11] Douglass, *Narrative*, 40–41.
[12] Du Bois, *The Souls of Black Folk*, 214.

For instance, Toni Morrison believes that education "implicitly and explicitly introduces expectations of normalcy, of standard cultural practices, and of aesthetic valuation...tacit instructions for social and political relations, naturalizing racism, too, in all its subtle forms."[13] Robert Stepto asserts that the Black subject is "made aware for the first time that he or she is colored" while in school, particularly since "the schoolhouse episode is a staple event in African-American narratives no doubt because it is remembered or imagined as a formative *first scene* of racial self-awareness."[14] Bergner takes it a step further, noting that scenes of racial discovery are not just visual events, in that "characters assume a racial identity not so much by seeing skin color as by *learning* its cultural significance."[15] Being raced in school offers the first lesson for Black students: in the American calculus of race, Whiteness is the pillar of superiority and privilege. To enjoy some of the privileges, Black students who are able to pass begin to do so in school.

Before these critics shared their meditations on the importance of school for subject formation, Frantz Fanon published his own theories in *Black Skin, White Masks* (1952). Fanon's premise is that Blacks seek Whiteness due to the psychological effects of colonialism, which he explores through sexuality, language, behavior, and education, among other domains. According to Fanon, the classroom is critical to racialized subject formation because "if there is a traumatism, it occurs here [in school]."[16] This is due to the type of education forced onto Black students, one which erases their history in favor of a whitewashed one that equates Blackness with negativity and malice.[17] Another reason lies in the fact that the classroom is the first space where Black and White children interact with each other and learn the significance of their racial difference. With this first interaction, Black children become "abnormal at the slightest contact with the white world."[18] He also argues that

---

[13] Quoted in Elam, *The Souls of Mixed Folk*, 28.

[14] Stepto, *A Home Elsewhere*, 27, emphasis mine.

[15] Bergner, *Taboo Subjects*, xv, emphasis mine.

[16] Fanon, *Black Skin, White Masks*, 127.

[17] Toni Morrison uses this language of trauma as well. According to her, "everybody remembers the first time they were taught that part of the human race was Other. That's a trauma. It's as though I told you that your left hand is not part of your body." For more on Morrison's remarks on school and race, see Bonnie Angelo, "The Pain of Being Black: An Interview with Toni Morrison."

[18] Fanon, *Black Skin*, 122.

schools contribute to the cultural trauma that provides a racial neurosis for Black subjects.

Black Skin, White Masks is groundbreaking for its application of psychoanalysis in understanding racism and colonialism. Up until its publication, psychoanalytic scholarship on colonized subjects justified colonialism by reiterating stereotypes that were imbedded in classical psychoanalysis. Fanon, however, "provides a theoretical model for adapting psychoanalysis to study political, economic, and gendered forces of racialization."[19] Indeed, he modifies Freud's inquiry, "what does a woman want," to ask, "what does the Black man want," to contend that the childhood trauma that Freud uses as a starting point for his theories, is a trauma of racism and colonialism, specifically for Black children. Bergner reminds us that Fanon's "study of colonial race relations inaugurates a politicized psychoanalytic discourse of race," though he does not write from an African-American standpoint specifically.[20] He argues that colonization caused Black subjectivity to be predicated on an inferiority complex, thereby leading to a perpetual desire to imitate White colonizers.

What Fanon accomplishes, then, is to revise psychoanalysis popularized by Freud (itself predicated on Freud's own anxieties with race) to create a theory specifically for Black subjects. Though Fanon was well aware that psychoanalysis had its limitations with addressing race, he strategically uses specific elements of the theory to advance his own theory of Black subject formation. My book is equally invested in using key elements of psychoanalysis to posit theories of subject formation specifically for racial passers. For example, Fanon believes that the desire to become White stems from racialized childhood trauma, which explains why some Blacks would endure drastic measures to "whiten the race [and] save the race."[21] A hypothetical "denegrification serum" would allow the "Black man [to] whiten himself and thus rid himself of the burden of this bodily curse."[22] He creates a theoretical space for racial passing which Sigmund Freud could only allude to. This chapter continues Fanon's line of inquiry that school is a place of subject formation for the Black subject by arguing that learning about race in school has a deep

---

[19] Bergner, *Taboo Subjects*, xxix.
[20] Bergner, xxix.
[21] Fanon, *Black Skins*, 91.
[22] Fanon, 91.

traumatic effect on African-American youth and, as a result, the ones who are able to racially pass do so. They endure what I call a "race-learning," in that learning about race in school encourages them to jump the color line. Though this also happens with real racial passers (such as Anatole Broyard, who will be discussed in chapter three), I begin with the abundant examples of fictional passers to show the influence that formal education has on racial education.

Fanon was hardly the only twentieth-century psychoanalyst who theorized subject formation after studying youth. One of Anna Freud's disciples, Erik Erikson, devoted the second half of the twentieth century to formulating the *Stages of Psychosocial Development*. According to Erikson, there are eight stages of psychosocial development, with each one corresponding to specific relationships, stages, strengths, and rituals. Erikson names each stage a "Psychosocial Crisis," a phrase I want to emphasize because he notes a conflict in each stage, which parallels the racial conflicts that passers typically endure. Before diving into Erikson's theories, we must uncover the two main areas that influenced his theorization: children and race. For the former, he often observed children at play in order to advance his theories, believing that children at play predict their behaviors as adults. In looking back at his works, he recalls his "first paper" published in the United States, "Configurations in Play" (1937), in which he observed children at play and analyzed their behaviors.[23] He further notes that inhibition is lost during the play age, especially since children at play demonstrate "the lifelong power of human playfulness in all the arts. In playfulness is grounded, also, all sense of humor, man's specific gift to laugh at himself as well as at others."[24] Observing children at play thus became the impetus for the rest of his theories of development, collected as *The Life Cycle Completed* (1982).

Erikson not only saw the importance of analyzing the behavior of children, but he was also sympathetic to matters of race and ethnicity. He deeply understood all the events happening around him while he researched and published, arguing that medical centers welcomed psychoanalysis in the 1930s and 1940s in part because of "growing world turbulence."[25] For instance, he published the provocative essay "The Concept of Identity in Race Relations: Notes and Queries" in 1966—at the height of the Civil Rights

---

[23] Erikson, *The Life Cycle Completed*, 22.
[24] Erikson, 77.
[25] Erikson, 11.

Movement. As the title attests, he posits his ideas about identity development for African-Americans. Citing Du Bois, James Baldwin, and Ralph Ellison, Erikson highlights "an absence of identity or the prevalence of what we will call negative identity elements" in the works of these critics. Invoking Fanon, Erikson believes those who belong "to an oppressed and exploited minority" often fuse the negative images "held up by the dominant majority," with their own "negative identity."[26] He also raises questions about integration, wondering if "desegregation, compensation, balance, [and] re-conciliation," would truly "save the Negro at the cost of an absorption which he is not sure will leave much of himself left?"[27] Erikson thus views Black identity as an absence or lack, particularly given the history of slavery and racism that defined the United States.

Erikson's critics have further discussed race and ethnicity throughout his writings. For instance, Aerika Brittian asserts in her article "Understanding African American Adolescents' Identity Development: A Relational Developmental Systems Perspective" that "issues of race may complicate the search for an adaptive identity," citing Erikson's aforementioned article from 1966.[28] Perhaps the most important "adaptive identity" is that of racial passing, since the subjects of my own research all attempt to create an adaptive identity using their lighter complexion. More recently, in 2018, Moin Syed and Jillian Fish published "Revisiting Erik Erikson's Legacy on Culture, Race, and Ethnicity," in which they demonstrate a deep understanding of Erikson's legacy of race and psychoanalysis. Among their many assertions, Syed and Fish observe "that Erikson's work suggests that historical trauma serves as an ideological setting for the identity development of marginalized groups."[29] Indeed, Erikson's widely cited text *Identity: Youth and Crisis* (1968) contains a chapter devoted to the matter of race and ethnicity. According to Syed and Fish, members of an "oppressed and exploited minority" often internalize society's negative views and develop self-hatred.[30] This is borne out by an examination of racial passers, whose identity development is complicated by

---

[26] Erikson, "The Concept of Identity in Race Relations," 155.
[27] Erikson, 160.
[28] Brittian, "Understanding African American Adolescents' Identity Development," 175.
[29] Syed and Fish, "Revisiting Erik Erikson's Legacy," 276.
[30] Syed and Fish, 303.

slavery and its racist legacy; specifically, they develop their negative identity characteristics after realizing their position as "oppressed members" in a White-dominated society.

Erikson made these assertions through his extensive arguments on the structural nature of race and identity, meaning he "focused extensively on the legacy of colonialism and slavery and how they had constrained African American identity options."[31] By highlighting the lingering effects of slavery and colonialism, he stands in sharp contrast to the more recent, yet short-sighted idea of "postrace," which argues that we are now beyond racism. On the contrary, Erikson noted that slavery and colonialism are "ongoing oppressive forces that shape opportunities for positive development" as Syed and Fish summarize.[32] Fanon influenced Erikson's theorization, but as Syed and Fish note, it was Erikson himself who clearly demonstrated "how being systematically undermined informs identity development," especially for those in societies dominated by Whites.[33] These examples serve to contextualize his ideas about identity formation, as well as situate him alongside the work of Fanon. Like Freud before him, Erikson had race in mind when developing his psychoanalytic theory of the Stages of Psychosocial Development, yet he was far more explicit in utilizing race in his research than his predecessor. Fanon, writing out of a decolonial context, took it a step further and centered race in his theorizations. Indeed, Fanon "transposes psychoanalysis…to a register where it would account for race as one of the fundamental differences that constitutes subjectivity."[34] He argues that racial passers redefine what it means to get an education, since they are sent to school to learn race as a constitutive aspect of identity.

Both Erikson and Fanon are essential to understanding the impetus behind characters jumping the color line. Building on their perspectives, I develop my own theory of race-learning by exploring the ways in which education is traumatically raced in school by closely reading Charles Chesnutt's *The House Behind the Cedars* (1900), James Weldon Johnson's *The Autobiography of an Ex-Colored Man* (1912), Jessie Fauset's *Plum Bun: A Novel Without a Moral* (1929), and Danzy Senna's *Caucasia* (1999). The preconditions

---

[31] Syed and Fish, 278.
[32] Syed and Fish, 278.
[33] Syed and Fish, 280.
[34] Bergner, *Taboo Subjects*, 2.

for passing traditionally include light skin color, silence, stealth, and a desire for middle-class respectability. This chapter adds education, literal and symbolic, as a formative and traumatic site for twentieth-century passing narratives. By exploring this range of passing narratives through the lens of school, I make the case that formal education allows for a racial education, which inevitably leads to passing. Moreover, racial passers seem to be stuck in stage five of Erikson's Stages of Psychosocial Development, *Identity versus Role Confusion*, as they attempt to determine which identity to assume. Although trauma theorists have dominated literary study over the past two decades, work on the intersection of trauma and racial passing remains scant.[35] This chapter adds to the scholarship of passing and race by asserting that racial passing is the manifestation of a severe racial trauma at school.

Just as duality hovers over the lives of those who jump the color line as part of their education into race, it informs my own theory. Indeed, my goals for this chapter are twofold: primarily, I upend the conventionally held notion that passing is only a form of resistance. Readers of these narratives take for granted that characters jump the color line strictly to avoid dealing with racial prejudice, especially during the Jim Crow era. For instance, the Ex-Colored Man observes a lynching in a pivotal scene that critics often adduce as evidence that his passing begins only after witnessing it. He notes his "shame" with belonging to a race in which bodies can be burned, mutilated, and discarded at public spectacles and begins pondering "the Negro question" as a result.[36] Harryette Mullen believes this is precisely the point where the Ex-Colored Man's race-shifting begins. He does not explicitly use the language of passing, however; his rhetoric is of one who will remain passive about the ways in which people will categorize him.[37] She believes that he crosses the color line because this is "preferable to the loss of life of the Black man

---

[35] Critics like Jennifer L. Griffiths and Anne Cheng have written exemplary texts on the intersection of trauma theory and race. However, when it comes to trauma and the subcategory of racial passing, little has been said. My argument for this chapter, then, is that the classroom is a site of trauma for Black children who have no other choice but to pass. For more on race and trauma, see Griffith's *Traumatic Possessions: The Body and Memory in African-American Women's Writing and Performance* (2010); and Cheng's *The Melancholy of Race: Psychoanalysis, Assimilation, and Hidden Grief* (2001).

[36] Johnson, *Autobiography of an Ex-Colored Man*, 497–98.

[37] Mullen, "Optic White: Blackness and the Production of Whiteness," 76.

burned alive, whose horrific public execution by a white mob determines the narrator's decision to pass…and escape the stigma of Blackness."[38] However, as Randall Kennedy rightly observes, "passing long hovers in the background" of the plot.[39] This "hovering" begins in school for the Ex-Colored Man, as well as the protagonists analyzed in this chapter. For them, passing is not only a choice but is the logical end result of the trauma of race-learning. My secondary goal in this chapter is to advance a new theory for the different ways in which men and women begin passing, which also becomes useful for reassessing the real and fictional narratives in the remainder of this monograph. Parents actively thwart discussions of race for their sons, which explains why being rendered Black at school is such a pivotal moment for them. Black girls, however, first hear about passing long before race becomes a problem in school. According to *Plum Bun* and *Caucasia*, daughters learn about passing as a response from their mothers, but this knowledge is not concretized until they become raced in the classroom. Redefining traditional views of passing in this way helps us to expand our understanding of the connections between school and race: education emerges as one area where African-Americans pass.

Racial passing requires a long-term willingness to achieve the ideals of Whiteness. Looking carefully at each protagonist's diction suggests that physical violence cannot be the sole impetus for passing because this latter phenomenon comes first, vis-à-vis education. This logic complicates the beginnings of when African-Americans pass by asserting that it is not simply violence but racial hypervisibility that initiates it. According to Erikson and Fanon, the reason that African-Americans struggle to completely function in society is due to a subconscious belief that all things rendered Black, including skin color, are inherently wrong. The epistemic violence of education predates the threat of any physical violence for racial passers, explaining why they search for mirrors and books for validation of their Blackness after their race-learning.

In arguing that Black subjects are afflicted with divided identities, Fanon turns to Du Bois's *Souls of Black Folk* to create a psychoanalytic extension of the "double consciousness." Each character's double consciousness develops in more ways than Du Bois could have predicted: John Warwick, the Ex-Colored Man, Angela Murray, and Birdie Lee all transition into another

---

[38] Mullen, 87.
[39] Kennedy, *Interracial Intimacies*, 311.

world instead of inhabiting both the Black and White ones. They share the rhetoric of duality to represent their collective movements while seeking answers about their phenotypes. In twentieth-century passing narratives, race-learning in school propels Black children to pass if their lighter complexion allows for it. Brando Skyhorse, Teresa Wiltz, and Trey Ellis did not begin passing in a vacuum; they had many literary precursors of school-inspired passing narratives from which to draw. Continuing Fanon's and Erikson's line of thinking, this chapter explores the psychoanalytic underpinnings of race-learning, by arguing that it is the initial trauma (and not physical violence) that leads to passing.

"We Knew He Was Colored": Trauma and Passing for John Warwick and the Ex-Colored Man

Twentieth century fictional and nonfictional racial passers follow a similar trajectory: education yields racialization. This is first evident in two passing novels published in the early twentieth century, Charles Chesnutt's *The House Behind the Cedars* (1900) and James Weldon Johnson's *The Autobiography of an Ex-Colored Man* (1912). These Black writers were invested in psychoanalysis—the nascent field which "was originally explicated in Sigmund Freud's 1899 text, *The Interpretation of Dreams*."[40] Chesnutt's *House* is the story of John and Rena Warwick, the children of Molly Walden—a free, mixed-race woman—and her nameless and absent White benefactor. Fathers are notoriously absent or aloof in the lives of racial passers. Equally absent are discussions of race. *The House Behind the Cedars* does not include any lessons about race passed down from Molly to her biracial children, which raises the question of whether she remained silent out of complete oblivion about Blackness or purposely equivocated on race in order to hide the implications of their Black ancestry.

John Warwick provides no answers to this question in the first section, which focuses entirely on his racial passing in the post-Reconstruction south. The novel begins with John returning to his maternal home in North Carolina after residing for several years in South Carolina. Yet his visit is hardly one to reaffirm family ties: he returns home only because "he needs a caretaker

---

[40] Ahad, *Freud Upside Down*, 3.

for his now-motherless son and promises to Rena the wide world of white opportunity."[41] This "white opportunity" is a euphemism for his true goal, which is to "convince [his] sister Rena to return with him to South Carolina to pass and seek her fortune as a white gentlewoman."[42] Molly perceives a problem based on the secrecy shrouding her son's surprise trip and her suspicions that her daughter might never return. Though the text does not initially clarify the reasons for John's secrecy, the narrative clues suggest that whatever has transpired previously can barely be spoken of, lest it compromise John's now privileged position which forced him to cut his familial ties in the first place.

John's race-learning helps to explain his furtive movements, since it demonstrates his gradual realization of race which develops in two scenes. Part one of his race-learning occurs at school when he first learns that he is Black.

> He was informed one day that he was Black. He denied the proposition and thrashed the child who made it. The scene was repeated the next day with variation,—he was himself thrashed by a larger boy. When he had been beaten five or six times, he ceased to argue the point, though to himself he never admitted the charge. He [referring to God] must have meant him to be white.[43]

This opening section exemplifies several key elements of passing narratives. For one, John returns home without anyone knowing about it, thus establishing a shroud of secrecy that hovers over his movements. Those who jump the color line always remain in stealth; a return home is a dangerous endeavor because it increases the likelihood of racial discovery. His race-learning suggests that he previously considered himself White; nobody taught him about his Blackness. John realizes that there is something different about him, which sets him apart from his White peers. This "difference" is one that he does not initially perceive, responding violently to his classmate's revelation. The violent thrashing symbolizes the nameless student's attempt to beat it into John that he is indeed Black and John's vehement denial of the Blackness that he literally tries to beat back. Being beaten several times does not convince him that he is Black; instead, he believed it was God's will for him "to

---

[41] Ryan, "Rena's Two Bodies," 39.
[42] Belluscio, *To Be Suddenly White*, 140.
[43] Chesnutt, *House*, 373.

be white."⁴⁴ Indeed, even after several fights, he continues to contradict his peer and does not admit to being Black.

At first, it might appear that John's refusal to continue fighting suggests passive acceptance of his Blackness, yet he requires further proof and seeks racial validation by examining himself in a mirror. This move is telling, since the mirror emerges as an important area of focus for Lacanian psychoanalysis. Jacques Lacan delivered a speech entitled "The Mirror Stage as Formative of the I Function" (1949), in which he argues that the mirror stage occurs when a child first sees himself in a mirror. Before this point, the child does not understand the separation between himself and the world around him. He considers himself fragmented after being aware he has hands and feet, but not aware they are connected to the rest of his body. Seeing the reflection in the mirror, however, shows him his complete body for the first time, providing him with the sense that all his body parts are connected and he can move them at once. He also discovers the division in the world between what he can move and what he cannot. This stage underscores his conception of himself as different from everything and everyone else.

Though Lacan is speaking about a stage in a child's development, passing narratives both preempt and literalize this stage. Lacan's hypothesis is compelling, but it does not "address the implications of racial difference."⁴⁵ In an essay that maps the mirror stage onto racial development for *The House Behind the Cedars* and *The Autobiography of an Ex-Colored Man*, Sheehy observes that when passing figures view their reflections in mirrors, it "marks a point at which the enigmatic American dialogue of race is resolved into a single human being."⁴⁶ For John Warwick, what the outside world sees is merely a construction that contradicts how he sees himself as he processes the trauma of being raced in school. The image mirrored back to him is strange and frightening; as such, a splitting occurs where he sees himself as White according to God's mandate, despite being rendered Black by his classmates. There is a lack of phenotypical markers to "prove" his Whiteness to his classmates, thus the visual validation becomes a primary indication of his doubt regarding his race after being called out at school. The mirror, which John turned to in search of phenotypical verification, is not what it purports to be

---

⁴⁴ Chesnutt, 373.
⁴⁵ Sheehy, "The Mirror and the Veil," 401.
⁴⁶ Sheehy, 402.

for passing characters. Instead of being a site of identity consolidation and unity, it is one of ambivalence, identity confusion, and further splitting. In short, the mirror stage for passers develops into an actual mirror that reveals their complexion and forces them into a racial consciousness.

John follows up this mirror image in the second part of his race-learning, where he retreats into his mother's library. While there, he enjoys Molly's "small but remarkable collection of books," which includes the works of Henry Fielding, Walter Scott, Cervantes, Milton, Shakespeare, the Bible, and Pilgrim's Progress.[47] Molly is completely illiterate yet encourages her children to attain the education she never received. As a result, this library does not serve her as well as it serves her son, for he turns to it in ways that she cannot. Much like seeing mirror images, turning to literature is typical of passing narratives: it not only furthers the education of Black youth who belatedly discover their Blackness, but also suggests that they seek validation through literature after failing to gain visual validation by examining their reflection in the mirror. Those who jump the color line interpret literature just as they themselves are often (mis)interpreted by society. In John's case, his voracious appetite for books motivates him to pursue a legal career. During a lengthy exchange in which the formidable Judge Archibald Straight attempts to read John's dedication to his newfound desire to be a lawyer, Straight dismisses him with "You want to be a lawyer....You are aware, of course, that you are a Negro" (378); "You are Black, and you are not free;" and "[You are] Black as ink, my lad…[because] one drop of Black blood makes the whole man Black."[48] The diction of ink inadvertently anticipates a similar image used several decades later by Fanon, when he argues that "the Other fixes me with his gaze, his gestures and attitude, the same way you fix a preparation with a dye."[49] Though the theorist specifically refers to the person on the train who proclaims "Look! A Negro!" when seeing him, the concept underlying this exchange applies to Chesnutt's novel and passing narratives as a whole: perceptions of skin color are written onto the skin regardless of the actual color of the skin. Judge Straight is the "other," who hyperbolically assigns the darkest skin color, or the "dye," to the future lawyer by rendering his phenotype "Black ink." This imagery also anticipates the title of Philip Roth's novel, *The*

---

[47] Chesnutt, *House*, 373–74.
[48] Chesnutt, 379.
[49] Fanon, *Black Skin*, 89.

Human Stain, in that Blackness is portrayed as a tangible "stain" that passers seek to erase.

Judge Straight educates the wide-eyed John on the impediments he would face as a Black attorney. Not only is it illegal for "men of color to practice the law," it is also taboo because "public sentiment would not allow" for this transgression of the social order.[50] John maintains his stance, arguing that his light complexion is tantamount to unequivocal Whiteness, thereby ignoring his Black ancestry. Only after learning about the one-drop rule does he fully begin to comprehend the meaning of his race. While John views his actual body as the source of his identity, Judge Straight teaches him that his body only has meaning in what the social order ascribes to him. He uses it as justification for his new identity, when he proclaims, "From this time on, I am white," before brokering a deal to clean Straight's office in exchange for studying his legal books in stealth. This scene ends with the eighteen-year-old John leaving his family indefinitely, prompting Molly's sorrowful prediction that "he's gone over on the other side"—her euphemism for both the other side of the Carolina border and of the color line.

This second scene reveals the extent of John's race-learning, which prompted his racial passing. In the first scene at school, John angrily defends his Whiteness with his classmate through fighting; in this second scene, his belligerence is replaced initially by obstinance, then acceptance about what his skin should mean regardless of its actual color, in light of his conversation with Judge Straight. Additionally, the use of the mirror is not just a literary trope but also a meta-commentary on John's progression, since instances from his pre-passing stage are revised for his passing phase as the two parts of his life begin to mirror each other. Apprenticeship was the primary means of attaining a legal education in the nineteenth century, and the school setting from the first scene becomes the more intimate venue of a legal office. Judge Straight serves as John's educator for his dual apprenticeships into the law and into race.

The narrative's use of apprenticeship helps readers situate John as an example of Erikson's fifth stage of Psychosocial Development. Each stage is characterized by a specific age range, a psychosocial crisis, virtues, and significant relationships. Stage Five, for instance, is the adolescent stage and corresponds with puberty, when youth face the psychosocial crisis of *Identity versus*

---

[50] Chesnutt, *House*, 380.

Identity Confusion when they attempt to discover their true identity. During this stage, they seek models of leadership, often through peer groups and out-groups, and their basic strength is fidelity. Furthermore, "an identity formation is impossible without some role repudiation, especially where the available roles endanger the young individual's potential identity synthesis."[51] Erikson notes that "adolescence and the ever more protracted apprenticeship of the later school and college years can, as we saw, be viewed as a *psychosocial moratorium*: a period of sexual and cognitive maturation and yet a sanctioned postponement of definitive commitment."[52] As the scene above suggests, John fits within the *Identity versus Identity Confusion* stage, for he has to be convinced that he is indeed Black. Being thrashed by his classmate was not enough; neither was looking at his reflection in the mirror. Only after Judge Straight repeats the phrase 'you are Black,' is John convinced of his race. He then decides to repudiate his Blackness and render himself White. In doing so, he seeks a leader in Judge Straight, or as the text accurately puts it, an *apprenticeship*. Ostensibly, John becomes an apprentice to learn about the law, but it also teaches him about race as he seeks a (White) model of leadership he cannot find in his home. When seen through Erikson's terms, then, John's introduction to the legal profession further motivates him to pass—the ultimate manifestation of Stage Five, when the existential questions include "who am I and who can I be?" as youth engage in an identity crisis.

John's legal apprenticeship inevitably includes knowledge of the law, explaining one reason why he is surrounded by Straight's books, yet books are also symbolic for racial passers. While John views the legal library as "the portal of a new world, peopled with strange and marvelous beings," he also understands the transformative impact reading has on him: after reading all the books, "the blood of his white fathers, the heirs of the ages, cried out for its own, and after the manner of that blood set about getting the object of its desire."[53] John reads about other people's lives through literature, which inspires him to contrive his own life through his White ancestors. He then follows up by speaking with Judge Straight, who allows John to "surreptitiously read the law books."[54] Though reading in stealth is a slave trope, John's end

---

[51] Erikson, *The Life Cycle Completed*, 74.
[52] Erikson, 75, emphasis in original.
[53] Chesnutt, *House*, 374–75.
[54] Chesnutt, 381.

goal is to forge a White identity for himself through passing—which is also tethered to slavery. The library of his youth is replaced by Straight's legal repertoire, suggesting that the realization of Blackness is incomplete unless it entails a search for literary validation. To endure a race-learning then, means African-Americans discover their Blackness in school and in books, thereby explaining why racial passing is often juxtaposed to multiple types of reading.

The retreat into literature is a step towards passing, which John views as a "rational decision" yet one that "collides with the social realities of race and has inevitable familial consequences."[55] For John Warwick, proximity to his family can complicate his time as a lawyer and as a racial passer, thus, he metaphorically kills off his relatives to thwart the potential of racial exposure. Erikson addressed the desire to repudiate one's family when theorizing Stage Five of Psychosocial Development, by arguing that this stage includes youth transferring "the need for guidance from parental figures to mentors and leaders."[56] One of the effects of jumping the color line is the complete denial and removal of one's family, a theme that appears throughout passing narratives as a measure of safety and practicality. The novel itself takes it a step further by killing John off. Midway through the narrative, he drops out of it completely and his story is replaced by Rena's story. John has to exit the narrative because of his identity crisis, especially when seen through an Eriksonian lens.[57] He deals with the dilemma of neglecting his Blackness to assume the identity of a White lawyer, while the narrative allows him space to contend with this identity confusion by prioritizing Rena's story. In doing so, the text

---

[55] Wilson, "Reading *The Human Stain* Through Charles W. Chesnutt," 140.

[56] Erikson, *The Life Cycle Completed*, 73.

[57] Melissa Ryan notes that John "vanish[es] from the novel as if he had never been" (40), while William Andrews dismisses John altogether. In *The Literary Career of Charles W. Chesnutt*, Andrews claims that the novel consists of two unconnected halves: "what might be entitled 'Rena in White Society'…[and] what might be called 'Rena in Black Society'" (151). Ryan and Andrews are less concerned with the question of what happens to John after he travels to "the other side" of both the Carolina border and the color line, but Chesnutt insists that Rena's story helps to complete the mirroring of John's life. For more on the role Rena plays in the story, see Melissa Ryan, "Rena's Two Bodies: Gender and Whiteness in Charles Chesnutt's *The House Behind the Cedars*"; and Daniel Worden, "Birth in the Briar Patch: Charles W. Chesnutt and the Problem of Racial Identity."

affirms that John remains stuck in Stage Five, without offering much closure on his racial identity.

Like her brother, Rena's race becomes a problem primarily in school. After learning about Rena's Blackness, her fellow teacher applicants—who are preparing for a teacher's examination—protest having to sit with her, forcing Rena to complete the examination two hours after the White teachers. While she passes the test, she fails to pass as White. Years later, she renounces passing to embrace her Blackness while teaching at a Black school, prompting the mother of one of her White suitors to urge her to pass again: "If you choose to conceal it, no one would ever be the wiser."[58] This brother and sister tale demonstrates the connection between hypervisible race and school; the former is made explicit in the latter.[59] John Warwick can only pass after learning the significance of his Blackness, as his interactions in the schoolyard and in the office of Judge Straight attest. Understanding race is traumatic for him, and he must shift from Black to White as a result of not wanting to deal with being hypervisible. In parallel academic contexts, both his bully and mentor remind him that being Black is a major impediment, not only as a phenotypical marker but also as a social transgression; they instill Whiteness in him as the ideal. This differs for Rena though. By the time she enters her classroom, her pedagogy is less important than her phenotype, as passing is not the result of her hypervisible Blackness but predates it. Chesnutt portrays Rena as a counterpoint to her brother, since her classroom scene is less focused on her learning about race and more about it being conspicuous to her future colleagues. Thus, he forces readers to grapple with the question of gender, in that both mixed-race Warwick siblings endure completely different racial experiences through school. As will be discussed later in this chapter, African-American women are explicitly encouraged to pass while their male counterparts learn about this through their education.

John Warwick is the first fictional example of a male passer who realizes his Blackness as a student. Even before readers get to the plot, Chesnutt's title serves as our primary indication that covert activities will ensue: references to

---

[58] Chesnutt, *House*, 427.

[59] According to Belluscio, Rena "feels obligated to help less fortunate Blacks, so she becomes a schoolteacher, a profession significant not only because it was one of the only white-collar options for Black women in the postbellum South but also because it implicitly involved a commitment to social and political activism" (217).

the Lebanon cedar appear in the Bible, as it was used to build King Solomon's Temple and to seal David's house, while the height and longevity of cedar trees represent strength. Since cedar trees are tall evergreens, a collection of them can partially or completely hide anything behind them. The novel's title, *The House Behind the Cedars*, thus informs readers up front that cedar trees are obscuring a home in which clandestine activities occur. Within the first few pages of seeing the protagonists pass, we see that the house behind the cedars is a house of racial passers.

Because of his European roots, Charles Chesnutt himself was light enough to pass as White, yet he saw himself as an African-American. Nevertheless, elements of his own life story informed the novel and his other narratives about life on the color line. Through John, Chesnutt sets up a logical progression of "identity crisis leads to passing," a trajectory also taken up by his contemporary, James Weldon Johnson. *The Autobiography of an Ex-Colored Man* was first published anonymously in 1912 to a poor critical reception. In 1927, Alfred A. Knopf republished it, listing Johnson as the author. This version generated a wider readership because it reappeared during a time of increased interest in the lives of African-Americans—the Harlem Renaissance. Despite its title, the text is not a strict autobiography but is a *roman à clef*, a novel depicting real people and events with fictitious names. As with *House*, the title indicates what will transpire within: it is the life story of someone who was "colored" but is no more. How this "man" became "ex-colored" is the plot of the narrative—a plot that centers on race-learning.

This race-learning begins at school for the protagonist.[60] As a young boy in elementary school, the unnamed Ex-Colored Man stands up in class at the request of his teacher, who wants all the White students to rise. She then scolds him by telling him to remain seated because he is actually Black.[61] In response, he slowly comprehends the weight of his phenotype:

> I sat down dazed. I saw and heard nothing. When the others were asked to rise, I did not know it. When school was dismissed, I went out in a kind of stupor. A few of the white boys jeered me, saying:

---

[60] The remainder of this chapter uses "narrator" and "protagonist" interchangeably when discussing the Ex-Colored Man, since the main character serves both roles in this novel.

[61] Johnson, *Autobiography*, 400.

"Oh, you're a nigger too." I heard some Black children say: "We knew he was colored."[62]

Afterwards, he rushes home to examine himself in a mirror and notices his Blackness for the very first time during his literal self-reflection. Recalling previous criticisms about his complexion, he then runs downstairs to ask his mother if he is indeed a "nigger."[63] Though his mother evades the question, one thing that is obvious is the similarity between the Ex-Colored Man's development and John Warwick's. He does not fight the way John does, but his status as an African-American becomes explicitly clear in the classroom; this time, it is the instructor who initiates race-learning and not his classmates. In response, he questions himself with the help of a mirror, where he seeks "visible evidence of his identity—a sign or mark which might brand him indisputable as either Black or white."[64] Much like John, the Ex-Colored Man assumes he can verify how others view him and possibly reconcile it with how he sees himself, but the reflection he sees raises more questions than answers.

Indeed, his reactions after seeing himself suggest that seeing a reflection in a mirror is important in the development of racial passing. The Ex-Colored Man's classmates see something that he cannot determine; there is an imaginary Black shadow hovering over him, which is vastly different from what he can comprehend himself. According to Sheehy, the image that the protagonist sees "must remain fragmented, [he] must deny some part of what he sees in the mirror, leaving him finally with the unresolvable choice between living either as a physically 'white' Black man or as a secretly 'Black' white man."[65] This scene is the beginning of his racial passing, in which he vacillates between Blackness and Whiteness because he is traumatized at being relegated to the former. The first manifestation of this irresolution is his questioning of his mother on whether he is Black, when he crudely renders himself "a nigger." Instead of offering a concrete response, she "tremblingly" replies that his father "is one of the greatest men in the country—the best blood of the South is in you."[66] But the narrator is less concerned with his father's

---

[62] Johnson, 400–401.
[63] Johnson, 401.
[64] Sheehy, "The Mirror and the Veil," 401.
[65] Sheehy, 404, emphasis mine.
[66] Johnson, *Autobiography*, 402.

prominence and more interested in comprehending the meaning of the term "nigger," not realizing that the two are intertwined. In her analysis of the *Autobiography*, Heather Andrade reiterates this by indicating that his mother's nebulous reaction only serves to "assure the narrator's confusion surrounding his racial identity is never resolved."[67] Not only is his White father absent from the narrative, which is the same case for John Warwick, but he also realizes that his sheltered youth did not prepare him to understand his Blackness until it was made hypervisible. The Ex-Colored Man remembers being raised as a "perfect little aristocrat" who dressed well, played the piano well, and divided his time between "music and school books."[68] He often invented games to keep himself occupied, since he lacked playmates and avoided friendships with his peers at church. His mother teaches him his "letters, figures…hymns…and some old Southern songs," in an effort to prevent him from "straying too far from the place of purity and safety."[69] In other words, the narrator did not learn about race in his youth, which affects his reactions to it in school, suggesting that knowledge of race at home might have eased the transition into hypervisible Blackness at school.

The Ex-Colored Man looks back on that day as a crucial one, the day in which the nascent seeds to pass were planted in him. As he articulates, "I have often lived through that hour, that day, that week, in which was wrought the miracle of my transition from one world into another; for I did indeed pass into another world."[70] What he describes is his newfound double consciousness, which Johnson certainly had in mind when he wrote his novel. His invocation of "passing" into a different world is a very provocative one; had the Ex-Colored Man been thinking strictly about his double consciousness, which involves inhabiting two worlds, then he could have used the language of duality. Instead, he takes it one step further by noting his transition into another world, and not simply occupying multiple subjectivities. "Passing into another world" is his euphemism for transgressing racial boundaries, a long-term result of his race-learning.

After the trauma of learning about his race in school, he distances himself from other Black students: "But I do know that when the blow fell, I had

---

[67] Andrade, "Revising Critical Judgments," 261.
[68] Johnson, *Autobiography*, 395–97.
[69] Johnson, 395–96.
[70] Johnson, 403, emphasis mine.

a very strong aversion to being classed with them"—"them" refers to the "Black and brown boys and girls" at his school.[71] Hearing an oration on Touissaint L'Ouverture, which he admits has a Du Boisian "double effect" on him, eventually motivates him to enjoy being Black, and he starts having "wild dreams of bringing glory and honour to the Negro race."[72] Like John, he reads books after being raced in school, but unlike Chesnutt's protagonist, the Ex-Colored Man only reads up on notable Black men throughout history, including L'Ouverture, Frederick Douglass, and Alexandre Dumas. This is after reading the Bible, *Pilgrim's Progress*, and *Natural Theology*, among others, when his mother has to purchase other books to feed his literary appetite after being raced. He is uncertain how to proceed because of the trauma inherent in learning about his Blackness, which his classmates and teacher seemed privy to all along. This uncertainty translates into an attempt to reconcile the White world he thought he inhabited with the Blackness he belatedly finds himself. As such, he initially detaches himself from his classmates before exhibiting pride at Black men who distinguished themselves throughout history.

Like John, the Ex-Colored Man initiates a point that Fanon expounds upon decades later. Learning about Black antiquity, Fanon realizes that Black men have been successful for millennia. He summarizes his epiphany with "the white man was wrong, I was not primitive or a subhuman; I belonged to a race that had already been working silver and gold 2,000 years ago."[73] Fanon reconciles his own feelings of colonized inferiority by studying Black achievements that history overlooked. With Johnson's narrator though, his racialized duality lasts longer as he wavers between the "attraction and repulsion to both Black and White identities."[74] He then spends the rest of his life in a futile attempt to navigate the color line, as he is afflicted with a delayed comprehension of his Blackness in post-Reconstruction America. This forces him to maintain a part of his subjectivity in a place he cannot access because dissociation is his sole recourse in contending with the trauma of race. Despite his mother's deep love of parenting and domesticity, neither of these categories can assist her in teaching him what it means to be Black. School, not his

---

[71] Johnson, 404.
[72] Johnson, 417.
[73] Fanon, *Black Skins*, 109.
[74] Belluscio, *To Be Suddenly White*, 152.

mother's ideal home, is where the Ex-Colored Man learns the most important lesson which she actively avoided: race.

The protagonist's story parallels John Warwick's in yet another psychoanalytic way: both racial passers remain stuck in Erikson's *Identity versus Identity Confusion* stage. As Erikson notes, Stage Five of his theory of Psychosocial Development includes the search for "a lasting sense of self [which] cannot exist without a continuous experience of a conscious 'I,' which is the numinous center of existence."[75] When the Ex-Colored Man examines himself in the mirror, it is a result of his White identity being shattered after being unceremoniously raced at school. He searches for the unified "I" that Erikson defines in his theorization, yet he is unable to detect it, as evidenced by his inquiry to his mother. He does not just ask her if he is "Black" but uses the negative identity term of being a "nigger too" in his inquiry. By doing so, the Ex-Colored Man offers the first indication that he will remain in the fifth stage of Erikson's theory. He is still in this stage a few years later, when he works for the anonymous benefactor who assumes responsibility for his music career. Though by this point, the Ex-Colored Man is physically an adult, the benefactor's purpose in the narrative is to help readers further situate the protagonist's psychosocial development within this stage. If Stage Five entails "transfer[ring] the need for guidance from parental figures to mentors and leaders," as Erikson makes clear, then the Ex-Colored Man turns from seeking guidance from his mother to the mentorship of his benefactor.[76] The benefactor, like Judge Straight in *House*, supports the protagonist's role repudiation by encouraging him to pursue his career as a White musician. In short, John Warwick and the Ex-Colored Man have parallel experiences in their adolescence, as defined by the dilemma of *Identity versus Identity Confusion*; they remain in a state of confusion as they fluctuate between Blackness and Whiteness while presenting themselves as White.

Additionally, they are both tethered by school, which is the site of their racial repudiation and underscores the Ex-Colored Man's impetus for leaving his home in bucolic New England. In choosing between attending college at "Harvard or going to Atlanta," the narrator ostensibly selects the latter institution due to its affordability. His true motivation for traveling to Atlanta University is his "peculiar fascination" with the South, invoking the

---

[75] Erikson, *The Life Cycle Completed*, 73.
[76] Erikson, 73

euphemism for slavery, "the peculiar institution," as he travels to the all-Black Atlanta University.[77] In a reverse migration from north to south, the Ex-Colored Man dismisses the Black people he encounters while travelling, including the "big, fat, greasy-looking brown-skin man" and the African-Americans in the streets who utterly disgust him with their "unkempt appearance, the shambling, slouching gait and loud talk and laughter."[78] He scorns African-Americans, hiding his repugnance as a defense mechanism to ward off the trauma of being rendered Black. Rejecting members of his own race is one way to distinguish himself as White while he passes, while also highlighting the identity confusion that characterizes racial passers.

As a consequence of his race-learning, the Ex-Colored Man's movement between Black and White culminates in college. Rather than sympathize with African-Americans who still suffer from the aftereffects of slavery and the Civil War, he is invested in classifying them based on rigid categories. Expounding upon these categories, he complains about the three classes of Blacks he observes in his travels: "the desperate class," the class consisting of those "connected with the whites by domestic service," and finally, those who are "independent workmen and tradesmen."[79] His interests lie in creating subjective and monolithic groups within which to box African-Americans, placing them within subjective categories that only he deems as appropriate. The narrator seems incapable of categorizing Blacks via any other interactions, thereby overlooking intraracial alliances.

Continuing his hasty categorization, the protagonist asserts:

> It is my opinion that the colored people of this country have done four things which refute the oft advanced theory that they are an absolutely inferior race, which demonstrate that they have originality and artistic conception, and, what is more, the power of creating that which can influence and appeal universally. The first two of these are the Uncle Remus stories, collected by Joel Chandler Harris, and the Jubilee songs, to which the Fisk singers made the public and the skilled

---

[77] Johnson, *Autobiography*, 420. It is important to note that James Weldon Johnson graduated from Atlanta University in 1904. It is now Clark Atlanta University.

[78] Johnson, 422.

[79] Johnson, 434–36.

musicians of both America and Europe listen. The other two are ragtime music and the cake-walk.[80]

This scene offers critical insight into the protagonist's attitude towards Blackness. By his own admission, he relegates Black achievement to "artistic conception." In citing creative endeavors as evidence that African-Americans are not at all inferior, he conspicuously omits their academic achievement. He is clearly aware of the intelligence and foresight of the likes of W. E. B. Du Bois and Booker T. Washington, as well as the oratorical prowess of Frederick Douglass, but they are glossed over in favor of artistic endeavors. To exclude these men and others of their stature highlights the Ex-Colored Man's contention that creativity is the sole thermometer of Black achievement, especially since the protagonist's own development is inextricably linked to education. He thinks this list helps to undermine racist perceptions of African-American inferiority, yet by focusing exclusively on artistic achievements, the protagonist mainly reiterates long-held stereotypes about the limited ways Blacks can prove their humanity, mainly through music, dance, and racist folktales featuring passive slaves on a plantation. He makes these claims while studying at Atlanta University, which affirms the tethering of his race-learning and book learning is now complete.

While we might attribute the Ex-Colored Man's emphasis on judging Black achievement through the arts as an extension of himself—for he too is studying to be an artist (musician)—this does not mean his attempt at revising stereotypes is successful. Instead, it reveals his role repudiation in accordance with Erikson's theory, vis-à-vis his difficulty with African-Americans due to his traumatic race-learning. He positions himself as a White man and, to use Erikson's terms, loses a sense of fidelity to his race. To readers of Johnson's writing in the 1920s, the Ex-Colored Man's revelations are nothing new, since the author himself offered similar observations in his preface to *The Book of American Negro Poetry* (1922), published five years before the republication of *Ex-Colored Man*. In Johnson's preface, he makes a more compelling case that literature and art are the two criteria that should be used to judge the success of a group of people. He uses this preface to assert that much of the creative output in the United States derives from African-Americans. The implication is that contrary to conventional views on Black Americans, they did not deserve to be stereotyped as inferior since their creativity

---

[80] Johnson, 440–41.

proves otherwise. While the Ex-Colored Man is engaged in a race-learning, the novelist is more interested in race-teaching. He cites myriad examples of renowned Blacks to undermine perceptions of Black inferiority, while implicitly questioning the logical basis of racism. Johnson knows that the education most Americans received omitted Black achievement, which he tries to rectify in his preface. He thus opens a space for Fanon to argue, three decades later, that observing transhistoric Black history provides a thorough, accurate, and nuanced negation to racial inferiority. Moreover, the narrator serves as a prime example of Erikson's concept of "negative identity." According to the theorist, those who belong to oppressed groups seek to emulate the groups oppressing them: "There is ample evidence of 'inferiority' feelings and of morbid self-hate in all minority groups" especially Black Americans who suffered from the long-term results of slavery.[81] Despite this self-hate and suffering that defined Black life for most of American history, Erikson points to literature for the answer: "the literature abounds in descriptions of how the Negro, instead, found escape into musical or spiritual worlds or expressed his rebellion in compromises of behavior."[82] The Ex-Colored Man employs elements of both. He was able to "find escape" from American racism by passing as White both in the United States and in Europe, a process made easier by having a White patron support his career as a musician. There is no stronger "compromise of behavior" for light-skinned African-Americans than racial passing, where they can use their lighter complexion to navigate America's racism. In doing so, the Ex-Colored Man, John Warwick, and many others who jump the color line, prove they are stuck in the psychosocial crisis of Identity Confusion as they repudiate their Blackness in favor of a feigned Whiteness.

The penultimate chapter of Johnson's novel details a brutal lynching the protagonist witnessed. It has such a profound effect on him that he decides to leave the South and relocate to New York City to "let the world take me for what it would."[83] This vague statement is his way of passively passing—allowing others to interpret his race in any way they chose. Although he mentions this racialized violence as the impetus to pass as White, he first began passing long before seeing the lynching. To watch a Black man hanging, even

---

[81] Erikson, *The Life Cycle Completed*, 155.
[82] Erikson, 155.
[83] Johnson, *Autobiography*, 499.

from afar, supports his claim that nobody in town knew he was "a colored man."[84] His passing began in adolescence. He does not label it himself, yet Fanon and Erikson help us to see that passing defined him long before he verbalized it after seeing the lynching. When the teacher told him to sit down and his snickering classmates called him "nigger," it became a source of trauma, leading him to seek answers in the mirror and in literature. He tried to discover whether or not he was Black by reading both his reflection and the fictional lives in the library of his home. The problem is that his mother's focus on an idyllic youth omitted conversations on race, and he entered school seeing himself as White before enduring his race-learning. He then embarks on dual journeys—a psychological one where his Identity Confusion makes him vacillate between Blackness and Whiteness, and a physical one where he leaves New England to attend a Historically Black college in Atlanta. When the Ex-Colored Man determines to remain passive about his identity, he is announcing a long-established endeavor to himself, since readers observed the beginnings of his race shifting long before the lynching occurs. His racial passing parallels that of John Warwick, who also endures a traumatic classroom race-learning that inspires him to search for answers in literature and in a mirror, yet neither one provides him with concrete conclusions about his race. With his mother's silence about race, coupled with his father's absence, John learns the limitations of being Black from Judge Straight. His racial passing as a lawyer leads him to traverse North and South Carolina, before he is moved out of the novel altogether.

    The Ex-Colored Man seems to have taken a literal and figurative page out of John Warwick's book. Both protagonists process the trauma of being rendered Black by looking at their reflections in the mirror and realizing a split between what they see and what the world sees. The "real" is the skin color others see that racial passers cannot, but what is more socially determinative is the skin that others comprehend. These racial passers waver between the two skin colors that they are stuck between—Black and White—upon encountering their reflections as part of their race-learning. Race-learning is hardly a problem that only Black boys endure: Black girls also learn about race, but in a different manner than their male counterparts. Whereas mothers do not always educate their sons about the meaning of their Blackness, they teach their daughters about it before they get to school. As *Caucasia* and

---

[84] Johnson, 496.

Plum Bun suggest, race-learning for girls is a longer process that entails passing as a generational inheritance from their mothers, criticism about their Blackness in school, and Eriksonian elements of play.

"All the Good Things Were Theirs": Racial Passing as a Generational Inheritance

Jessie Fauset's passing novel *Plum Bun: A Novel Without a Moral* (1929) was published two years after the reprint of Johnson's novel. Her semi-autobiographical text is the story of Angela Murray's racial passing. Fauset suffered through classroom humiliation similar to Angela's: she recalled her first day of high school when White children from her youth "refused to acknowledge [her] greeting."[85] She considered Du Bois her "teacher, mentor, and friend" and represented him in the book as Van Meier.[86] Additionally, she studied at the Sorbonne in Paris, then travelled to Harlem to join her peers as the literary renaissance flourished, which is the inverse of Angela Murray's travels.[87] Since Fauset's "own life story enter[s] the novel in a number of ways," the points of convergence raise the question of whether or not the text itself is passing.[88] If this fictional text is more autobiographical than it purports to be, it reverses the trajectory of *The Autobiography of an Ex-Colored Man*, which is a novel published as the protagonist's first-person account. Fauset said that her novels are "taken from real life" and that the "stories are literally true."[89] Although she was an Ivy League-trained teacher and editor for Du Bois's *The Crisis*, her work as a novelist solidified her reputation during the Harlem Renaissance.

Scholars reevaluating her work, however, describe Fauset's fiction as flawed in many ways, as evidenced in literary criticism by Cheryl Wall, Deborah Barker, Mar Gallego, Houston Baker, and Cherene Sherrard-Johnson, among others. Over the past two decades, they have dismissed her novels as unconvincing and anachronistic, citing her Victorian conservatism, sentimental styles, overly dramatic plot structures, underdeveloped

---

[85] Sylvander, *Jessie Redmon Fauset*, 27.
[86] Wall, *Women of the Harlem Renaissance*, 41.
[87] Wall, 38–53.
[88] Japtok, *Growing Up Ethnic*, 71.
[89] Quoted in Starkey, "Jessie Fauset," 219.

characterizations, affected diction, and reliance on fairy tales and romance.[90] They view these last two categories as Fauset's most egregious weaknesses since fairy tales and romance are not traditionally associated with African-American writing. As Ann Douglas argues, Black writers employing "white material" have faced heightened scrutiny about where they stand when it comes to representing the race.[91] Many of the commentators take for granted that she employs conventional narrative forms in her work, such as the bildungsroman, but Angela Murray's nuanced maturation into race is hardly comparable to the generic coming-of-age novels that precede *Plum Bun*. The same could be said of Birdie Lee, who is the protagonist of Danzy Senna's novel *Caucasia*. This novel takes place in 1970s Boston during school integration. Unlike the idyllic Murray household, the Lee home in *Caucasia* is rancorous, with Sandra and Deck constantly fighting and cursing in front of their daughters, Birdie and Cole. In writing about the literary tradition of passing novels, Ralina Joseph argues that *Caucasia* "references and pays homage" to a range of texts, including Fauset's *Plum Bun*, which is plausible given the similarities that will be discussed.[92] On a stylistic level, *Caucasia* does not include the overly stilted diction that critics dismiss as a flaw in Fauset's text. Both texts, however, feature light-skinned Black girls for whom passing is a response to learning about race from their mothers and being raced in the classroom. Building on Lacan, Fanon, and Erikson helps us to explore the ways in which Angela Murray and Birdie Lee demonstrate that race-learning and racial passing are gendered.

The first step to race-learning for female passers is observing the ways in which their mothers navigate race as a result of their families being divided along lines of complexion. What initially appears as a stable nuclear family in the Murray home, for example, is actually one divided by skin color. Angela and her mother, Mattie, are both light-skinned, while Virginia shares her darker skin tone with her father, Junius. Mattie uses her phenotype to her advantage by passing in restaurants, hotels, and department stores, among

---

[90] See, for example, Houston Baker's *Workings of the Spirit* (1993), Cheryl Wall's *Women of the Harlem Renaissance* (1995), Deborah Barker's *Aesthetics and Gender in American Literature* (2000), Mar Gallego's *Passing Novels in the Harlem Renaissance* (2003), and Cherene Sherrard-Johnson's *Portraits of the New Negro Woman* (2007).

[91] Douglas, *Terrible Honesty*, 86.

[92] Joseph, *Transcending Blackness*, 70.

other places.⁹³ She takes pride in pretending to be White, while also passing as wealthy in the process. Passing on the weekends in particular helps Mattie to forget that for the remainder of each week, she is a domestic worker with middle-class aspirations. Planning weekend family trips is simple for the Murrays: each parent accompanies the daughter with the matching complexion—Junius and Virginia shop together because of their darker skin color, while Mattie and Angela follow suit using their lighter complexion.

The familial divisions become explicitly clear when Mattie and Angela refuse to speak to Junius and Virginia in public. In admitting her guilt, Mattie states:

> "I was at my old game of play acting again to-day, June, passing you know, and darling, you and Virginia went by within arm's reach and we never spoke to you. I'm so ashamed."

> But Junius consoled her. Long before their marriage he had known of his Mattie's weakness and its essential harmlessness. "My dear girl, I told you long ago that where no principle was involved, your passing means nothing to me. It's just a little joke; I don't think you'd be ashamed to acknowledge your old husband anywhere if it were necessary."⁹⁴

The Murrays dismiss Mattie's passing as mere amusement: Junius calls it a "little joke" while Mattie herself renders her racial duplicity an "old game."⁹⁵ A joke is meant to be harmless, and he claims that he is not slighted at all by his wife's ignoring him nor does he take it very seriously. Yet both Mattie and Junius realize that acknowledging each other in public is also tacit acknowledgment of her Blackness—a dangerous endeavor given the racial customs for most of the twentieth century. A visibly dark man conversing with a phenotypically White woman could have elicited any number of questions about his intentions as well as her safety, to say the least. Rendering Mattie's silence as a "little game" is highly ironic, considering the danger in which both characters could have found themselves if they were discovered.

Mattie is portrayed as selfish and shallow while Junius appears dismissive and naïve, but to focus exclusively on the parents in this exchange overlooks Angela's role. She is with her mother when the other half of her family passes

---

⁹³ Fauset, *Plum Bun*, 15–16.
⁹⁴ Fauset, 19.
⁹⁵ Fauset, 19.

by, yet she too avoids speaking to them. The only thing she can express is relief that "Papa didn't see us" because it would mean publicly acknowledging their shared Blackness.[96] Had she not known any better, she could have hailed Junius and Virginia out of respect. However, Mattie has already shown Angela the way to publicly pass as White: strictly evade African-Americans even if it means ignoring and disrespecting her immediate family. While Mattie admits wrongdoing to her husband, she does not explain anything to Angela afterwards, implying that if she does this again, she expects her daughter to remain quiet and follow suit. The first step in Angela's understanding of race is realizing her freedom to do anything required to prevent her Blackness from being revealed—a belief instilled by Mattie Murray who is anxious about raising Black children in racialized America. In this first step, knowledge about race for Black girls begins in the family, contrasting with the boys who first learn about it in the classroom and not from their mothers. By the time they enter the classroom, Black girls already know about race and are less shocked to encounter it. In the case of *Plum Bun*, Mattie's anxiety about race forces her to pass alongside her daughter; this racial anxiety is the impetus for mothers initiating the race-learning of their daughters.

Angela's racial affiliation with White people and self-hatred develop as she joins her mother on their trips to businesses and across the color line. As a result, Angela's "clearly formed conclusions," include the realization that "the great rewards of life—riches, glamour, pleasure—are for white-skinned people only."[97] This reiterates her previous point that "colour or rather the lack of it seemed…[to be the] absolute prerequisite to the life" which she dreams about constantly.[98] According to Gallego, Angela's "sole desire is to pass into the white race which, she believes, has all the positive values she aspires to."[99] Japtok echoes this sentiment in his assertion that Blackness restricts the young Angela, who hopes to have a life better than her parents.[100]

Angela's inclinations are reaffirmed not only by Mattie's racial passing and public interactions with her family, but also through her education. Each school Angela attends reminds her that passing is a way to avoid the ignorance

---

[96] Fauset, 19.
[97] Fauset, 17.
[98] Fauset, 13.
[99] Gallego, *Passing Novels in the Harlem Renaissance*, 158.
[100] Japtok, *Growing Up Ethnic*, 75.

of her classmates and enjoy the privileges that Whiteness bestows. For instance, in high school, she is chosen to be the assistant to the student newspaper. The defeated student, Esther Bayliss, slanders Angela by cautioning her peers against "trust[ing] subscription money to a coloured girl."[101] After hearing this shocking allegation, the newspaper's editor angrily proclaims "Angela, you never told me you were coloured!"[102] Angela maintains her defensive stance, yelling "Tell you that I was coloured! Why of course I never told you that I was coloured! Why should I?"[103] This scene is repeated, with variation, when Angela enrolls in the Art Academy years later. A career in art enables her to create—an extension of a duplicitous life already predicated on creativity—so it is no coincidence that she aspires to being an artist. In art school, Esther Bayliss appears again, this time as a model who refuses to pose for Angela's class because of the latter's Blackness. Nobody responds to what they consider an unfounded rant, yet once their instructor intervenes and discovers Angela's race (after observing her family on Opal Street), he confronts Angela the next day. She repeats her response from high school: "Coloured! Of course I never told you that I was coloured. Why should I!"[104] Indeed, why should she divulge her race, knowing that it would hinder her mobility, which her mother instilled in her during their weekly excursions in her youth?

Both school incidents share the spectacle aspect of Angela's racial unveiling, and this scene is the adult version of what she endured in high school. Since Mattie makes it explicitly clear that passing as White comes with social benefits, Angela does so in part because she intends to befriend her White classmates in high school. She considers her life "dark and tortured," with having White friends as her only respite.[105] When Angela exclaims "why of course I never told you that I was coloured," she initially sounds as though her silence should be completely obvious to her accusers because she has upward mobility in mind.[106] Yet given her previous passivity when her father and sister walked by on the street without speaking, this is a continuation of

---

[101] Fauset, *Plum Bun*, 43.
[102] Fauset, 43.
[103] Fauset, 44.
[104] Fauset, 44–45.
[105] Fauset, 38–39.
[106] Fauset, 44.

her silence on race. In high school, Angela's reticence about her Blackness has less to do with a desire for her classmates' money and more with her mother's teaching. Esther remains the culprit in art school, disclosing Angela's Blackness to her teacher and peers, thus making the risks much higher: Mr. Shields expels Angela from class based on her racial deception.

From a reader's perspective, Shields's action is not as surprising as his students' inaction. Nobody stands up for Angela when Esther suggests that her race disqualifies her from being an artist, as though "she were as good as a white girl."[107] Regardless of how open-minded artists purport to be, there is no guarantee that accepting African-Americans would fall under their tolerance, which Angela realizes when her art career in Philadelphia ends prematurely. Her increasing knowledge of race is not just about it being called out, but it also entails learning the ways in which Blackness can serve as an indicator of tolerance, especially in academic settings. After realizing she would not be welcomed in professional school, Angela relocates from Philadelphia to New York City, introduces herself as Angèle Mory (a French version of her birth name which foreshadows her move to France at the narrative's conclusion), enrolls in art classes at Cooper Union, makes predominantly White friends, and dissociates from her sister Virginia. In short, the dual scenes of race-learning motivate Angela to begin passing full-time as an adult.

In commenting on Angela's ordeal in art school, the narrator remarks, "she felt as though she were rehearsing a well-known part in a play."[108] This image of play explains why she says the phrase "Of course I never told you that I was coloured" twice: the scene of her racial unveiling occurs twice, and she repeats the line in response as though she has memorized it from a script. Wall draws our attention to Fauset's affinity for "theatrical tropes," as evidenced by the form of her final novel, *Comedy: American Style* (1933), but the image of "play" is especially apropos in *Plum Bun* where Angela is the main character, Esther is the antagonist in the first section, and the central problem is that of racial passing—especially who gets to determine when to reveal Blackness and on what grounds.[109] The "well-known" part for Angela, is that she is always pressured to reveal herself even when it otherwise goes unnoticed. There is another definition of "play" at work in this novel: as a

---

[107] Fauset, 72.
[108] Fauset, 72.
[109] Wall, *Women of the Harlem Renaissance*, 80.

verb, "play" also refers to the behaviors of children who participate in activities mainly for fun and recreation. Images of children and play dominate the text, beginning with the novel's title, which is excerpted from the children's nursery rhyme "To Market, To Market": "To Market, to Market / To buy a Plum Bun; / Home again, Home again, / Market is done." This nursery rhyme epigraph is the first indication of the importance of children and play in the novel. Indeed, Mattie justifies not speaking to her husband as "play acting," and when Virginia moves to Manhattan and sees Angela speaking with a White man, she greets her sister with "I beg your pardon, but isn't this Mrs. Henrietta Jones?"[110] Jones's name refers to a game they played as children. This time, it serves as Virginia's cautious acknowledgement to her sister that she has finally arrived, to which Angela plays along, proclaiming that she is not Mrs. Jones. This is Virginia's way of making a covert introduction lest she outs Angela as Black, further conjoining passing, games, and children. Moreover, a "*Plum Bun*" is a pastry in which dark raisins or prunes are baked within white flour. The Whiteness of the pastry cannot obscure the dark ingredients within it, just as Angela's light complexion is often insufficient in containing the Blackness she sought to hide.

Angela and Virginia's "Mrs. Jones" skit developed as a childhood joke, yet passing is hardly a comical matter considering the level of danger Angela is in: acknowledging Virginia in public is an implicit admission of her Blackness. This same logic prevented Mattie from acknowledging both Virginia and Junius in Angela's youth. Angela's racial transgression has its roots in her childhood through Mattie's excursions, which first divided the Murray family based on skin color. Many twentieth-century theorists viewed childhood as a pivotal time to make predictions about adulthood. For example, in *The Play of Animals* (1896, translated 1898), philosopher Karl Groos noted that playing introduces children into the adult world, while Jean Piaget believed that the verbal and physical realms of children help them conceive of adult life. For Erikson, play was equally pivotal to the development of his ideas. As mentioned previously, his first article published in the United States was based on his observations of children at play. He notes that studying children at play is essential "for the art-and-science of psychoanalysis."[111] Indeed, the third stage of his Psychosocial Development is the Play Age, which features a

---

[110] Fauset, *Plum Bun*, 159.
[111] Erikson, "The Concept of Identity in Race Relations," 22.

crisis of *Initiative versus Guilt* and the significant relationships we maintain are primarily with our immediate family. Angela and Virginia are clearly enjoying this stage during their "Mrs. Jones" skit, which also serves as a precursor to the identities they take on as adults. We might wonder, then, whether the guilt mentioned in Erikson's theorization is translated as Angela's guilt for not speaking to the darker-complected half of her family. By passing as White, Angela Murray practices the identity her mother created for herself and imparted on her as a child, while being raced in school helps her to internalize it. Thus, when the narrator reads Angela as "rehearsing a well-known part in a play," it invokes the dual connotations of "play" in the narrative: she is acting in the drama that is her life as a racial passer, as a result of observing her mother's "old game" of pretending to be White.

This language of performance also defines a modern passing narrative, Senna's *Caucasia*, particularly Birdie's play acting with her sister, which foreshadows her behavior as an adult. According to Jones, "Birdie's transformation [is] a performance" and her parents remain oblivious to the racial fluctuation.[112] Birdie will not be accepted at school until she learns "the cultural markers of Blackness."[113] The similar diction and tone used by critics of *Plum Bun* and *Caucasia* suggest that racial passing is indeed a performance that entails sustaining a false identity for others. Both Angela and Birdie pretend to be something they are not in academic settings, with the help of their mothers' motivations and a strong sense of racial anxiety. Added to this is Sandra Lee's alleged illegal activity, which also provides an impetus for another level of racial performance in *Caucasia*.

Birdie's mother, Sandra, is a progressive White woman who hides criminals and activists in her basement and who was married to Deck Lee, a Black anthropology professor. Together, they have two daughters—Cole, who is dark-skinned, and her lighter-skinned sister, Birdie Lee. Sandra home schools them, justifying it as a way to shelter them "from the racism and violence of the world."[114] After initially acquiescing to it, Deck decides that placing them in the Nkrumah Black Power School would be a more feasible alternative. Yet Sandra disagrees: "Come off it, Deck. I mean, I guess the school makes some sense with Cole. But Birdie? Look at her sometime, really look at her.

---

[112] Jones, "Tragic No More?," 92.
[113] Jones, 91.
[114] Senna, *Caucasia*, 26.

Try to see beyond yourself and your goddam history books. She looks a little Sicilian."[115] Her entreaties are futile, because Deck is determined to send his children to Nkrumah, a school predominately for Black children and appropriately named after Kwame Nkrumah.

At the heart of this exchange are two prevalent images for racial passers: education and sight. This appears through the convergence of Deck's intellectualism and the contrasting skin tones in his daughters. When it comes to their education, Sandra is less interested in making a political statement and more concerned with her husband's inability to clearly see his daughters. By telling him to look beyond the history books, she simultaneously mocks his erudition and asserts that he spends too much time analyzing and not enough time parenting. According to her logic, if he would spend more time in the latter position, then he would realize that Nkrumah, a school for Black children, is not a feasible educational environment for a phenotypically non-Black girl like Birdie to attend. Birdie also ascertains this problem with sight; when Deck visits each week to see his daughters, Birdie does not believe that her father sees her at all, rendering Cole as her father's "special one…his prodigy—his young, gifted, and Black."[116] Cole is his favorite child because she is physical proof that Deck did not get too whitewashed while studying at Harvard. He fears that his Ivy League pedigree might have made him White, but the darker-skinned Cole contradicts this notion. In other words, Deck's schooling has initiated his own racial anxieties. As a result, he prefers Cole because she is dark-skinned just like he is, which is underscored by the fact that the name "Cole" is a homonym for "coal," and it is easier for them to be in public without others questioning their relationship. Birdie resembles her mother, implicitly undermining Deck as a pro-Black academic, while making it difficult for him to treat her like he does Cole. Nevertheless, Deck is the first person to misread Birdie because of his laser focus on his scholarship instead of parenting. As John Warwick and the Ex-Colored Man suggest, racial passers often turn to books in search of themselves when they are confronted with Blackness, which explains why Birdie writes a narrative in her youth that vaguely resembles her life—she wants to correct the image of herself after being woefully misread by everyone else.

---

[115] Senna, 27.
[116] Senna, 55.

In the meantime, she is challenged with inferring the meaning of "Sicilian" based on her mother's admonition. To her, the word sounds "dirty off [Sandra's] tongue."[117] When preparing for bed, she again speculates on why she is rendered "Sicilian" and not her sister, deciding to examine her sister's "reflection behind me."[118] Yet she can only guess that there is a correlation between this unnamed difference and the "Sicilian" label from her mother as she gazes into a mirror in a futile attempt to read herself. The answers do not appear in any books or in her reflection, as "Sicilian" is just one term that will be used to (mis)read her during her adolescence; it helps to define her race-learning, which she becomes aware of primarily through her parents' conversation about school.

Once Birdie begins Nkrumah, her knowledge about race becomes much more explicit, as does her transition to Erikson's *Identity versus Identity Confusion* Psychosocial Stage. While waiting for history class to begin, a student asks if she is "a Rican or something?" Another one sarcastically states, "I thought this was supposed to be a Black school."[119] When a boy throws a spitball at her, he interrogates her by asking, "what you doin' in this school? You white?" Her classmates misread her because of her ambiguous complexion, leading them to stare at her constantly. However, instead of responding, Birdie finds solace in the "dried lumps of bubble gum," indicating that countless other students have sat there and have "lived through this moment."[120] She continues to feel the dried gum under her desk, moving her "fingertips…as if trying to read Braille."[121] Not only is this Birdie's method of coping with racialized humiliation, but the Braille reference symbolizes her inability to critically read her own racialization, especially given her inexperience in conventional classrooms. Just as she tries to read during the taunts, her classmates are eager to "read" her, though their attempts to place her either as "[Puerto] Rican" or "white" are unsuccessful. Her complexion is foreign to them, leading to the multiple levels of (mis)reading at Nkrumah. This persists beyond the classroom: in the bathroom, one of Birdie's classmates pulls her

---

[117] Senna, 27.
[118] Senna, 29.
[119] Senna, 43.
[120] Senna, 44.
[121] Senna, 44.

straight hair, and asks "Why you so stuck up? You think you're fine?"[122] Her peers read her as someone who pretends to be someone she is not, due to her skin color and hair texture. They attempt to fix her in the limited categories with which they are familiar. On her first day in the Black Power school, the girl who looks anything but Black becomes the object of everyone's gaze, as her race is questioned publicly and extensively.

Birdie's classroom experience parallels many other racial passers in school, yet they are conspicuous because of their Blackness, while Birdie's misreading derives from her perceived non-Blackness. Unlike the Ex-Colored Man, for instance, Birdie has a response to the question of her race—Sicilian—but the teacher walks in before she articulates it.[123] She suggests that her mother was successful at rendering her as other, comparable to Angela's decision to pass at Mattie Murray's urging. Birdie internalizes Sandra's category by contemplating a fictional Italian ancestry, foreshadowing the different identities that both women will assume when they start passing. While teenagers, both real and fictional, often endure taunts from their peers, the added element of race means that the insults are particularly sharp in *Caucasia*.

She realizes that the only way to survive Nkrumah is to create a new identity for herself, or as Joseph puts it, Birdie must pretend to be Black, which is "the first iteration of passing in *Caucasia*."[124] The irony is that later in her youth, she must pretend to be Jewish, but while in an all-Black school, she must first assume what she thinks is a Black identity to remain inconspicuous. To initiate this, she changes her hairstyle, begins wearing lipstick, and talks about boys. She blames the racial dynamics of Nkrumah for teaching her "the art of changing…a skill that would later become second nature to [her]."[125] Birdie has fond memories of playing dress up with Cole in their youth, but at Nkrumah, it is no longer a "game" since she must "erase the person [she] was before" to become someone else and appease her peers.[126] This change takes on extra expediency because she is not just transitioning into girlhood, but into what she perceives specifically as Black girlhood. She assumes that making herself resemble her peers is a guaranteed way of

---

[122] Senna, 46.
[123] Senna, 44.
[124] Joseph, "Tragic No More?," 76.
[125] Senna, *Caucasia*, 62.
[126] Senna, 62.

becoming less conspicuous, and the act of putting on makeup literalizes Paul Laurence Dunbar's poem "We Wear the Mask." Much like the speaker of the poem, who believes we all wear a metaphorical mask that "hides our cheeks and shades our eyes," Birdie's physical mask of makeup has a comparable effect of hiding the White skin that her classmates detest.

Picking up where Fanon leaves off in *Black Skin, White Masks*, Birdie Lee tries to be Black linguistically as well. In one of her rituals, she stands before "the bathroom mirror, practicing how to say 'nigger' the way the kids in school did it, dropping the 'er' so that it became not a slur, but a term of endearment, *nigga*."[127] She also repeats Deck Lee's Afrocentric theories in school, garnering the praise of her pro-Black instructors when she criticizes Black people who act like "jigaboos" on television.[128] Moreover, she speaks to Cole using the made-up language Elemeno, thus providing another way for her to reaffirm her Blackness with her visibly Black sister. Much like other elements of their play, Elemeno is a language shared only between the sisters, proving that existing language is insufficient in capturing their specific form of communication and their identity formation. In short, Birdie Lee practices "acting Black" through her speech to prove her authenticity, since passing as Black—not White—can lead to peace for the conspicuously non-Black-looking girl at the Black institution. Her knowledge of race develops just as her book knowledge grows.

Playing dress up and communicating with Cole is no longer a mere game, because she must truly play dress up to aid her new identity creation to survive Nkrumah. According to Erikson, the "play age entrusts the vastly increased sphere of initiative to the capacity of children to cultivate their own sphere of ritualization; namely, the world of miniature toys and the shared space-time of games."[129] He further notes that children at play "permitted the illusion of also mastering some pressing life predicaments."[130] In other words, it is at this stage when children create their own rituals with each other, in preparation for the rituals of life. In conversing with each other in Elemeno, then, the Lee sisters not only prevent others from comprehending their world, but they also set the stage for their adulthood. More to the point, Birdie's

---

[127] Senna, 63, emphasis in original.
[128] Senna, 72–73.
[129] Erikson, *The Life Cycle Completed*, 48.
[130] Erikson, 50.

ability to pass linguistically in her youth—by switching between talking "Black," Elemeno, and English—foreshadows her mastery of the "life predicament" that all passers face: how to jump the color line while code switching and maintaining her stealth.

Much like "play," the image of a "game" resonates throughout passing narratives, especially given the juxtaposition between the severity of passing and the lightheartedness suggested by seeing it as a "game." This contrast appears regularly throughout *Caucasia*, especially after Sandra runs from the law. Whomever she has been hiding forces her to run at a moment's notice, tersely summarized as "then and there…we were parting."[131] Sandra and Birdie prepare to run together, while Deck, Cole, and Deck's girlfriend Carmen plan their departure for Brazil. Sandra, like Deck, only brings the daughter with the matching phenotype, thus dividing the family along lines of complexion. The narrator never clarifies the specific reasons that force Sandra to start running, other than her hiding someone and involvement in covert activities, but her ambiguity gestures to a larger point about race: the main problem in the novel is not that Sandra hides strangers in her home; contributing to the racialized division of her family is far more dangerous for their already unconventional interracial family unit.

By splitting her family up this way, Sandra's behavior is reminiscent of Mattie Murray's in *Plum Bun*. Both of these mothers run from their race, which influences their daughters who most closely resemble them: Mattie runs from her Blackness to pass as White, while Sandra runs from her Whiteness to pass as Jewish. Sandra's mother comes from old Puritan stock, dating back to Cotton Mather, and she tries to instill White pride in Birdie at every opportunity. Thus, Birdie is perplexed that her mother wants them both to pass as Jewish, wondering if this is "just another one of her [mother's] games to get us out of a bind."[132] The stakes for this "game" are significantly higher than for Mattie Murray's "old game of play acting:" if Sandra and Birdie fail at their contrived Jewish identity, they risk having both their race and alleged crime uncovered, while Mattie only has to worry about the public scorn of

---

[131] Senna, *Caucasia*, 120.
[132] Senna, 128.

her friends and family, which can be more embarrassing and damaging than legal action.[133]

According to Erikson, "adults have the power to use playfulness for most destructive purposes; play can become a gamble on a gigantic scale, and to play one's own game can mean to play havoc with that of others."[134] This is certainly borne out in the behaviors of these racial passers, when the "game" of racial transgression can have serious consequences. Mattie admits her game, but Sandra does not. Instead, she makes Birdie pass as well, citing her daughter's "straight hair, pale skin, [and] general phenotypic resemblance to the Caucasoid race."[135] Sight is essential once again, in that if anyone recognizes Sandra and Birdie together, they see two generically White women, since Birdie does not appear to have a trace of Black ancestry. Passing also emerges as a passed down inheritance in this novel, as Sandra initially encourages Birdie to choose whether she wants to be "Puerto Rican, Sicilian, Pakistani, [or] Greek" before ultimately rationalizing that "Jewish is better, I think."[136] Birdie's fictional life includes being "the daughter of an esteemed classics professor and so-called genius named David Goldman."[137] With these new identities, the protagonist becomes "a half-Jewish girl named Jesse

---

[133] The use of Jewishness as their new identity is an interesting move. In many canonical passing narratives, including *Running a Thousand Miles For Freedom*, *The Autobiography of an Ex-Colored Man*, and *Passing*, the characters pass generically as White. In *Caucasia* however, mother and daughter adopt Jewish identities, therefore suggesting that in contemporary iterations of passing, there are more expansive ways to pass instead of living generically as White. Furthermore, their passing as Jewish is a curious choice considering they know nothing about this religion at all. Kathryn Rummell believes that Birdie "does not have to bone up to rabbinical law because she can reject the cultural/religious aspect of her new race" (7). She can reject it to an extent but must always live in fear of someone discovering it. The irony is that the success of their new identities is contingent upon *not* being around actual Jews who would question their religiosity for ignoring traditional holidays or not maintaining dietary restrictions. In failing to consider these potential impediments, they prove that passing as Jewish is a movement to the unknown for them both. The overall purpose of passing revolves around assuming an identity that is completely foreign and exotic to the one held before, even if it means remaining on high alert about meeting people who would undermine one's allegiance to it.

[134] Erikson, *The Life Cycle Completed*, 51.
[135] Senna, *Caucasia*, 128.
[136] Senna, 130.
[137] Senna, 130.

Goldman, with a White mama named Sheila—and the world was our pearl."[138] She begins passing at eight years old and continues to do so for four years as they traverse New England. Birdie's movement is not just physical but also psychological—travelling forces her to move from racial ignorance to someone who gradually questions her Blackness. Indeed, her move into adolescence also corresponds with her move around New England as a racial passer, when she fluctuates between her fidelity to Blackness and racial repudiation.

By the end of the narrative, Birdie aims to unite her family and discover the reasons behind the seemingly arbitrary familial divisions. To this end, she travels from New England to California in search of Deck Lee, who has spent the past several years writing his magnum opus about race while they were running from it. She tries to explain the type of life she suffered while he did his research, proclaiming "I passed as white, Papa," but he remains unfazed. In her most critical commentary on race, Birdie turns the tables on her father by lecturing him, instead of having the anthropology professor lecture her:

> *You left me.* You left me with Mum, knowing she was going to disappear. Why did you only take Cole? Why didn't you take me? If race is so make-believe, why did I go with Mum? You gave me to Mum 'cause I looked white. You don't think that's real? Those are the facts.[139]

This separation that he participated in contradicts his stance on the alleged fiction of race. If he genuinely believed that race is created, then he would not have allowed his family to be divided because of skin color. By referring to her ideas as "the facts," Birdie suggests that her lived experience is far more convincing than his research project, which provides one last backhanded critique of his inability to read critically. She now comprehends the relevance of race within her own family—an epiphany neither Deck Lee nor anyone at the Nkrumah School predicted.

The separation was part of his research to determine how well his mixed-race daughters would survive. They did, which proves to Deck that race is a complete "illusion, make-believe," "a costume," which can be "switched" easily because "we're all just pretending."[140] Deck is nonchalant because he, too, sees this as a mere game; he claims to be an expert on race but contributes to

---

[138] Senna, 131.
[139] Senna, 393.
[140] Senna, 391.

the racial separation of his family. While Cole and Birdie were pawns in his research experiment, Sandra Lee was gaming the system as a Puritan-descended White woman passing as Jewish, with her "Jewish" daughter in tow. Birdie Lee is caught in the middle, for she was forced to play the game of Blackness in Nkrumah and the game of Jewishness with her mother while in hiding, despite what others invariably read as her Sicilian or Puerto Rican appearance. Birdie is ultimately "disappointed by her mother's resignation to live out what was supposed to be a passing game in New Hampshire" and detests Deck's indifference about their reunion.[141] Much like passing reflects a confusion of identity, it also reflects a slipperiness of language: both "play" and a "game" are used as verbs and nouns. The multiple levels of passing, play, and discretion in *Caucasia* raise a pertinent question: who, exactly, is gaming whom?

Reading, Writing, Arithmetic, and Race

The terms "play" and "games" denote children, thus reaffirming that passing begins in youth instead of adulthood. Psychoanalysts can appreciate this connection, since they cite the importance of analyzing childhood to better comprehend adult behaviors. For instance, Freud spent his entire career asserting that neurotic disturbances stem from our childhood histories, while Fanon argued that observing "children at play" is important since "playing can be seen as an initiation to life."[142] Fanon also asserted that neuroses for Blacks derive from "indirect or cultural forms of oppression or trauma" instead of acts of physical violence—such as "the lynching of one's father."[143] This type of physical racialized violence is often viewed as the impetus for racial passing, but as this chapter has shown, the epistemic violence of being rendered Black in school is far more traumatic; school is the first time Black children become raced. The cultural trauma that Fanon mentions broadly refers to the racist values that are instilled in Black children beginning in school—a place where students and teachers call out Blackness. Because "racial drama is played out in the open," it becomes a traumatic event for Black children whose knowledge of race was minimal or non-existent beforehand.[144] They create

---

[141] Ahad, *Freud Upside Down*, 153.
[142] Fanon, *Black Skins*, 10.
[143] Quoted in Hook, *Fanon and the Psychoanalysis of Racism*, 117–18.
[144] Hook, 121.

new identities for themselves in response to this epistemic violence. Whereas race-learning is the only step to jumping the color line for Black boys, it is merely one step to passing for Black girls since passing is a generational inheritance for them. In rendering racial passing as strictly an adult phenomenon, we overlook the roles that parents and education play, and the ways in which they influence race-learning. The education-yields-racialization relationship explored in this chapter demonstrates that Black children learn the four R's in school: reading, writing, and arithmetic and *race*.

The stages that these nascent passers go through map directly onto Erikson's Theory of Psychosocial Development. In summarizing his ideas on the life cycle, he states:

> We play roles, of course, and try out for parts we wish we could play for real, especially as we explore in adolescence. Costumes and makeup may sometimes be persuasive, but in the long run it is only having a genuine sense of who we are that keeps our feet on the ground and our heads up to an elevation from which we can see clearly where we are, what we are, and what we stand for.[145]

These lines aptly define the behaviors of racial passers, for whom "costumes and makeup" serve merely temporary goals. Indeed, it is the "genuine sense of who we are" that passers frequently ask themselves once they navigate the color line. Angela and Birdie learn about passing in the Play Age, which explains why the games they play with their sisters entail creating new identities, even if temporarily. When Angela and Virginia perform the Mrs. Jones routine, Angela proclaims she is not "Mrs. Jones," thus creating an identity for herself defined specifically as the *absence* of an identity. When Birdie talks to her sister in Elemeno, they speak in a language that only they can comprehend, thereby engaging in a type of linguistic passing. In both cases, they create fleeting new identities for themselves; their childhood games pale in comparison to the adult games they foreshadow however, which include passing, stealth, and constant movement. Whereas Birdie and Angela advance out of the Play Age and into other phases of development, John and the Ex-Colored Man remain in Stage Five—Adolescence—when Identity Confusion defines their lives as racial passers. This is evidenced by each character's need for "models of leadership," which shifted from parents to White mentors and

---

[145] Erikson, *The Life Cycle Completed*, 110.

benefactors, exemplifying their move from Blackness to Whiteness. This racial shift is solidified by John's excision from *The House Behind the Cedars* and the Ex-Colored Man's self-imposed exile from the United States in *The Autobiography of an Ex-Colored Man*. Both protagonists were forced out, in order to deal with the Identity Confusion that hindered them.

One important goal for this chapter is to demonstrate the ways in which psychoanalysis can help cultivate a thorough understanding of the gendered distinctions of passing, which plays out across a wide range of narratives. As the rest of the book makes clear, real and fictional passing narratives often tether psychoanalysis and race-learning, suggesting that racial passing begins long before physical violence occurs in adulthood. Yet this comparison would be incomplete without exploring the differences across the texts as well. *The House Behind the Cedars*, *The Autobiography of an Ex-Colored Man*, and *Plum Bun* take place in different geographic areas but during a similar time frame, the late nineteenth and early twentieth century. John Warwick and the Ex-Colored Man are in constant danger as Black men in the South, especially when the latter travels to Atlanta University to study. Thus, passing for them is first a response to race-learning in their youth, and then a way to circumvent the dangers of being Black in the Jim Crow South. However, in Philadelphia, Mattie Murray passes to advance her social mobility and teaches Angela to do the same, while the White Sandra Lee passes as Jewish and tells Birdie that their success is contingent on her following suit. Ostensibly, the latter two pass believing federal law enforcement wants to arrest Sandra for hiding criminals and illegal weapons, yet Deck eventually reveals that this was all part of his research project on whether or not his biracial children would survive as "Canaries in the Coal Mine."[146] Birdie's passing occurs in the backdrop of Boston's school desegregation in the 1970s and 1980s, when she must move between Boston and New Hampshire. Ahad further distinguishes *Caucasia* from other passing narratives by indicating that "Birdie passes as white in appearance only; her act of passing is not confused with the appropriation and privileging of white identity," especially since her goal is to be seen as Black to finally receive her father's love.[147]

Given the geography and time period of the novel, Birdie's life is not in much physical racialized danger in these idyllic New England settings, as it

---

[146] Senna, *Caucasia*, 392.
[147] Ahad, *Freud Upside Down*, 143.

was for John and the Ex-Colored Man during the Reconstruction. Moreover, Birdie Lee is forced to pass because of her mother's wishes, while Angela Murray actively wanted to live as White to achieve social privileges. While I agree with Ahad that Birdie does not pass in the specific manner that other characters in this chapter pass, she does pass nevertheless: she assumes several of the behaviors of traditional racial passers, namely, learning about the fluidity of her physical appearance from her mother and the public humiliation of being raced in school. She also uses books, a mirror, and play as components of her race-learning, while remaining reticent when subjected to racist comments even though they clearly make her uncomfortable. Eventually, she forgets what her father looks like and can only see her surrogate father: "my father was fading on me. Not the Jewish father. I could see David Goldman clear as a day....it was my real father, Deck Lee, whom I was having trouble seeing."[148] Her true Black father is now being replaced by her non-biological one, which recalls the biological fathers that are conspicuously absent from passing narratives. Though Birdie's passing might be perceived as "in appearance only," her actions suggest that she has internalized her mother's desire to be Jewish at the expense of embracing her Black ancestry for much of her youth.

Despite these differences, the overwhelming similarities offer a powerful take on the nuances of jumping the color line. For instance, all racial passers go on quests to new locations. Travelling is a very old phenomenon in literature; the quest narrative is a story of a character's journey toward a precise goal, dating back to the *Epic of Gilgamesh* and Homer's *Odyssey*. The quest is usually for self-knowledge, which explains why those going on the journey are often adolescents: a youthful journey offers questers time for growth. For racial passers, the quest is not about a generic desire for growth and education, for they embark specifically on *racial quests*. Racial passing leads the Ex-Colored Man to traverse Atlanta, New York City, and Paris, among other areas. He travels to Atlanta to attend college, while Angela Murray moves from Philadelphia to New York City, to pass full-time and attend art school, before relocating to Paris in the narrative's denouement. Birdie Lee moves from Boston to New Hampshire, learning about race in the process, and then to Berkeley, California, in search of her Blackness vis-à-vis her father. Underscoring

---

[148] Senna, *Caucasia*, 188.

all three is education, for their race-learning inspired their journeys, which eventually taught them about their Blackness.

The only character from this chapter with movements we have limited knowledge of is John Warwick, whose important quest begins *The House Behind the Cedars* but who is removed from the plot. Perhaps he ends up in a big city, based on the actions of other racial passers. As the locations above make clear, racial passing entails constant movement, especially to large metropolitan areas. The quest narrative often entails travelling from the country to the city, but the racial quest narrative necessitates relocating to a major city—a practical move given that the population density of a large metropolis affords racial passers much more anonymity as they forge new identities for themselves. Relocating to a big city allows racial passers more opportunities to assimilate within the large population, and far fewer possibilities to be recognized by someone who knows them as Black. When Virginia Murray first arrives at Pennsylvania Station, for instance, she does not even announce herself, opting instead to use the Mrs. Jones game to continue Angela's anonymity. That this interaction occurs in New York City is due to the fact that most racial passers travel there at some point, for it is one of the most populous cities in the United States. Even when racial passers reside in other densely populated cities, such as Philadelphia (*Plum Bun*) or Chicago (as in the case of Nella Larsen's *Passing*, Vera Caspary's *The White Girl*, and Anita Reynolds's memoir *American Cocktail: A Colored Girl in the World*), they still travel to New York City for ultimate anonymity.

In addition to its population, New York City's reputation as a "melting pot" and bastion of liberal thinking appeals to racial passers. This explains why the city plays a major character in their lives. After all, it was the home of the Harlem Renaissance, as well as Bohemian and avant-garde writers. When Angela and Virginia Murray first arrive in New York City, Virginia chooses to live near African-Americans in Harlem, while Angela first chooses downtown Manhattan, where she can fit in more easily with her White neighbors. It is hardly a place to see the type of racialized violence that terrorized the South. This is not to suggest that racism was nonexistent in New York City, but African-Americans who travelled there were able to escape some of the explicit racial atrocities that defined the segregated Jim Crow South. Thus, for passers who travelled north in the twentieth century, escaping physical racial violence was one reason they started to pass; the violent act of attending school is equally important for their decision. After being raced in school, they search for themselves through books and mirrors, before moving to major cities in search of obscurity and eventually more knowledge about race. This quest is not only physical but also psychological, as they travel to a populous city to take a trip into Whiteness, before travelling back home to affirm their rediscovered Blackness.

According to Hook, "the Black subject is often forced into the recognition of their own Blackness," which leads to a keen desire to achieve Whiteness.[149] Taking this to be true, we can see that school is the place where this "recognition of Blackness" first occurs, especially given parental interactions, or the lack thereof. Mothers do not teach their sons about race, thus John and the Ex-Colored Man first encounter it as a trauma only when they begin their formal education. Girls, on the other hand, begin school already knowing about race because their mothers demonstrate that passing affords many privileges, but once in school, they learn how easy it is to be rejected because of Blackness. Whereas Black men are defined by their classroom race-learning, race-learning for their female counterparts entails discovering how to circumvent racism long before it is called out during the formative years of their education.

Education in the United States has long been fraught with humiliation and pain for several generations of African-Americans. In an often-discussed scene, Du Bois remembers learning of his Blackness in school: after a girl refuses to accept his card, he realizes "with a certain suddenness that [he] was different from the others… shut out from their world by a vast veil."[150] Her refusal to accept Du Bois's card prompts him to ruminate on his racialized selfhood, leading him to create the metaphor of the veil for his prescient theory of double consciousness. In the twentieth century, some White teachers denigrated high achieving Black pupils and kept them separate from their White counterparts. For instance, after Malcolm X's English teacher tells him that being a lawyer is "no realistic goal for a nigger," he distances himself from his White classmates and contemplates other career options.[151] Adrian Piper recalls an elementary school teacher who felt compelled to verify her race with her parents before demoting her to remedial classes "in anticipation of low

---

[149] Hook, *Fanon and the Psychoanalysis of Racism*, 127.
[150] Du Bois, *The Souls of Black Folk*, 214.
[151] Malcolm X, *The Autobiography of Malcolm X*, 43–44.

achievement."¹⁵² Even a young Barack Obama, whose ascendancy to the White House allegedly symbolized a utopian postracial America, had to endure degrading racism on his first day in an American school in 1971. After his teacher forced him to reveal his father's tribe, one of his classmates made "a loud hoot, like the sound of a monkey," prompting Robert Stepto to argue that "even at a young age, these children know intuitively that racism's project is to primitivize the other."¹⁵⁴ Not only does this scene reflect the bigotry afflicting these children from their youth, it also reveals that Obama's introduction to the American school system entailed an introduction to race. As these examples indicate, "education" for real and fictional Black students, means race is as embedded in the curriculum as the alphabet and multiplication table.

The White education, however, is vastly different. Douglass highlights the illegality of slave literacy when Mr. Auld forbids his wife from continuing his reading lessons. As a result, he asserts that slavery is "injurious" to both slaves and masters, prompting him to resume reading in stealth.¹⁵⁵ Similarly, Harriet Jacobs argues that slavery effects both Whites and Blacks. It "makes the white fathers cruel and sensual; the sons violent and licentious; it contaminates the daughters and makes the wives wretched."¹⁵⁶ While Douglass and Jacobs agree that slavery provided an education into racism for White slave owners, twentieth-century literature also portrayed White children learning how to classify and dominate others through race. For example, in Flannery O'Connor's short story "The Artificial Nigger," when young Nelson fails to accurately describe a Black man, his uncle Mr. Head replies, "that was a nigger." Toni Morrison cites this conversation in her argument that the boy's "education is now complete" since the protagonist's primary goal is to teach racism to his nephew.¹⁵⁷ In *Rising Out of Hatred: The Awakening of a Former White Nationalist*, Eli Saslow narrates the education of Derek Black, a former White nationalist who was homeschooled and studied a curriculum he designed himself. He learned computer coding (which allowed him to build a White nationalist website), read world history from the 1914 Encyclopedia

---

¹⁵² Piper, "Passing for White," 258.
¹⁵⁴ Obama, *Dreams From My Father*, 60; Stepto, *A Home Elsewhere*, 42.
¹⁵⁵ Douglass, *Narrative*, 43–44.
¹⁵⁶ Jacobs, *Incidents*, 52.
¹⁵⁷ Morrison, *Origin*, 24.

Britannica (which sanguinely referred to the KKK as a "fraternal organization"), and thus "best reflected the family's beliefs about race.[158] Whereas African-Americans get an education into race, for many Whites, education includes learning explicitly about racism.

A widely accepted belief today is that race is a social construct instead of a biological one, yet it continues to be invoked as a discriminatory tool. The need to separate Blacks from Whites says more about the latter group of people than the former. I agree with Morrison's contention that slave masters worked very hard to prove the savagery of the enslaved, yet they, and by extension racist Whites, were the ones exhibiting barbarity in their gross mistreatment of the powerless.[159] As James Baldwin contends in *I Am Not Your Negro*:

> What white people have to do, is try to find out in their hearts why it was necessary for them to have a nigger in the first place. Because I am not a nigger. I'm a man. If I'm not the nigger here, and if you invented him, you the white people invented him, then you have to find out why.[160]

In vilifying African-Americans, racists primarily prove their own version of humanity and power over African-Americans, instead of "proving" biological differences based on phenotype. Understanding this fact is pivotal in comprehending racial passing; for if the color line did not exist in the first place, the White education into racism and the Black education into race would also cease to exist. As the next chapter argues, in addition to mirrors, books, play, games, and their psychosocial development, racial passers must also contend with multiple deaths: the physical death of their Blackness and the symbolic death of their families.

---

[158] Saslow, *Rising Out of Hatred*, 11–12.
[159] Morrison, *Origin*, 29.
[160] Peck, *I Am Not Your Negro*.

CHAPTER 2

PASSING AND FREUD'S DEATH DRIVE

"Then Everything Was Dark":
The Color of Death for Racial Passers

In *Reimagining the Middle Passage* (2018), Tara Green observes that "Death, for some, can be a morbid subject that many would hope to avoid. Yet, it is a theme that emerged in the creative work of African descendants and that is traceable to the Middle Passage."[1] The Middle Passage was the first site of the death of Black people en masse, as enslaved Africans either jumped, succumbed to illness, or were killed during their forced displacement from the continent of Africa to the Americas. Their descendants in the United States still die at an alarming rate today, as evidenced by the frequent killings of unarmed African-Americans which spurred the Black Lives Matter movement. Claudia Rankine elaborates on Black death in her appropriately titled essay for *The New York Times*, "The Condition of Black Life is One of Mourning." By evoking the Middle Passage and the untimely murders of Emmett Till, Michael Brown, and Tamir Rice, among others, she argues that African-Americans are unaware of how or when they will die, forcing Black families to remain in a constant state of "mourning and fear that remains commonplace."[2]

This "mourning and fear" persisted throughout Barack Obama's historic presidency. As Michael Eric Dyson argues, African-Americans feared for Obama's death, especially given the assassinations of Black leaders before him (Malcolm X, Dr. Martin Luther King Jr., Medgar Evers) and the attempts on the lives of Al Sharpton and Jesse Jackson. The election of Obama's successor "is a form of death" to his accomplishments, as his vitriolic comments about race and the systematic dismantling of his policies made clear.[3] The tone of Dyson's essay resembles a eulogy for Obama's legacy, reminding readers that we do not have to mourn his body, but we must mourn his body of work

---

[1] Green, *Reimagining*, 39.
[2] Rankine, "The Condition of Black Life."
[3] Dyson, "How Black America Saw Obama."

instead. Part of the anxiety about Obama's death stems from the tragic mulatto image, which is an archetypical biracial figure who dies because of his or her inability to fit within a Black-or-White world.[4] Even though Obama was the first biracial president, White commentators often rendered him the first Black president, as an attempt to view his Blackness as vindication of America's racist past. This was a futile endeavor, yet one which raised concerns that the visibility of the first Black president—the most powerful politician in the world—could lead to his death.

Just as death remained prominent during Obama's presidency, it also hovers over the lives of those who descend from the mulatto figure—racial passers. Not only does the tragic mulatto stereotype foreshadow the death of racial passers, but creating a new identity also entails killing off the old one, including family members. Such is the case throughout twentieth-century passing narratives, including Alice Dunbar-Nelson's short story "The Stones of the Village," Vera Caspary's novel *The White Girl* (1929), and Nella Larsen's novella *Passing* (1929).[5] In these texts, protagonists symbolically kill their families before hastening their own deaths, which is problematized by the confluence of sexual impropriety and racial deception. The goal of this chapter is to explore the different ways in which twentieth-century passing narratives contend with death, guided by the following questions: How do male and female passers die differently? How do race and sexuality complicate the demise of racial passers? How is passing as White tethered to passing away? How does death in these narratives underscore the futility of jumping the color line?

Psychoanalysis provides some answers to these questions, especially since Freud's theories influenced turn-of-the-century African-American writers,

---

[4] Reginald Watson argues that the tragic mulatto first began in French literature in 1815, before appearing in American literature in Lydia Maria Child's short stories "The Quadroons" (1842) and "Slavery's Pleasant Homes" (1843). The very first novel published by an African-American, William Wells Brown's *Clotel* (1853), centers on the mixed-raced daughter of Thomas Jefferson and his slave, Currer. In the denouement, Clotel is forced to jump into the Potomac River to escape slave catchers. Child and Brown employed the mulatto image as an abolitionist tool, to highlight the horrors of enslavement.

[5] Scholars believe Dunbar-Nelson wrote her short story in the first decade of the twentieth century, but it was not published until 1988 as part of *The Works of Alice Dunbar-Nelson*, vol. 3, a collection edited by Gloria Hull.

including Pauline Hopkins and Alice Dunbar-Nelson; the latter of whom was an avid reader who kept copious notes on the books she studied. As apparent in Dunbar-Nelson's reading journal, "sex and sexuality were subjects that would interest her for many years. A number of her readings in non-fiction, satire, and prose writing indulged this quiet exploration, which included titles like Sigmund Freud's *Three Contributions to the Theory of Sex* (1905)."[6] Harlem Renaissance writers maintained a keen interest in Freudian psychoanalysis as well: Nella Larsen, for instance, "suffused" her work with "new ideas about human psychology" that Sigmund Freud and Otto Rank "popularized" in the 1920s.[7] This included Larsen's keen "attention to the concepts of repression, psychological doubles, and anxiety in *Passing*."[8] As Ahad summarizes, "Since the beginning of the twentieth century…there have been a coterie of Black writers and scholars who have maintained an interest, and I would argue an investment, in psychoanalytic thought."[9] While Dunbar-Nelson and Larsen have a documented history of reading and interpreting Freud, Caspary does not, but it is hard to imagine her not being influenced by his ideas since they were popular at the same time as her writing career. Perhaps these writers' interest in psychoanalysis stems from Freud's own "investment" in psychoanalysis and race; as explained in the introduction to this book, one contributing factor to his psychoanalytic theories was his anxiety over race.

The other was his sexuality. For several years, Freud maintained a very close relationship with fellow Austrian doctor Wilhelm Fliess, whom he considered as a father figure. Eventually, their relationship developed into something more; as Freud wrote to Fliess, "I can write nothing if I have no public at all, but I am perfectly content to write only for you."[10] According to Matory, "Freud and Fliess regularly examined each other's noses as they explored the theory that noses are erogenous zones neurologically connected to the penis."[11] These examinations raise the question of whether or not they occurred during a furtive love affair, when Fliess's nose seemed to stand in for his penis. It was also during this time frame in the last decade of the

---

[6] University of Delaware, "Introduction," *Alice Dunbar-Nelson Reads*.
[7] Davis, *Nella Larsen: Novelist of the Harlem Renaissance*, 310.
[8] Ahad, *Freud Upside Down*, 40.
[9] Ahad, 3.
[10] Jones, *The Life and Work of Sigmund Freud*, 196.
[11] Matory, *The Fetish Revisited*, 153.

nineteenth century, when Freud was the most productive in his research and scholarship as he was motivated by his relationship with Fliess. Indeed, Fliess helped Freud to create his theories based on the notions that people are born bisexual, and sexual impulses became the primary factor in his research on human development. Moreover, in 1895, Freud allegedly stopped having sex with his wife.[12] Taken in tandem with each other, these behaviors imply an illicit connection between the founder of psychoanalysis and his mentor—a "homosexual affair [that] seems to have been critical to the development of psychoanalysis."[13] Freud was well aware that his relationship undermined the image he sought to create; he sought a "monumental patriarchal image of himself that he wanted to survive him," which a homosexual relationship at the turn of the twentieth century would have complicated.[14] As a result, he desired that the letters that transpired between him and Fliess get destroyed and prevented his friend Arnold Zweig from writing his biography.[15] Based on his reactions to both race and sexuality, he did not want any details of his life in print lest they revealed his closeted homosexuality or his status as a Jew with possible African blood.

Matory surmises that "Freud was internally divided and deeply ambivalent about himself and his people," which profoundly influenced his theorization "that the self is shaped by ambivalent motives."[16] Accordingly, psychoanalysis is important to help us understand "people's ambivalence toward one another and of its expression through symbolism, projection, condensation, inversion, and…displacement."[17] In short, Matory insists that Freud's racial and sexual ambivalence made their way into his theorization, which we can then use to theorize the behaviors of others. While he believes this ambivalence is symbolized by Freud's fetishizing of the penis, I argue that this ambivalence is also borne out in his observations on the death drive. Though ideas of the death drive circulated throughout the nineteenth century, Freud first published his perspectives on the theory in *Beyond the Pleasure Principle* (1920), in which he argues that human behavior is driven by many internal

---

[12] Matory, 118.
[13] Matory, 118.
[14] Matory, 118.
[15] Jones, *The Life and Work of Sigmund Freud*, 186, 507, 510.
[16] Matory, *The Fetish Revisited*, 118.
[17] Matory, 128.

drives, including a sexual instinct. According to him, human nature dictates that we must avoid everything that is not pleasurable, but he is ambivalent about what he defines as pleasurable and what's not. When faced with unpleasurable events, we repeat them to return to "inorganic life to restore an earlier state of things."[18] The death wish, or death instinct, is our inherent desire to return to the inorganic state from which life emerged.[19] In other words, it is easier to die than to continue revisiting events that are traumatic—such as racial or sexual ambiguity.

Freud revised his terminology throughout his life but ultimately concluded that the human death instinct is as prevalent as our need for sexual satisfaction.[20] Yet this need for sexual satisfaction is constrained by the nuclear family, according to Freud. Hence, in order for organisms to survive, the death instinct is "projected outwards into the objects that surround it, these are inevitably the mother and other family members."[21] The death drive not only entails a reaction to a family's repression of sexuality, but also a reaction to the family in the form of anticipating their demise.

This theory of the death drive is particularly applicable in understanding the motivations toward death that define people similar to Freud: characters in African-American literature who transgress boundaries of race and sexuality. I invoke Freud's theory not as a rigid analytical framework for passing, but as a way to provide answers to the questions that passing narratives raise, chief among them is why are racial passers compelled to die and symbolically kill off their relatives. For instance, in Dunbar-Nelson's "Stones," Victor Grabért pretends that his entire family is dead before he dies while waving away help when he chokes; in Larsen's *Passing*, Clare Kendry dies by jumping out the window, years after her parents' deaths; and in Caspary's *The White Girl*, Solaria dies by ingesting poison after metaphorically killing off her family. After becoming "blackened," all three protagonists hasten their own deaths as a result. Whether in the form of waving away medical help or consuming poisonous pills, these deaths are not only suicide, but also include speeding up the process of dying after protagonists become raced. Moreover, each passing narrative draws our attention to the mouths of the protagonists:

---

[18] Freud, *Beyond*, 308.
[19] Freud, 315.
[20] Freud, 148–49.
[21] Dalal, *Race, Colour and the Processes of Racialization*, 38.

lips say or consume something they should not, which further hastens their demise. Of course, the mouth is a prominent image in Freud's *Three Contributions to the Theory of Sex* (1905), where he observed its use for both sexual pleasure and for taking in nourishment. According to him, infantile sexuality predicts future sexuality; specifically, infants sucking a breast or a thumb proved to Freud that sucking is the root of all later sexuality. Freud was personally interested in Fliess' nose, yet his scholarship and racial passers are focused on the mouth vis-à-vis the dual purposes of communication and consumption.

For female passers, part of the impetus behind their deaths is sexuality—a topic in which Freud maintained an intense lifelong interest. Racial passers often become sexual passers as well, and according to Boisseron, "Given that the light-skinned passing subject is the result, at one point in the lineage, of a sexual encounter between a Black and a white, it is undeniable that racial passing somehow exposes the (historically marked as "controversial") practice of miscegenation."[22] Gubar makes a similar case in *Racechanges: White Skin, Black Face in American Culture* (1997). In exploring the ways in which White Americans pretend to be Black throughout literature and art from the twentieth century, she concludes that "racechanging imagery deploys sexual iconography to create a host of provocative connections and tensions between conceptions of race and those of gender."[23] Hence, racial passers are often conspicuous for their depiction as a "traitor of the Black community" and also because passing "was enabled by the sexual 'deviation' of miscegenation," which explains the tendency to "treat racial defiance within the realm of sexual deviance."[24] Boisseron also calls out the "compelling need" that encourages critics and writers "to dig out the sexual secret behind the story of racial passing."[25] For twentieth-century passing narratives, racial passing and taboo sexuality are conjoined, as evidenced by the dual images of colors and lips that this chapter explores.

Turning to Freud's death drive helps readers to uncover the connections between race, sexuality, and death in racial passing narratives. All three areas influenced his creation of psychoanalysis, as well as influenced the behaviors

---

[22] Boisseron, *Creole Renegades*, 38.
[23] Gubar, *Racechanges*, 11.
[24] Boisseron, *Creole Renegades*, 39.
[25] Boisseron, 48.

of racial passers. Specifically, this chapter asserts that twentieth-century passing characters hasten their own deaths, rendering it far more feasible than maintaining racial and sexual indiscretions. Suicide is the ultimate manifestation of the death drive for passing subjects. They take an active role in their deaths, unlike their nineteenth-century predecessors who could not fit within the Black or White categories and were forced to succumb as victims of a slave-based society.[26] Twentieth-century racial passers were impeded by race and sexuality on multiple levels, thus prompting them to accelerate their deaths. Freud's premise for the death drive—that humans strive for pleasurable experiences but seek inorganic matter when this cannot be attained—relates to racial passers, who seek pleasure and the benefits of being White while hiding their race, especially from their romantic interests.

Many scholars have written about African-American death in recent years, yet the focus on death in racial passing narratives remains scant; they are often limited by the tragic mulatto image.[27] Since the passive tragic

---

[26] In Brown's *Clotel*, the title character commits suicide by jumping into the Potomac River *not* because she wants to, but because she has to. She is surrounded by slave catchers on the Long Bridge and has no other choice but to jump into the river to prevent recapture. In the context of twentieth-century passing subjects, Clotel initially seems to fit within my schema, but the main difference is that she is forced to kill herself during slavery, whereas the twentieth-century passers in this analysis kill themselves when presented with their racial passing and evidence of their sexual lies, before their inorganic Blackness is resurrected. They suffer a racial paranoia that Clotel lacks. For her, passing and suicide were to save her life. It is very telling that the etymology of "Currer" comes from the Latin verb "currere," which means "to run." Clotel runs from her past, just as racial passers often run from reminders of their Blackness. According to Sollors in *Neither Black Nor White*, "nearly a score of plays and novels on the subject of the quadroon girl and her tragic mystery" were published between 1845 and 1855 (224). In the second half of the nineteenth century, the image appears in novels where racial passing ensues or hovers as a possibility, including Frank J. Webb's *The Garies and Their Friends* (1857), Harriet Wilson's *Our Nig* (1859), and Frances Harper's *Iola Leroy* (1892).

[27] Among the scholarship on death, Sharon Holland's interdisciplinary monograph *Raising the Dead: Readings of Death and (Black) Subjectivity* (2000) argues that there is a deep connection between Black subjectivity and death. Specifically, examining "the space of death" provides a timely and logical metaphor for comprehending the intersection of discourses and Black bodies. Karla Holloway's *Passed On: African-American Mourning Stories* (2002), includes analyses of music, film, literature, and archival research, to argue that African-Americans in particular suffer from untimely

mulatto appears primarily—but not exclusively—as a nineteenth-century phenomenon, I argue that the more appropriate term to describe the hastened demise of twentieth-century racial passers is "active death." This active death differs from their literary predecessors who were agent-less victims of nineteenth-century fictions. Highlighting this important distinction helps us to better understand the tethering of racial passing and sexuality in modern passing narratives and to further explore Freud's relationship to race. Instead of using the death drive as a theoretical apparatus, I use it to provide compelling answers to the related issues of sexuality, race, and death with which racial passers must grapple. This chapter is not invested in a one-to-one comparison of the texts; it is far more generative to contrast the different ways in which passing ensues. By closely reading Dunbar-Nelson's "The Stones of the Village," Caspary's *The White Girl*, and Larsen's *Passing*, through the lens of psychoanalysis, this chapter argues that twentieth-century racial passers want to die as White, but actually die blackened (as a manifestation of inorganic matter) after being encumbered by race and sexuality.

The death drive is used to hide racial and sexual transgressions, which are never truly hidden in the first place. Sigmund Freud's obscuring of race and sexuality parallels that of racial passers in twentieth-century African-American literature. As a result of his racial and sexual neuroses, he created psychoanalysis, which several writers then invoked to create characters who also suffered from matters of race and taboo sexualities. I use "taboo sexualities" broadly to refer to sexual relationships that have not been rendered normative in the Western literary imagination, including interracial relationships and same-sex relationships. The lives of racial passers are peppered with many examples of taboo sexualities. In short, racial passers are invested in preventing Blackness and transgressive sexuality from springing to the surface, which

---

deaths more frequently than any other group, and as a result, "Black culture's stories of death and dying were inextricably linked to the ways in which the nation experienced, perceived, and represented African America" (6). Abdul JanMohamed examines death another way. In his book, *The Death-Bound-Subject: Richard Wright's Archaeology of Death* (2005), he argues that the history of slavery and Jim Crow has led to a "death-bound-subject" who appears throughout African-American Literature. From birth, this subject knows of his impending demise. JanMohamed's goal is to "comprehend the 'normal' effects of the threat of death on the formation of subjectivity" (2). He proves this thesis by applying Lacanian psychoanalysis to the canonical and minor texts of Richard Wright's corpus.

is best understood by psychoanalysis—a theory created by a man who influenced many Black writers because he too sought to conceal his race and sexuality.

His "Lips Were Ever Sealed":
Indicting Passing in "The Stones of the Village"

Although Alice Dunbar-Nelson established her career as a political activist, journalist, educator, and writer, literary critics have been reticent in praising her work. Her contemporaries often compared her to male counterparts, such as her first husband Paul Laurence Dunbar and fellow local color writer George Washington Cable. More recent scholars criticize her conventional writing style and the ostensible racelessness of her work. Jordan Stouck argues that the main problem with her writing is that her "activism contrasts with her rather conventional narrative forms."[28] Gloria Hull notes that her writing is separated from her firsthand experience being Black, despite her role in helping to create "a Black short-story tradition."[29] Kristina Brooks, however, believes that the problem lies in "the reader's response to characters whose race does not verifiably adhere to one side of the Black-white binary."[30] According to her, focusing on Dunbar-Nelson's seemingly ambivalent characterizations is pointless since readers are the ones at fault for not seeing through racial dualities.

Though critics often question Dunbar-Nelson's portrayal of race, her writings are actually deeply critical of racism as evidenced by her depiction of Creole characters. She was Creole, which had a contested meaning in early twentieth-century New Orleans, since White residents often excluded those of African descent from their conception of Creoles. White writers in particular, including Grace King and George Washington Cable, created Creole fiction that excluded an African presence, while historian Charles Gayarré argued that "the Creoles of Louisiana…have not, because of the name they bear, a particle of African blood in their veins."[31] Alice Dunbar-Nelson's fiction rejected these assertions. In her essay "A Creole Anomaly" (1897), she asserts that Creoles are of French, Spanish, and African descent. Almost two

---

[28] Stouck, "Identities in Crisis," 271.
[29] Hull, *The Works of Alice Dunbar-Nelson*, xxxi–xxxii.
[30] Brooks, "Alice Dunbar-Nelson's Local Colors," 8.
[31] Quoted in Domínguez, *White by Definition*, 144.

decades later, she notes that the blood of Louisiana Creoles contains "mixed strains of everything un-American, with the African strain slightly apparent."[32] This latter essay places more importance on the African presence in Creoles than in the first, which indicates her evolving ideas on the visibility of Blackness in Creole ancestry. Nevertheless, Dunbar-Nelson always maintained that "Creoles identifying as white would adamantly reject the idea of African descent," according to literary scholar Caroline Gebhard.[33] One such Creole who attempted this rejection is Victor Grabért, the protagonist of her short story "The Stones of the Village."

Victor is a light-skinned Creole raised by his darker-skinned grandmother in turn-of-the-twentieth-century Louisiana. He passes as White to earn a college degree to become a lawyer, but his racialized subjectivity is revealed at the end of the narrative as he anticipates a coveted judgeship. The text follows a conventional plot of a person who passes, achieves professional status, and loses it when his racial duplicity unravels.[34] In the process, death and lips arise as prevalent images, as they did for Freud: Victor pretends that his family is all dead, and his own death entails choking on a mysterious Black substance.

Given the theories about Creoles that Dunbar-Nelson highlighted in her essays, she employs Victor to meditate on the outcome of a Creole rejecting his African ancestry in "Stones." In it, she posits that passing as White is a futile endeavor, because racial passers will have to encounter reminders of the Black past they previously warded off. Despite the various ways racial passers hoped to escape their past, their death scenes remind them of the

---

[32] Dunbar-Nelson, "People of Color in Louisiana, Part I," 367.

[33] Gebhard, "Masculinity, Criminality, and Race," 338.

[34] Despite this conventional storyline, it is different from similar passing narratives from the same time period. It contrasts with Charles Chesnutt's *The House Behind the Cedars* because we are afforded a complete picture of Victor's life in Dunbar-Nelson's story, whereas John mysteriously drops out of Chesnutt's narrative midway through it. John, like Victor, becomes a lawyer, but his narrative gets replaced by his sister's passing story, making his fate unclear. Frances Harper's *Iola Leroy*, is less a passing narrative and more a "refusal to pass" narrative. Both Iola Leroy and Dr. Latimer are mixed-raced professionals, who refuse to use their lighter complexions to pass, though the possibility hovers over the entire text. Some of their acquaintances perceive them to be passing, while others wonder why they are not passing. At the end, Latimer marries Iola and they vow to help African-Americans.

impracticality of jumping the color line, with Victor Grabért as a prime example. During Victor's dying scene, where he is reminded of Blackness one last time, Dunbar-Nelson indicts racial passing as an ineffective endeavor because passers cannot truly escape their Blackness. In accordance with Freud's theory of the "death drive," Victor has an active death as he hastens his own demise.

Critics reevaluating Dunbar-Nelson criticize the alleged "racelessness" in her writing.[35] Her fiction, however, is not devoid of race after all; instead, her subtle use of literary devices, such as imagery, irony, and foreshadowing, reveal her as highly critical of racism and the prevalence Americans place on racial distinctions. She employs irony to question the logic of racism and to foreshadow Victor's demise throughout the narrative, while juxtaposing the literal and symbolic deaths of several characters. Everyone dies by the end of "Stones," but the protagonist's death is the most conspicuous because he hastens his own demise and is reminded of Blackness in the process. Since the other characters do not die in this manner, Dunbar-Nelson uses them as foils for Victor's death. Her narrative does not focus on one theme over another; it tethers racial passing and death to criticize the futility of the former. Despite Victor's Creole heritage, he suffers from intense paranoia about the African part of his ancestry specifically, which forces him into a state of constant disavowal and fear. He constantly worries that others will discover he is part Black, thus explaining why he symbolically kills off his family by pretending they are all dead. Thus, the first collective death in the narrative is that of Victor's immediate family, to negate his racialized ancestry.

Freud asserted that the nuclear family prevented sexual gratification, implying that this can be one reason why the death drive is not limited to a self-destructive behavior; getting rid of others can lead to sexual gratification. Yet the passing characters in this chapter suggest that killing off their immediate

---

[35] For example, Violet Harrington Bryan renders Dunbar-Nelson's fictional treatment of race "ambivalent" ("The Myth of New Orleans," 71) but also asserts that her gradual use of racial themes coincided with changes in her personal life that made race more problematic for her ("Race and Gender," 133). Bryan also notes that "The Stones of the Village" treats race "more explicitly" than her earlier work ("Race and Gender," 138). Jordan Stouck believes that "Stones" reveals a "crisis of identity in which race is simultaneously overdetermined and denied" ("Identities in Crisis," 270), while Marylynne Diggs renders it "a perfect example of the narrative of passing, secrecy, and the fear of detection" ("Surveying the Intersection," 13).

families will achieve racial gratification. Victor's nuclear family consists of his grandmother, whom he affectionately calls Grandmère, but he chafes under her strict parenting; she provides food and shelter but is emotionally distant during their life in poverty. Grandmère has a darker complexion than Victor, which brings about bullying from the children in the neighborhood. He endures "derisive laughs and shouts, [and] the taunts of little brutes, [who are] boys of his own age."[36] These boys harass him for having Black ancestry, as evidenced by Grandmère's darker phenotype. Moreover, she forbids him from speaking Creole and from playing with the other children. They relegate him to a "nigger" before completely refusing to interact with him. Even though he is light-skinned, his grandmother's complexion gives him away as not being fully White. As a result, it leads him to anticipate her death, while the narrative also meditates on the deaths of others in his life.

As difficult as life is for him, he has no choice but to cope with her detached demeanor. She is his only relative, because neither of his parents is around to raise him: "For his mother had died, so he was told, when he was but a few months old. No one ever spoke to him about a father."[37] Victor is unsure about his mother's death because the details remain ambiguous, as the phrase "so he was told" attests. It leaves open the possibility that maybe his mother did not die at all, or that she died in a manner that was different than he initially thought. With the death of his mother, the parenting responsibilities would logically fall to his father, yet his nameless father is omitted from the narrative, creating more ambiguity. Throughout the text, he is referred to as "a father" and not "Victor's father," and the indefinite article in the former title implies that his father is distant and/or impersonal. Regardless of the specific details, he is killed off and not mentioned at all. In doing so, the symbolic and actual deaths of Victor's parents foreshadow his own death, both of his Creole past and of his eventual White present. Passing subjects cannot have any reminders of their raced relatives if they intend to live as White. To achieve the benefits of racial gratification, close relatives must die.

The narrative revisits the image of death with Victor's employer, whose demise is equally ambiguous. Grandmère sends Victor to her friend Madame Guichard in New Orleans, so that he can "mek one man of himse'f."[38] While

---

[36] Dunbar-Nelson, "Stones," 3.
[37] Dunbar-Nelson, 4, emphasis mine.
[38] Dunbar-Nelson, 6.

there, he finds employment in a bookstore, where he works for three years until the bookstore owner dies, "and his shop and its books were sold by an unscrupulous nephew."[39] The details of his death remain unclear, but a lawyer takes over his affairs, telling Victor that his future is set: the late owner has left behind a will that provides money for his former apprentice, with the only stipulation that he attend Tulane University.[40] Victor must decide between admitting to having a mixed-race genealogy and being denied the chance to attend college because of it, or remaining silent about his race to become college educated.[41] He chooses the latter, rationalizing his decision by realizing that Madame Guichard "was not near" and "Grandmère would have willed it so."[42] His deceased employer was not aware that he was Black, and probably would have dismissed Victor if he found out. Instead, he leaves Victor the privileges of Whiteness as a racial inheritance—books, money, and the means to attain a college education.[43]

Because of the benefactor's generosity and his subsequent racial passing, the protagonist earns a law degree from Tulane University, then avoids references to his past during a successful legal career. While vacationing in Switzerland, he discovers that Grandmère "had been laid away in the parish churchyard. There was no more to tell."[44] Instead of mourning the death of his caretaker, he simply says of "Poor Grandmère" that he will "take a look at her grave" when he returns to America.[45] The details of her death are ambiguous, much like Victor's parents during his youth. He finds out about her

---

[39] Dunbar-Nelson, 8.
[40] Dunbar-Nelson, 9.
[41] Dunbar-Nelson, 9.
[42] Dunbar-Nelson, 9.
[43] The Ex-Colored Man and John Warwick, the respective protagonists of *The Autobiography of an Ex-Colored Man* and *The House Behind the Cedars*, also turn to books after they become raced. Additionally, Anatole Broyard worked in a bookstore when he returned from World War II. Victor follows a similar trajectory, though his race-learning lasts longer: his peers ridicule him, he is sent away first, and while away, he immerses himself in books by working in a bookstore. He had "grown pale from much reading. Like a shadow of the old book-seller, he sat day after day pouring into some dusty yellow-paged book, and his mind was a queer jumble of ideas" (Dunbar-Nelson, 8). If immersion in books is a prerequisite for passing, then Victor proves this by becoming lighter through reading.
[44] Dunbar-Nelson, 11–12.
[45] Dunbar-Nelson, 12.

death after her burial, thereby suggesting that it was insignificant. Victor treats her more as an afterthought, proclaiming his intention to merely "look at her grave" instead of mourning her.

Victor's nonchalance is further highlighted once he returns home:

> But he did not go, for when he returned to Louisiana, he was too busy, then he decided that it would be useless, sentimental folly. Moreover, he had no love for the old village. Its very name suggested things that made him turn and look about him nervously. He had long since eliminated Mme. Guichard from his list of acquaintances.[46]

Victor thus vacillates from his initial inclination to visit his grandmother, to not being interested at all, rendering it a waste of his time. He associates Grandmère with his youth in the village, a place he loathes because it conjures up memories of the endless taunts he endured and of his subsequent race-learning. As much as he hates the past, Madame Guichard is the second person to raise the protagonist, but he symbolically kills her off by omitting her from the cohort of people he considers "acquaintances."[47] By this point in the narrative, the three people who influenced Victor have been killed off: Grandmère, Madame Guichard, and the benefactor, which is all unsurprising in the context of the death drive. The death instinct is often "turned outward on to the external world" and directed primarily to one's family, with the ultimate goal of survival.[48] Grandmère's actual death is juxtaposed with Guichard's metaphorical one, since their demises are essential for Victor's survival and development: reminders of his youth must be disavowed to ensure that his past will not complicate his life as a passing subject.

Despite the disregard for the women who raised him, they influence him in ways he does not realize. For instance, during Victor's youth, Grandmère silenced him at least twice—once to admonish him for wanting to play with other children, and again to forbid him from speaking Creole in favor of English, which resulted in "no language at all."[49] Victor internalized his grandmother's rebukes by maintaining his silence into adulthood. He believes that silence would advance his legal career, as evidenced by his failure to support a prisoner who is called a "nigger" even though he initially feels inclined

---

[46] Dunbar-Nelson, 12.
[47] Dunbar-Nelson, 12.
[48] Dalal, *Race, Colour and the Processes of Racialization*, 37–38.
[49] Dunbar-Nelson, "Stones," 5.

to defend him. On one hand "the lawyer was tingling with rage and indignation," even though "the affront had not been given him."[50] However, he tersely asks "What have I to do with them?...I must be careful."[51] This rhetorical question underscores the distance Victor seeks between himself and African-Americans, as he second-guesses his initial inclination to speak up on behalf of the slighted prisoner. Even as he attempts to separate himself from African-Americans, he still has a particular proximity to it which he cannot fully escape. His indignation at the "affront" indicates how he receives it as a man with Black ancestry though living completely as White. Caroline Gebhard cites this scene as evidence that Victor has become an "ardent segregationist" by this point in his life.[52] However, if he truly disavowed his African ancestry, he would have remained oblivious or unsympathetic to the remark. Victor is instead protectionist—choosing not to speak up—to thwart the possible exposure of his racial background. The Black psychoanalyst Charles Gibson would agree: "the average 'passer' considers this prejudice as a necessity toward retaining his employment—a means of proving himself 'pure white'."[53] In choosing silence, Victor also draws readers' attention to his lips, a body part that becomes more prevalent as the narrative unfolds. In this scene, his lips are sealed to highlight his desire to feign Whiteness; while in the denouement, his lips darken and close for the final time. Years after he chooses silence lest his lips reveal Blackness, these lips are forced into perpetual silence as he turns Black. Victor's silence, as well as his interactions with those who influenced him, all assert the power of the death drive for racial passers, while also foreshadowing the narrative's end.

By relegating the Black prisoner to a category of "them," Victor renders himself as superior not just because of differences in class but also in phenotype. This observation also applies to Victor's relationship with the women who raised him, since "them" is a veiled reference to Grandmère and Guichard—one of whom died and the other of whom is killed symbolically. It is no surprise that his recollection of the prisoner is followed by firing his Black office manager in favor of a "round-eyed Irish boy," which implies that passing as White entails divesting oneself of all racial markers and hiding them as

---

[50] Dunbar-Nelson, 13.
[51] Dunbar-Nelson, 13.
[52] Gebhard, "Masculinity, Criminality, and Race," 343.
[53] Gibson, "Concerning Color," 423.

internal.[54] This is an attempt to expunge any mark of Blackness from his life. The narrative sets this up to critique its flawed logic with Victor's death scene, when his Blackness physically re-emerges.

According to critic Michael Tritt, Victor is "victim to culturally-created prejudices" during his childhood.[55] This trauma is one reason he passes and forcefully kills off his past, yet he must consider its long-term effects when he courts Elise Vannier, a White woman. Dating her brings about the morally fraught dilemma of lying about his family history. Whereas Elise comes from a large family and expects Victor does as well, he admits that "not one" of his relatives is living.[56] It is true that his family members are dead but what remains unclear is whether Madame Guichard, his surrogate mother, is still alive. He knows that Elise's family "would want to know all" about Victor's genealogy, but lying is his way of appeasing them and protecting himself. For Victor, having no family is a more viable option than having one with Black ancestors. Otherwise, with a trace of Black lineage, he would be unable to court her.

Victor violates the rules of miscegenation by being in an interracial relationship, yet the court of public opinion would be harder to navigate; acknowledging this interraciality could incite physical violence against him. This dilemma places Victor in the difficult situation of lacking "family ties [that are] so important in validating lineage."[57] Victor and Elise appear as foils for each other: while her family "had traditions" and "a long line of family portraits" to show off, Victor had neither, and would "have destroyed" Grandmère's picture if one existed, "lest it fall into" the wrong hands.[58] Given his desire to live as White, he is anxious that someone might discover his heritage and expose his racial background.

To remind readers of the futility of passing, the text raises the question of whether fatherhood would undermine Victor's duplicity: "If ever I have a son or a daughter, I would try to save him from this."[59] "This" refers to Victor's ancestry, which is not completely White like Elise's. He does not name

---

[54] Dunbar-Nelson, "Stones," 13.
[55] Tritt, "The Force," 2.
[56] Dunbar-Nelson, "Stones," 15.
[57] Stouck, "Identities in Crisis," 283.
[58] Dunbar-Nelson, "Stones," 16.
[59] Dunbar-Nelson, 17.

it as such because verbally referencing it would invoke an identity he renounces; instead, he upholds the silence that his late grandmother enforced on him in his youth. Fathering children raises the possibility that they would be born with dark skin, forcing him to admit to Elise that he has Black ancestry instead of a purely White one. Cognizant of this risk, Victor sheepishly admits to himself that his "blood is tainted in two ways."[60] When discussing race in America, the image of blood is of primary importance, even if the logic is deeply flawed. The "one-drop rule" stipulates that anyone with merely one drop of Black blood is African-American by default. At the time "The Stones of the Village" is set, Louisiana laws defined being Black as having as little as one thirty-second of "negro blood."[61] Aware that blood is not a racial marker at all, the invocation of the one-drop rule questions its irrationality to keep Blacks and Whites separated. This racial mythology between Blacks and Whites challenges readers to reconsider the absurdity of using it as a racial indicator. Moreover, Victor's belief in it underscores a major flaw with the reasoning behind the one-drop rule: fearing that his children might look Black does not mean that their children (his future grandchildren) will come out completely White either. Victor engages in multiple types of duplicity with Elise: he pretends that he does not have a family history and that he is completely White. Yet each of Victor's efforts to forge a new identity is useless—claiming that he has absolutely no relatives, destroying existing pictures of them, and remaining vigilant about having children will not make Victor's true Black ancestry disappear. To his dismay, his "blood" will always remain "tainted" and no amount of racial repudiation can resolve it.[62]

The other way in which Victor perceives his blood as "tainted" is through socioeconomic class because he is conscious of the stark class

---

[60] Dunbar-Nelson, 17.

[61] Domínguez, *White by Definition*, 2.

[62] One of Dunbar-Nelson's contemporaries was the historian Charles Gayarré, with whose work she was familiar. In 1885, Gayarré delivered a speech at Tulane University, where he argued that, even though there are 250,000 Creoles living in Louisiana at the time, they do not have "a particle of African blood in their veins" (3). Tulane University was Victor's alma mater in "The Stones of the Village," and he certainly did not acknowledge the "African blood" in his ancestry either. It is possible that Victor serves as a stand-in for Gayarré in Dunbar-Nelson's story, but whether that is the case is ultimately uncertain. Nevertheless, the references to blood remind readers that it is hardly a scientific justification to maintain segregation.

differences between him and Elise: whereas he endured an impoverished upbringing, Elise hails from a very wealthy family. Much like her bloodline, Elise inherited wealth from her family, and would pass both on to their children if they become parents. Victor, however, was unable to attain any wealth and will only be able to pass on his African-infused Creole ancestry to them. The confluence of their different class statuses and races becomes explicitly clear in references to slavery. When they must decide upon where to spend their summer vacation, Elise complains that her father wants to go to their plantation, but she prefers to travel elsewhere. She then asks Victor "haven't you some sort of plantation somewhere?" as she recalls a mutual friend of theirs who once mentioned it.[63] Elise wonders why Victor "never spoke of it, or ever mentioned having visited it."[64] The reason he has not mentioned this plantation previously is because it is a complete fiction, much like his life. He claims that his family owned a plantation several generations ago, yet the image that comes to mind instead is of the "little old hut" that he grew up in, which is far from the fictional plantation. With this image, Elise assumes that Victor comes from a family of slave owners and is thus wealthy. If his family were on a plantation, they might have worked on one instead of owning it.[65] The irony in this scenario highlights its possibility: fathers are noticeably absent from the narrative, which helps to explain why Victor appears unaware of much of his family history.

He does not know of his family's origin because they were the victims of what Boisseron renders the "sexual deviance of miscegenation."[66] I prefer the more capacious term "taboo sexualities," which allows for the range of sexual boundaries that racial passers and their families transgress. Somewhere in the protagonist's family history, the taboo of miscegenation occurred, thus allowing him to be light-skinned enough to pass as White.[67] That the

---

[63] Dunbar-Nelson, "Stones," 14–15.

[64] Dunbar-Nelson, 15.

[65] Of course, the location of this story is New Orleans which was "the South's busiest slave marketplace," according to Richard Campanella (*Lincoln in New Orleans*, 111). He also notes that "a visitor to New Orleans arriving any time prior to the Civil War could not help but witness an entire cityscape of slavery" (324). What this means then is that the characters in the story would have had deep involvement in, or at least knowledge of, New Orleans slavery, despite Victor's avoidance of the issue.

[66] Boisseron, *Creole Renegades*, 39.

[67] Boisseron, 39.

narrative is conspicuously ambiguous about Victor's origin might be the result of racial mixing in his lineage, supported by the references to slavery and his lighter complexion. Invoking slavery suggests that Victor is a product of someone's unexpected/unwanted sexual practices, further tethering sexuality and racial passing. In Victor's case, though there is no textual evidence of his own sexual passing, he continues to obscure his identity during his marriage to Elise, a marriage that further allows him to live as a White man based on his proximity to her.

Yet this proximity to Blackness is his main concern, especially once they have children. Slavery hovers over Victor and Elise's marriage: when they welcome a son, Vannier, she specifically wants a Black maid whom she renders an "old mammy" and a "darkey."[68] Victor adamantly detests this notion, couching his distaste through hatred for African-Americans generally. He believes that Black staff would "frighten children" or would be "shiftless and worthless and generally no-account."[69] These stereotypes might initially indicate his completion of racial passing in that his success as a passing subject is evidenced by his inability to remember that some of his ancestors were Black. What is more likely the case, though, is that fear of being raced is getting too close for him to deny it, as his marriage to Elise elicits his most vitriolic actions against African-Americans. Employing a Black nanny would force Victor to face the Blacks in his lineage, and he does not know how to reconcile his desire to avoid his own people with his intention to live as White. A Black domestic working in their home raises the probability that his race would be revealed if she detects his racial deception more easily than a White person. As Gibson observes, "there is an indescribable something which enables a Negro to spot a passer sometimes."[70] As his marriage to Elise attests, he has perfected the ability to conceal his true heritage from Whites, which means that employing a Black nanny could be a dangerous endeavor if she discovers his secret. Though articulating racist sensibilities undermines Elise's desire to have Blacks in their home, it allows Victor to continue suppressing his past and live as White.

Despite his desire to excise African-Americans from his life, Victor is unable to completely accomplish this task due to his profession as a lawyer.

---

[68] Dunbar-Nelson, "Stones," 20.
[69] Dunbar-Nelson, 20.
[70] Gibson, "Concerning Color," 423.

When a Black litigant arrives at his office seeking legal representation, Victor flatly denies the man's request because he views Blacks as having the "sheerest incapacity."[71] This racism is a façade; the real reason Victor refuses the client is because of the fear of discovery: "What could he have meant by coming to me...do I look like a man likely to take up his impossible contentions?"[72] The man's desire to have "the best civil lawyer in the city" is far from "impossible"; the only problem is that the praised lawyer happens to be passing as White. Considering Victor's response to having a Black nanny, his reaction to working with Black litigants is similar: being near African-Americans could increase his risk of racial discovery if he is not overly cautious. This is reminiscent of Freud's own distaste for Blacks, which he often assumed to maintain a distance between he and the "blackamoors."[73]

Victor's racial paranoia reaches its zenith with Mr. Pavageau, an African-American attorney. When Victor becomes a judge, he must decide a case that Pavageau argues, which centers on "a troublesome old woman, who instead of taking her fair-skinned grandchild out of the school where it had been found it did not belong, had preferred to bring the matter to court."[74] After Victor says that the law demands that the child's Black heritage renders him ineligible to continue at the school, Pavageau sarcastically says "Perhaps Your Honor would like to set the example by taking your son from the schools."[75] This case recalls Victor's own youth, as it sounds more like it could have been Grandmère and a young Victor as the litigants. Just like the boy at the center of the case, Victor was once a young child who faced trouble at school because of his complexion.

The protagonist's past and present are powerfully juxtaposed in this courtroom. We can assume that in this moment, Victor wants to see Pavageau's own death for articulating the Blackness of Victor's son. Victor is at once reminded of his youth because of the racial problems the light-skinned boy faces, while his own White-looking son (who is sitting in the audience) represents the future without visible signs of his Creole heritage. This contrast is underscored through irony, in that the court's precedent can be set by

---

[71] Dunbar-Nelson, "Stones," 23.
[72] Dunbar-Nelson, 23.
[73] Matory, *The Fetish Revisited*, 119.
[74] Dunbar-Nelson, "Stones," 25.
[75] Dunbar-Nelson, 26.

Victor, who should remove his own child from school if he is to follow the law that he himself seeks to enforce. When Victor is portrayed as "irritated," it has less to do with the unbearable heat and is more about his race: the juxtaposition of his past and his present means he will never be able to stop remembering that he is a White imposter whose racialized past is always on the brink of exposure.

After a private discussion where Victor discovers that Pavageau learned of his race from his aunt, Madame Guichard, they come to an agreement: Victor will treat Black litigants fairly, in exchange for the lawyer's silence.[76] The compromise appears reasonable, yet Victor's racial fears begin to engulf him, which foreshadows the concluding scene where it comes to the surface in full force. He is bedeviled by self-imposed questions such as "How did he know? Where had he gotten his information?," indicating that the past he thought was hidden was never too far gone in the first place.[77] This problem becomes clearer when Victor prepares for a banquet in his honor but is instead consumed by the deception he has sustained for decades. He feels inclined to call the guests "fools" who are unaware that "I'm a nigger—do you hear, a nigger!"[78] This phrase is ironic, considering his grandmother's directive not to play "with niggers" in his youth. In this penultimate scene, Victor struggles with the dual pressure of navigating between the Scylla of admitting his race on his own terms and the Charybdis of having someone else name it for him.

At the ceremony, he imagines that his late grandmother sits in the chairman's spot instead. He begins by addressing "Mr. Chairman" but she "looks at him sternly" as she recounts his life after he "sailed down the river to New Orleans."[79] The text does not reveal her words but suggests that they upset the protagonist because he responds with, "you don't understand—," before his speech abruptly ends. She may have chastised him for building his career on a farce, but the omission implies that her words do not matter, what matters instead is Victor's response:

> The words would not come. They stuck in his throat, and he choked and beat the air with his hands. When the men crowded around him

---

[76] Dunbar-Nelson, 29.
[77] Dunbar-Nelson, 27.
[78] Dunbar-Nelson, 31.
[79] Dunbar-Nelson, 32.

with water and hastily improvised fans, he fought them away wildly and desperately with furious curses that came from his Blackened lips....He arose, and stumbling, shrieking, and beating them back from him, ran the length of the hall, and fell across the threshold of the door.[80]

In this concluding scene at a banquet, Victor chokes not on food but on words—possibly the words defending his racial passing to the grandmother whom he has long forgotten. The Black ancestry that he attempted to suppress is still within him, now appearing as a danger springing forth from his lips. Readers might initially think that he dies because passing is too much for him to handle and he succumbs to the weight of his own duplicity, yet his death is more nuanced than this. Grandmère's image resurfaces precisely at the moment he is about to discuss his political agenda, therefore she represents his past while the speech is intended to outline his future. He would be unable to proceed without first addressing his present and his past—the racial duality that is responsible for his current success. We might be inclined to read Grandmère as a vision or hallucination, especially considering that "death is sometimes preceded by mysterious visions."[81] If fiction can imitate life, as Danticat notes, Grandmère is hardly a mystery considering the trajectory of this narrative: her resurrection in the denouement reminds Victor that he cannot move on because he is living a lie, and to punish him for not helping African-Americans advance despite his powerful position.

In this scene, the death drive reaches its apex. According to Freud, it is a self-destructive instinct and a desire to kill others—either physically or symbolically—to ensure survival. For racial passers, concealing elements of their past to create new identities for themselves entails turning it into inorganic matter and internalizing the loss. They need to ensure survival by silencing themselves and their families. When Blackness starts to come out, it is a dead, inert, and gruesome form of the self that emerges. Victor responds to this resurrected lost self by submitting to it, as evidenced when he blocks guests who come to his aid. "Water and improvised fans" are not enough to keep his racialized past from re-emerging to choke him, nor are they sufficient in preventing his racial exposure, which is his greatest fear. Victor confronts his suppressed Blackness immediately before he dies; not only does he engage

---

[80] Dunbar-Nelson, 33.
[81] Danticat, *The Art of Death*, 81.

with his Black ancestor, but his lips turn Black as he collapses on the threshold. He lived his entire life on a metaphorical threshold between Black and White, underscoring his hopes that the latter would win out. Regardless of his desire to be White, his left-behind Blackness resurfaces through the image of him dying with darkened lips, serving as a powerful condemnation of passing.

Indeed, lips are essential to his endeavors, as they are to Freudian psychoanalysis. Silence hovers over the entire narrative, beginning with Grandmère forcing Victor into silence during his youth, and it continues with reticence about his race in adulthood, as well as his nemesis's silence, which further concealed his race. Lips also symbolize intimacy, as Victor's lips are used for kissing his wife who was unaware that he was Creole and thus had Black ancestry. Dunbar-Nelson could have depicted any other body part that turned Black at the instance of his Black grandmother's reappearance, yet she chose to darken the lips specifically, raising the specter of taboo sexuality and racial passing. Though it is unclear how Victor is a product of a hidden sexual encounter, it is very clear that his relationship with his wife is built on an untruth to which she can never be privy. The last line of the narrative highlights the futility of passing: "The secret died with him, for Pavageau's lips were ever sealed."[82] So were Victor's. His own lips are the ones responsible for his death: long after beginning his racial silence, he chokes while trying to talk, refuses to drink any water, and allows his Blackness to physically consume him at the end. In short, Victor's death drive consumed him in the moment he was being racialized.

The death drive and silence in "The Stones of the Village" are essential for Dunbar-Nelson's indictment of racial passing. Indeed, death is foreshadowed throughout the text: as the ambiguous deaths of Victor's caretakers and employer attest, they allow him to achieve racial gratification. Leading up to Victor's death, the successful lawyer and family man frequently returns to the trauma of his youth when his peers derided him for being Black. He is cautious about interacting with Blacks, being unsure whether they will discover him and divulge his Creole heritage. Death literalizes the discovery that he has Black ancestry, and he dies hoping to prevent it from overtaking him. Dunbar-Nelson suggests that death is essential for racial passing to occur, thus explaining why all of Victor's immediate family dies before he can live

---

[82] Dunbar-Nelson, "Stones," 33.

completely under the guise of a White man. The deaths of his parents and grandmother ensure that nobody is around to witness, and therefore verbalize, Victor's Creole background. Passing itself is a form of death that entails burying one aspect of an identity in favor of another one, which is why silence is a motif throughout passing narratives. When Grandmère silences Victor for associating with "niggers," it foreshadows his entire life when he is silent around Blacks and about his own Blackness. He tries to avoid interacting with Blacks, but his lips Blacken as he speaks with his Black ancestor in the final scene. This imagery represents a final disapproval for Victor obscuring Blackness during his active death scene.

Jumping the color line proves ineffective because passers not only die but encounter their Blackness in the process. They actively hasten it, as Freud theorized. Nowhere in Dunbar-Nelson's oeuvre is the motivation for death more tangible than in "The Stones of the Village," where several deaths foreshadow the impending demise of the protagonist. By the end of the narrative, all the main characters are dead, yet Victor's demise is the most conspicuous because he is the only racial passer and the only one who welcomes his death. In doing so, he epitomizes Freud's theory of the death drive. Despite his desire to hide his race, it re-emerges to choke him and remind him of his long-term duplicity—Blackness comes up because it never fully disappeared in the first place. The "Stones" in the title of the story are weighted with dual meanings: they can refer to the literal and verbal stones hurled at Victor because his grandmother's darker-skinned complexion affirmed his Black ancestry, or the headstones that mark the literal and figurative deaths racial passers must endure in their quest to negate their Black past.

Though the criticism of "Stones" is scarce, its ending has received the most scholarly attention. Tritt notes that the threshold, which should represent accessibility and openness, becomes the point where "there is no freedom of entry for Victor," and he "succumbs to the debilitating psychological frailty…that has dogged him his whole life."[83] Hull believes that he dies from "psychosis [and] madness,"[84] as evidenced by the fact that "his mind completely snaps" after seeing the image of his late grandmother.[85] She further

---

[83] Tritt, "The Force," 8.
[84] Hull, *The Works*, xxxv.
[85] Hull, "Shaping Contradictions," 36.

observes that these traits help to define him as a "tragic mulatto."[86] Gebhard reads the contrast of the past, present, and future (since the banquet is to help position Victor to be a candidate for district judge) as evidence of the "intolerable strain" that racial passing has put on him.[87] However, employing the rhetoric of "succumbing" while insinuating that he goes "mad" overlooks the role he played in his own death; these perspectives locate Victor as lacking agency in hastening his demise, which racial passing complicates. Despite the complexity of this short story and subtle critiques of racism, it was not published during Dunbar-Nelson's lifetime; it first appeared posthumously in Gloria T. Hull's edited collection of Dunbar-Nelson's oeuvre in 1988. Dunbar-Nelson intended to expand "The Stones of the Village" into a novel, but Bliss Perry of *The Atlantic Monthly* convinced her that the American public was not quite ready for meditations about "the color line."[88]

This perspective would soon change. Walter White published *Flight* in 1926, followed by Jessie Fauset's *Plum Bun* (1928) and Nella Larsen's canonical novel *Passing* (1929). In 1927, Larsen herself encouraged her friend Dorothy Peterson to "write some poetry, or something" in response to a representative from Macmillan's, "who asked me to look out for any negro stuff and send them to him."[89] In 1933, Fannie Hurst's *Imitation of Life* became a bestselling novel, spawning two acclaimed cinematic adaptations twenty-five years apart. Macmillan's joined many other publishing houses in seeking literature by and about African-Americans during the Harlem Renaissance, to appease a White audience interested in Black life. Perry's premature assumption about the lack of readership for writings on race would have been outdated by 1929—Alice Dunbar-Nelson could have found a willing audience to read the novel version of "The Stones of the Village" steeped in Freud's theory of the death drive. Yet this void was filled by Larsen's *Passing* and the lesser-known novel *The White Girl* (1929).

---

[86] Hull, 37.
[87] Gebhard, "Masculinity, Criminality, and Race," 343.
[88] Hull, *The Works*, xxxvi.
[89] Larsen, "Letter to Dorothy Peterson," 165.

"The Most Painful Humiliation":
Solaria Cox's Fear of Racial Discovery

Literary critics have largely ignored Vera Caspary's second novel, *The White Girl* (1929). According to Caspary's admission in her 1979 autobiography, *The Secrets of Grownups*, this occurred because its publication led to rumors that it was written by an African-American woman who passed as White.[90] It was this mistaken logic that James Weldon Johnson sought to exploit by publishing *The Autobiography of an Ex-Colored Man* anonymously in 1912, hoping it would create a scandal and therefore sell more books. A. B. Emrys argues that *The White Girl* is a "sensation novel" because of the focus on "secrets and lies and its scandalous actions," while critiquing the sexual harassment of women.[91] Caspary is best known for her popular detective novel *Laura* (1942), which became a film in 1944. Since then, *Laura* has emerged as the primary popular and scholarly focus on her work, thus overshadowing her other texts.[92] As a White-authored novel about a Black woman who condemns sexual harassment, *The White Girl* contradicts what the American readership would have been accustomed to in 1929. Almost a century later, literary critics still grapple with the novel's complexity.

The White Girl features the concomitant images of family, sexuality, lips, and death to question the logic of racial passers and suggest that their demise is predetermined, similar to "The Stones of the Village." Caspary's protagonist is Solaria Cox, a light-skinned African-American woman who passes as White in early twentieth-century Chicago, and who is also motivated by Freud's death drive. The word "solaria" is the plural form of the noun "solarium," which has two definitions: it can be a room in a house with extensive glass that admits sunlight, or it can refer to a room that is furnished with tanning beds or sunlamps used to acquire an unnatural suntan. The irony of these distinctions is that solaria are used to produce darker skin, while Solaria Cox aspires to be anything but darker as a passing subject.

Her hatred for Blackness manifests itself in many ways, primarily through dissociating from her parents, Francia and Desborough. Solaria is displeased with her mother because of her seemingly backwards and uncouth demeanor, while she accuses her father of passively accepting his plight.

---

[90] Caspary, *Secrets*, 116.
[91] Emrys, *Wilkie Collins*, 103.
[92] Bakerman, "Vera Caspary's Chicago," 81.

Ashamed of Desborough's position as a janitor, Solaria wonders if "the blood of the Mississippi Coxes [is still] buried so deep in his veins?"[93] Since he performs his job "like a good servant," Solaria sarcastically assumes that the DNA of his enslaved ancestors—the Mississippi Coxes—motivates him to do manual labor several decades after slavery. Her logic is deeply flawed because she does not realize that as an uneducated Black man in the first half of the twentieth century, her father's employment opportunities are limited. Therefore, he must take any job that pays him, and though she considers his janitor position as an extension of slavery, he must have this job out of necessity and a lack of feasible options. The references to blood and enslavement also recall Victor Grabért: whereas Victor is afraid of passing on his blood to his children, Solaria is ashamed of the blood she carries from her enslaved ancestors.

Desborough suffers two heart attacks, with the second one being fatal. At her father's funeral, her mother's "ecstatic moaning and singing" disgusts Solaria, and she fears that White people are looking at "the negro's violent, showy grief."[94] She accuses Francia of making all African-Americans look bad by vocalizing her sorrow. After Desborough's death, Solaria is stuck at home with her mother, but this arrangement proves to be untenable: "There was no friendship between the two women, yet neither would acknowledge her hostility for the other."[95] What ultimately pushes Solaria over the edge is a heated exchange with her mother in which the latter grows angry that the former left her job with no other prospects for earning money. Solaria does not explain to her mother that she is compelled to quit after her supervisor sexually harasses her. Francia would not understand anyway, since her sole motivation is attaining money, believing that working for White people is the only way to achieve this goal. Once the argument between mother and daughter turns physical, Solaria decides to leave her childhood home, which foreshadows the remainder of the novel when she moves to a new location to prevent racial exposure. After this first altercation, she abandons both her mother and Chicago, effectually killing her mother off since she never speaks

---

[93] Caspary, *The White Girl*, 16.

[94] Caspary, 37. The text does not capitalize the "N" in the word "negro." Therefore, references to the term "negro" in this section of the book that are lowercase come directly from her text. There is no existing rationale that explains why Caspary made this stylistic choice.

[95] Caspary, 43.

to or about her again. She appears as an orphan: her father is physically dead and her mother becomes dead to her metaphorically.

This absence of parents should not surprise readers, since we saw a similar move in Dunbar-Nelson's short story. Just as Victor has to kill off his relatives in order to eventually pass, so does Solaria. This is especially the case when we consider Dalal's point, that in order for us to protect ourselves, we project the death instinct outside of ourselves, typically including "the mother and other family members."[96] Symbolically or physically killing off relatives is pivotal to human survival, which Freud addressed and Dalal expounded upon. In particular, racial passers employ the death drive to obscure their racial affiliation, which is aided by the people they chose to replace their "dead" relatives. Like Victor, the absence of blood relatives forces Solaria to find a surrogate mother when she leaves Chicago for New York City. Mrs. Seabury assumes this role when she allows Solaria to live with her as a boarder, after she presents herself as White. She continues to pass when she goes on a date with Oscar, Mrs. Seabury's son. Sitting apprehensively in the White section of a movie theater, Solaria fears being questioned for being in a section that is legally forbidden to her.[97] Trepidation becomes second nature to her, as she spends the rest of her life avoiding the inquisitive eyes of everyone she meets, lest she get revealed as Black. Nevertheless, Solaria stands out because of her attire: she dons a "simple Black coat drawn tight across her hips, [with her] severe Black hat pulled low over her carefully tinted face," which cause "shabby men and women [to] stare at her."[98] I quote substantially from *The White Girl* since most readers are unaware of this relatively obscure text and would miss the import of specific references that highlight the protagonist's relationship with race and with classical psychoanalysis. For instance, in the scene above when Solaria goes to the movie theater, her being smothered in Blackness is very telling: she is never fully able to dissociate from her race, as her attire and the subsequent stares attest. Even if she uses her light-skinned complexion to her benefit by passing, she becomes gradually accustomed to being conspicuous rather than shunning it. Moreover, when she appears in a dark theater clad in all black, this enveloping color foreshadows the conclusion, when her skin darkens as she commits suicide. In short, this all-

---

[96] Dalal, *Race*, 38.
[97] Caspary, *The White Girl*, 76.
[98] Caspary, 77.

encompassing Blackness that defines her night out prefigures the Blackness that will consume her at death.

Solaria deceives her associates into believing she is White, yet internally she knows that her Black heritage is always within her, hovering close to the surface as her paranoid references to blood make clear. When Al, an African-American man with whom she has been flirting, hugs and kisses her against her will, she is not angry with him as she is when her former supervisor did the same in Chicago. She instead blames herself for this encounter:

> It was the colored blood in her, the heritage from some forgotten ancestor that released these warm wild winds of passion. She was ashamed to cherish the memory of the kisses. She was sad to think that Solaria Cox who considered herself so dignified, so refined, should not have been able to control her feelings when a man laid his hard lips against her face and the jazz records played their restless accompaniment to the swift dancing in her heart.[99]

On one hand, she knows it is wrong to have this unwanted kiss forced upon her, yet on the other hand, she considers her "colored blood" as the reason she stealthily craves his affection. Solaria associates aspects of herself that she detests with qualities she considers innate to African-Americans. This forced kiss transpires with jazz as the soundtrack to her pensiveness, yet jazz is another aspect of Black culture that she scorns because it comes from a group of people she renounces. In suggesting that Solaria's African-American blood is responsible for her desire, Caspary situates her protagonist within stereotypical images of Black women in which they were considered lascivious. Her response to Al also highlights a provocative gendered twist for passing subjects. Whereas Victor is paranoid about inorganic Blackness in his professional life, Solaria's inorganic incorporated Blackness first resurfaces through her sexuality, as she enjoys physical intimacy while being turned off by the race of the man offering it. This is the first instance in the narrative that draws our attention to lips—Al's hard lips pressed against her unwilling ones that verbalize her "White" identity—which tethers race and sexuality through the most intimate bodily areas. This kiss also foreshadows the end of the narrative and of her life, in that she thinks about race when being kissed by a Black man, while her lips change and are used to consume poison. Racial passing and taboo sexuality emerge as united images in this text, due to the

---

[99] Caspary, 86.

unique circumstances that Black women have to endure while navigating racial and sexual stereotypes in the United States.

The reference to lips in this passage provides an example of Freudian psychoanalysis. In his *Three Contributions to the Theory of Sex*, the dual images of mouths and lips appear often. For instance, in the first contribution, "The Sexual Aberrations," Freud asserts that kissing "has received a sexual value among the civilized nations, though these parts of the body do not belong to the sexual apparatus and merely form the entrance to the digestive tract."[100] In the United States then, the mouth is viewed as the intimate parts for kissing, but according to Freud, the mouth is primarily for digestion. For Solaria—as it is for the rest of us—the mouth is for both the expression of intimacy and for digestion: she will ingest poison at the novel's end, long after Al's kiss. Today, this unwanted kiss takes on a different resonance in light of the #MeToo movement, but for Freud, the lips used for this kiss serve first for digestion.

When Solaria divorces herself from Blackness, it comes at the cost of ignoring her family. However, she can never completely avoid her heritage since the topic of blood is a constant problem in her life. When Fitz, the West Indian elevator operator, invites Solaria on a date, she irrationally thinks that he knows she is Black and is clandestinely trying to blackmail her into dating him. She creates an illogical mental narrative in which the elevator man, described negatively as a "barbarous dark figure in a badly fitting uniform" reveals to Mrs. Seabury that her White-looking boarder is indeed Black.[101] There exists no indication that he cares about Solaria's racial identity or would reveal it if he found out. Solaria's sole rationale comes from herself: "her dark blood made her subject to the insults of low-class colored men."[102] The references to a "dark" color are not only awkward textual descriptions, but also reveal Solaria's own obsession with color. She is concerned that someone else's "darkness" might rub off on her and potentially make her appear "Black" considering her current life as a racial passer. However, her fear of this nebulous dark color only sets the stage for her own color change. Additionally, the image of blood recalls Victor's disgust with his blood and underscores the fact that neither racial passer can completely disregard their Black

---

[100] Freud, "Three Contributions," 532.
[101] Caspary, *The White Girl*, 111–12.
[102] Caspary, 113.

ancestry despite their best efforts. Solaria believes that men who are romantically interested in her assume she is Black specifically because of her blood, as though they can see right through her façade of Whiteness and gaze into her DNA. What she renders her "conspicuous" Blackness appears primarily through her sexuality, further tethering racial passing and deviant sexuality.

The exchange with the elevator operator forces her to remember her family back home in Chicago, albeit fleetingly. When she discovers that her brother (a trained lawyer) must work as an elevator operator, and her mother was left destitute and must work as a "washer woman for white families," a nonchalant Solaria responds by dismissing them as mere "shabby people."[103] Instead of sending money to the relatives she has killed off, Solaria offers it to Fitz because the plight of her "blood" relatives is not as important as maintaining her racial deception. Her suspicion that he might reveal her race leads her to pay him five dollars to guarantee his silence. These regular payments inadvertently draw our attention to lips once again, for she wants to guarantee that his lips, like Pavageau's in "Stones," will remain "ever sealed."[104] He is completely unaware of Solaria's plan, and probably considers the money as tips for his service as an elevator operator, not as proverbial "hush money" to keep him from revealing her racial secret. Moreover, these monetary transactions expose Solaria's problems with her own lips, for she does not effectively communicate the explicit reason behind her payments. By this point in the narrative, the protagonist has lost all logic in ensuring that her innocuous suitor remains silent about her Black identity.

She stops buying his silence not because of the belated realization that her behavior is unreasonable, but strictly out of financial necessity. Solaria does not have enough money to pay Fitz one last time, which causes physiological and emotional effects on her:

> Her skin was like dry hot leather coated with icy rain drops. She heard the elevator creaking up and down its narrow canal. She paced the floor of her room until her feet ached. Standing beside the window she would glance down the steep shaft of the courtway and think how pleasant would be an endless sleep.[105]

---

[103] Caspary, 113–14.
[104] Dunbar-Nelson, "Stones," 33.
[105] Caspary, *The White Girl*, 116.

The scene is one of many indications of Solaria's death drive, in which she rationalizes death as an easier alternative than facing the Blackness she tries to hide that is still alive within her sexuality. Caspary includes Fitz in the narrative to introduce a tension between Solaria's fictional White identity and her hidden inorganic Black self. Instead of telling him that his invitations to date make her uncomfortable, she prefers to contemplate suicide, euphemized as an "endless sleep" that would result from jumping to her death in the courtyard.[106] Yet this does not paint the entire picture of her rationale; the resurrection of race through her sexuality instills more fear in her. Her death drive has more to do with negative perceptions of race and her own passing than with Fitz specifically. She fears that her employment, relationships with men, and her room at Mrs. Seabury's would be jeopardized. Referencing suicide again foreshadows her death at the end of the narrative, implying that she prefers it over being a sexualized Black woman. Yet she assuages her negative feelings by paying Fitz one final time, with her "gold chain, pearl earrings, [and] silver link bracelet."[107] To avoid Fitz—and the entire Black population in New York—she packs up and leaves her apartment. In doing so, Solaria follows a trajectory that many racial passers follow, in relocating often to prevent racial discovery.

After leaving, Solaria walks around a crowded New York City dejectedly, with "no sense of direction...[moving] as if she were hurrying somewhere."[108] Eventually, she escapes the crowds, and turns east at Fifty-Seventh Street, "walking slowly now, feeling the cold tingle in her fingertips."[109] If she continues to walk in this direction, she would eventually walk into the East River, which might indeed be her goal considering she pensively ambles throughout the city alone during Thanksgiving, a holiday that is typically spent with family. Her solitude is only broken by Eggers Benedict, a Black man who expressed romantic interest in her when they first met in Chicago. Now he is in New York pursuing a music career. She accepts the invitation to visit his studio but is profoundly discomfited being in close proximity to African-Americans: "Suppose someone should see her with a negro, someone she

---

[106] Caspary, 116.
[107] Caspary, 118.
[108] Caspary, 121.
[109] Caspary, 121.

knew. Suppose they should ask her to leave the hotel."[110] In response, when her friend Dell returns to New York City, Solaria begins living with her. Taking up residence in this White woman's home is her way of seeking shelter from her Blackness; relocating puts her at ease since she does not have to worry about Eggers, another Black man, disclosing her sexuality and race.

Though Solaria is desperate to obscure her blood relatives, she convinces herself that the image of blood implicates her as Black. When she mistakenly cuts her finger, it causes a "bright fountain of blood [to jet] out."[111] After admitting to Dell that Rita, a mutual friend of theirs, has been secretly dating her boyfriend, Basil, Rita retaliates by revealing the protagonist's own secret that she has attempted to conceal: "You've got nigger blood in your veins; that's what's biting you, Solaria Cox," as revealed to her by Oscar Seabury, Solaria's first lover in New York.[112] As the only White man romantically involved with Solaria, he is the one whom she least expects would disclose that she is Black, but in doing so, Oscar's revelation makes it clear that the Blackness she thought was hidden is always ready to spring to the surface. That it occurs with her lover again equates Solaria's sexuality with racial passing. In these scenes, her blood first becomes hypervisible to her peers in a literal sense after she cuts her finger. It prefigures the second scene in which she fears her racial passing is revealed where her blood is referenced as "proof" of her Blackness. Both "The Stones of the Village" and *The White Girl* feature blood prominently, forcing readers to reconsider the false science that the image invokes. Race is not determined by blood, as Charles Drew would prove through his research on blood transfusions during the Second World War. Victor and Solaria's reliance on it as a racial marker underscores the ineffectiveness of passing and the absurdity of maintaining a rigid color line.

Devastated by the news that her race is no longer a secret, coupled with Rita's indictment of her as nothing more than a "dirty nigger," Solaria responds in her typical fashion of wandering the city aimlessly, ending close to the river: "It would have been so easy to take one step, two steps forward into the shining water."[113] In the first example, after believing that Fitz has discovered her racial passing, she walks along Fifty-Seventh Street towards the East

---

[110] Caspary, 125.
[111] Caspary, 156.
[112] Caspary, 161.
[113] Caspary, 161–62.

River, yet is intercepted before arriving. In this example, the unambiguous "proof" that her race has been revealed motivates her to get closer to the river. The more people she perceives as seeing her as Black, the more likely she appears suicidal in the text. This image further literalizes the death drive, for she would be more at peace with death than being identified as Black.

Instead of death by drowning, Solaria decides to give life another chance after relocating, this time to a boarding house run by Mrs. Zimmerman. She still insists upon leaving, reasoning that "if necessary she would go back to being a negro. Anything was better than living this tortured uncertain life."[114] The novel juxtaposes her movement with a return to Blackness, contrasting with her previous actions in which she hoped movement would lead her away from it. This inclination is short lived though: the only place she goes to, reluctantly, is a party where she meets David Lannon, the last person with whom she would be romantically involved. She quickly falls in love with him but postpones meeting his mother lest she has Black servants.[115] Like Victor Grabért, Solaria is concerned that interacting with Black help could lead to her exposure. Solaria must remain extremely cautious to support herself—a task that could be Herculean if others discover that she is not the White woman she portrays herself to be. Moreover, she admits that inquisitive countenances from Blacks in general cause her to "blush" and exhibit a "swift change" that might confirm their suspicions, whereas the only physical effect of Blackness for Victor initially appears in his darkened lips.[116] Her blushing highlights the bodily ways in which Blackness re-emerges from her, contrasting with male passers.

David eventually stops showering Solaria with love, prompting her to assume that he has figured out her race. She imagines several scenarios in which her secret is revealed, while convincing herself that "to have it destroyed by such hideous unmasking would be the most painful humiliation she could possibly suffer."[117] Solaria has maintained the façade of Whiteness since relocating from Chicago to New York City and considers suicide at the mere notion—supported or otherwise—that someone knows of her true racial heritage. However, the stakes are now much higher, for she must consider

---

[114] Caspary, 168.
[115] Caspary, 178.
[116] Caspary, 178.
[117] Caspary, 196.

ramifications of discovery for both her career and for the White man she now adores. Based on her previous actions, the text suggests that she would not survive another "painful humiliation" of her Black background; having her mask thrown off for a final time would anger David and could potentially lead to her death.

As their relationship develops, her unmasking is less prevalent than the problems that arise from her masking. One issue is her dislike for David's mother, Mamie Lannon, an intrusive woman who mothers him as though he is still a small child.[118] On the surface, it appears that the lack of boundaries between mother and son is the sole impetus behind Solaria's aversion to their relationship. However, she is keenly aware that "she had no one except David to love her, but David had plenty of love in his life before she came."[119] This contrast indicates that Mamie's overbearing demeanor is not the primary problem, but it is the fact that Solaria does not have any relatives to show her the type of love that her partner receives regularly. She fails to realize that she has brought this upon herself, after metaphorically killing off her Black family to ensure that they do not ruin her chances of living permanently as a White woman. Had she not been preoccupied with forging a new identity for herself, then her circular argument would be moot—she could have enjoyed a healthy relationship with her family if she accepted being a Black woman. Solaria gradually understands that she cannot have it both ways. Nevertheless, she believes that blaming Mamie without being reflective of the true source of her jealousy is an easier alternative than admitting Blackness.

The other problem that arises in David and Solaria's courtship is that the latter is unwilling to be in the company of African-Americans, even at a distance, for fear of racial recognition. After dining with Mamie Lannon and Solaria, David invites them both to a jazz symphony concert performance by a "colored man" named Eggers Benedict—the same Benedict who was once interested in dating Solaria. Mamie refuses the tickets based on her lack of interest in a "dirty old nigger concert."[120] David understands that his mother represents a conservative, racist perspective that did not care for Blacks at all.

---

[118] For instance, during one of David's colds, Mrs. Lannon visits him and is "fierce in the intensity of her nursing," leaving the protagonist exasperated that someone else has taken responsibility for David's convalescence (Caspary, 213).

[119] Caspary, 213.

[120] Caspary, 267.

She admits that she is old-fashioned and can only see Blacks as "servants," since she only had "colored help in the house" during her adolescence.[121] Solaria's reasoning is more ambivalent: "I don't know. I just don't think I'd like it."[122] In response, he questions why she will not choose to attend a concert in which good music will be played, and he renders her ignorant for maintaining "this ridiculous prejudice."[123] She does not want to attend the jazz concert for the same reason she hesitates meeting Black servants: being surrounded by large groups of African-Americans increases the likelihood of discovery. After a heated argument, David concludes that they cannot have children because they are unable to provide "them [with] the right start."[124] He does not articulate the "right start" that would be a prerequisite for having children, making it difficult to speculate if it is due to his personal preference or impediments in their relationship. Nevertheless, Solaria responds by running home and crying, perhaps because of her desire to have children but inability to, due to David's unwillingness and fear of having Black children. Her actions raise the question of how can she desire children if she suspects that merely being around African-Americans can lead to her racial unveiling?

This dilemma preempts her death: the next scene depicts Solaria "on the couch wondering if she was still alive. She felt as if the ceiling were the roof of a crypt, her couch her coffin."[125] She believes that the impetus behind David's desire not to have children stems from his discovery that she "was the daughter of negro parents."[126] Without any concrete evidence to support it, Solaria rehearses her death after David's assertion, thus demonstrating that public knowledge of her Blackness will result in her death. David's wish to be childless with her is juxtaposed to her wondering if she is alive, fashioning herself as a corpse in a coffin. Solaria reads his decision not to father her children as "the worst insult a man could give to his wife," because it means she is "no better than his mistress."[127] In this scene, racial passing and taboo sexuality are again tethered: giving birth to the children of a White man would be the pinnacle of her subjectivity as a racial passer, for she can present those

---

[121] Caspary, 265.
[122] Caspary, 264.
[123] Caspary, 266.
[124] Caspary, 272–73.
[125] Caspary, 273.
[126] Caspary, 274.
[127] Caspary, 274.

children as concrete physical evidence of her Whiteness—a much better option than being "his mistress," cohabiting without the security of a legally bound family. Of course, she can have dark-skinned children too, but she temporarily disregards this risk to marry a White man, hoping to raise White children, and enjoying the rest of her life as a White wife and mother. She assumes that any other option could cause her death, as evidenced by the "crypt" and "coffin" imagery of her mortality.

The last stage in Solaria's life as a racial passer invokes the family she left behind. Though her brother Jackson wants to see her before traveling to Europe again, she fears that being seen with him would provide David yet another reason not to take her seriously. After vacillating, she reasons that "this dinner with Jackson…[will] be her last intercourse with any negro."[128] Considering the confluence of passing and sexual deviancy throughout the novel, Solaria's diction is illuminating: "intercourse" can refer to communication or sexual intercourse. The literal meaning of her phrase is that she will no longer communicate with any African-American to avoid raising racial suspicion. Proclaiming that she will have no other "intercourse" with African-Americans also implies that she will never be sexually intimate with them either, because the outcome has the potential to expose her Blackness. As a self-fashioned "White" woman, nothing would undermine her passing more than romantic involvement with a Black man, which adds to her caution about sexual deviancy.

Despite the circumspection that defines Solaria's movements, her Black past and White present appear simultaneously, thus initiating the end of her racial passing. Seeing Solaria hugging her brother offers David unambiguous and physical proof that she is Black—a realization that devastates the protagonist. She responds by dissociating from reality and entering a trance-like state: Jackson tries to speak with her, but she does not respond as they walk aimlessly together in midtown Manhattan.[129] The text does not explicitly clarify what she ponders while Jackson tries to reconnect with her, but this is precisely the point. Instead of dealing with the difficult convergence of Blackness and Whiteness, she opts to completely remove herself from reality by being present physically but not mentally. She chooses silence—keeping closed the lips that can reveal her race or sexual preferences. In the context of

---

[128] Caspary, 290.
[129] Caspary, 292–93.

the death drive, this disassociation suggests that she is now at a midpoint in her life between her seemingly buried Blackness and her living Whiteness.

The contrast between Solaria and Jackson underscores how little they have in common—he is a wealthy businessman who flaunts his Blackness, while a lucrative career eludes her as she tiptoes around her African-American heritage. Other than their bloodline, the one thing that unites them is their harkening back to slavery. In bragging about the opening of his southern style restaurant in London, Jackson proudly states that the "English people like us to be ourselves."[130] He further admits to running his "place...like an old Southern plantation," even though he has "[n]evah seen an old Southern plantation."[131] Although he scoffs at this assertion, his restaurant resembles a plantation, with the help of red table cloths and orchestra members who "dress as field hands."[132] He justifies his peculiar actions by admitting that throughout Europe, it is easier to fit into stereotypical Black images than to be an individual: "I have brains and money. But in my business I'm a jazz negro" who will gladly sing "about my mammy" any day if the need arises.[133] He taps into antiquated images of African-Americans instead of affirming Blackness in his place of business.

Resorting to slavery is a provocative endeavor for both siblings. For one thing, Jackson's rhetoric revises upon his sister's own use of the image of enslavement. In her first reference to it, she disparages their father for having to perform unskilled labor long after the legal end of slavery. Her brother, despite never visiting a plantation, represents one through his restaurant to capitalize on European perceptions of Blacks. Although Solaria wants nothing to do with "the blood of the Mississippi Coxes" because they were enslaved, Jackson embraces it.[134] As a result, the Cox siblings are both passing—Jackson hides his education and taps into images of enslavement to appease White patrons, while Solaria distances herself from their enslaved ancestors to forge a racial identity that is not the biological one of her birth. They offer contrasting perspectives on race: he performs what he perceives is Blackness and she fears that her sexuality will betray her hidden African-American identity.

---

[130] Caspary, 295.
[131] Caspary, 295.
[132] Caspary, 295–96.
[133] Caspary, 296.
[134] Caspary, 16.

Solaria evokes slavery again when referring to David. She believes that his knowledge of her racial passing would "always be a whip that he held over her" but she would be willing to endure any of his beatings or torture if it meant they would be married.[135] Furthermore, her humility is increasingly evident: "She felt now that she would cast herself on the ground before David and tell him she was joyous to be his slave."[136] The actual whip that slave masters once used can symbolize the information of Solaria's racial passing that she hopes would remain a secret. Just as slaves were forced into humility for their masters, she feels compelled to be humble for David, through diction that is filled with irony and sexual overtones. Although she has been adamant about shunning Blacks, she nevertheless adduces the most atrocious historical event that has happened to African-Americans to make her point: if becoming subservient to David is a prerequisite to marrying him, then she would gladly oblige.

By this point, Solaria has now removed herself from the present by returning to her family's past, rendering enslavement as an apt metaphor for her situation. This reference represents the reintegration of her Blackness (as seen through her sexuality) with her fictional Whiteness. She does not see that while slaves were forced into subservience, she has the freedom to choose independence instead, much like Victor Grabért. He refers to it by creating an identity for himself in which he symbolically kills off his Black family, thereby becoming a "genealogical isolate," to use Orlando Patterson's term.[137] Solaria is more explicit in using the language of enslavement to reveal the extent of her love for David, while evoking the long-held association of marriage and enslavement leading up to her suicide. In short, while the rhetoric of slavery marks Victor's social death, it serves as a precursor to Solaria's actual death. Both characters seek out death instead of being raced.

Solaria does not get the opportunity to test her theory that supplicating to David would prove beneficial for her; she chooses death instead. The day after Jackson's revelatory visit, she sits in her bathtub reading a love letter from David, which ends with the chilling proclamation, "I love you and would rather die than hurt you."[138] At first, the letter appears to contradict

---

[135] Caspary, 297.
[136] Caspary, 297.
[137] Patterson, *Slavery and Social Death*, 5.
[138] Caspary, *The White Girl*, 304.

her fears that David despises her because of her Blackness. However, she discards it after realizing that he wrote it before running into Jackson, and before realizing that she is Black. She rips up the letter, rendering them "yellow sheets," in a scene that recalls the Ex-Colored Man's "fast yellowing manuscripts" and Victor's "yellow paged books." The disintegrating papers sink to the bottom of her bathtub, symbolizing the split between her and David. Solaria then convinces herself that "David would never come back…David would not come back…David would not come back," sounding like a chant, as if repetition would help her to rationalize that her African-American heritage disqualifies her from becoming his wife.[139]

After staring "at her pale, delicate face," in the bathroom mirror, she notices that "a shadow had crept across it."[140] The novel closes with her suicide:

> She thought she saw the face change, the white skin seemed to darken, the lips to become thick and coarse. The face frightened her. She tried but she could not close her lids to shut out the reflection of the face. She could not turn away. Even as her hands reached for the large bottle at the end of the shelf, Solaria Cox was watching the face in the mirror.[141]

Hastened by her belief that David dismisses her after realizing her Blackness, Solaria kills herself, rendering death as the sole alternative to being rejected because of her race. The irony in this scene is that she spent her adult life feigning Whiteness, but being seen as Black by her White love interest precipitated her skin to change colors; her "white skin" goes from "pale" to a darker shade, so much so, that her own image in the mirror shocks her. Her lips that she once used to hide her race and highlight her sexuality also transform to become "thick and coarse," evolving to become the vessel through which she kills herself.[142] The denial of David's love is too difficult for her to bear and literally turns her Black, symbolizing the culmination of her racial passing and sexual deviancy. This concluding scene is resonant, for color, death, and lips—three images that define this passing narrative—converge to inspire her drive towards death. At the heart of the death drive is a desire for

---

[139] Caspary, 305.
[140] Caspary, 305.
[141] Caspary, 305.
[142] Caspary, 305.

self-destruction, which characterizes Solaria Cox's final days because she is no longer able to deny her African-American heritage.

After reading the novel's conclusion, we might be inclined to ask if Solaria ingests poison to stop the pain of her sexual rejection or the horror of her racial reflection. According to Freud's theories, the answer can be both. When describing the oral stage in "Infantile Sexuality," he argues that "the sexual activity is not yet separated from the taking of nourishment," in that the "sexual aim then consists in the *incorporation* of the object into one's own body."[143] He tethers sexuality and digestion in his theorization, believing infants get pleasure from the two. Freud also notes that those who are "physically abnormal, be it in social or ethical conditions...[are] regularly so in [their] sexual life."[144] Though he explicitly means sexual perversions, I believe "taboo sexuality" is far more relevant for both him and Solaria. The novel considers her sexual choices as taboo because she certainly transgressed sexual norms at the time. As an African-American woman in the decades before the *Loving v. Virginia* (1967) Supreme Court case, Solaria's relationship with David would have been deemed illegal, but she was able to get around it through racial passing and by tiptoeing around the matter of her race. Yet she believes that her meeting with Jackson initiates her racial undoing: if David saw them conversing, he might have assumed a romantic relationship, thus raising the question of incest where none existed explicitly. Perhaps this is why her description of it as "intercourse" resonates, for it adds another layer to her already taboo sexual behaviors. Solaria's sexuality is tethered to her race right up to her suicide—which she accelerates after believing her White partner discovers her Black ancestry. Her sexuality is never too far from her hidden race, yet Solaria attempted to conceal both.

In the only serious scholarly criticism on *The White Girl*, Emrys believes that the protagonist's suicide is "implied" given the seemingly ambiguous final sentence when she retrieves the large bottle from the shelf.[145] It is the same

---

[143] Freud, "Three Contributions to the Theory of Sex," 565, emphasis in original.

[144] Freud, 531.

[145] One of the critics who has written extensively on Caspary's work is Jane S. Bakerman. Her essays that reappraise Caspary's work, "Vera Caspary's Chicago, Symbol and Setting" and "Vera Caspary's Fascinating Females: Laura, Evvie, and Bedelia," surprisingly do not include any mention of Solaria Cox, even though she fits well within both texts. Her omission from "Vera Caspary's Chicago" is quite

bottle referenced in the previous scene: "The large bottle at the end [of the shelf] had a red label. 'Poison!' said the warm red letters."[146] She reaches for the last bottle after seeing her darkening reflection, and it is poison (instead of medicine) that she consumes. Emrys's suggestion that Solaria's culpability in her own death is merely "implied" parallels the critics who question the nature of Clare Kendry's death in *Passing*. Larsen's novella, also published in 1929, features similar images as *The White Girl*, and initial reactions for both works were divided primarily along racial lines.[147] This distinction suggests that, while many White Americans enjoyed reading literature by and about African-Americans during the Harlem Renaissance, racial passing narratives raised suspicions about who might be pretending to be White in their inner circles. Larsen's text has since overshadowed Caspary's novel to achieve canonical status, particularly since *Passing* "is distinguished by its deft presentation of the subject from the perspectives of two mulatto women of the 1920s."[148] The novella deepens and complicates the correlations between color, lips, and sexuality: these images relate to racial passers' reliance on Freud's death drive as a safer option after being "outed" as Black.

A "Nice Study in Contrasts": Colors, Mouths, and Death in Larsen's *Passing*

Larsen's *Passing* opens in medias res: Irene Redfield has received a seemingly anonymous letter, but she immediately perceives the sender as her childhood friend, Clare Kendry. This is based on the envelope's "illegible scrawl" and its resemblance to a similar letter she received two years prior to this one; both

---

peculiar, since Chicago plays a major role in Solaria's upbringing and her racialization, and she eventually decides to relocate. We do not know why Solaria is excluded from most criticism of Caspary, but I would argue that one reason lies in the difficulty in categorizing Solaria Cox, as she has traits of a New Woman and a racial passer. As a result, critics do not know how to analyze a female racial passer depicted by a *White* woman during the Harlem Renaissance, who rejects the advances of several men and does not easily fit within many notions of 1920s America.

[146] Caspary, *The White Girl*, 301.

[147] In her introduction for the Norton Critical Edition of Nella Larsen's *Passing*, literary critic Carla Kaplan asserts that White reviewers verbalized tepid praise when the book was first published, while Black reviewers praised the text (xiv). Similarly, in *The New Yorker*, Michelle Dean argues that *The White Girl* garnered praise from many "African-American newspapers, even as white papers mostly ignored the book."

[148] Madigan, "Miscegenation and 'The Dicta of Race and Class'," 387.

letters are distinguished by their "purple ink," "foreign paper," and covert appearance without a return address.[149] From here, the text offers vivid descriptions about the narrative's present and past. We discover Irene's recollections of her youth with Clare, including the day Clare's father, Bob Kendry, was brought home after his unexpected murder in a saloon fight. Clare received his corpse stoically at first, "with her *lips* pressed together...staring down at the familiar *pasty-white* face of her parent."[150] Her father's Whiteness contrasts starkly with Clare's "bright hair" which she began to pull once the reality of his death settled in.[151] Clare herself contrasts Whiteness and color in her letter to Irene, in which she laments being "so lonely for Irene" as she compares her current "pale life" with that of the "bright pictures" of the former life she left behind.[152] She ends her letter by implicating Irene for initiating a "wild desire" in her since their last encounter in Chicago.

This missive, furtive and unidentifiable, emerges as quite personal as Clare's recollections of and desire for Irene evidence. Her sentiments are couched in sexualized rhetoric, which Youman euphemizes as her ability to "flaunt the conventions that might restrict her."[153] These conventions include boundaries of race and sexuality that Clare crosses throughout the narrative. By opening her novella with a secret letter, Larsen hints at an illicit relationship, one that is so moving that it causes "brilliant red patches" to "flame in Irene Redfield's warm olive cheeks."[154] The very beginning of *Passing*, then, highlights the book's primary preoccupations—including color and sexuality—all of which contribute to racial passers' death drive.

Irene's attention to her beauty is palpable throughout the narrative. She first re-encounters Clare through her "slightly husky" voice, yet "her words were blurred" by the noise of the city when they meet at the Drayton Hotel in Chicago; moreover, she notices Clare's "wide mouth like a scarlet flower against the ivory of her skin."[155] Irene is intrigued by this strange woman but

---

[149] Larsen, *Passing*, 5. All citations come from the Norton Critical Edition of Larsen's *Passing*.

[150] Larsen, 6, emphases mine.

[151] Larsen, 6.

[152] Larsen, 7.

[153] Youman, "Nella Larsen's *Passing*," 338. Helena Michie further reminds us that "canonically, mysterious letters suggest love affairs" (414). Both of these articles appear in the Norton Critical Edition of Larsen's *Passing*.

[154] Larsen, *Passing*, 7.

[155] Larsen, 9.

cannot place her, not even her "odd sort of smile" jogs her memory.[156] The focus on Clare's mouth is what Irene initially uses to recognize her long lost friend to no avail. What at first emerges as a premature endeavor becomes fruitful for both women, as Irene eventually recognizes "the friendliness of that smile" as well as "that voice…those husky tones…a voice remotely suggesting England."[157] The moment of recognition occurs by centering Clare's lips, via the vivid description of her mouth's shape, smile, and especially her voice. As Freud articulates in his *Three Contributions*, the mouth is for both nourishment and sexuality, but in *Passing*, it is primarily a source of hiding both race and sexuality. The attention to Clare's mouth suggests Irene's attraction to her, even if she denies it to herself, thus symbolizing an act of repression. This is a distinctive admission, since racial passing is often predicated on sight, yet *Passing* complicates this by focusing primarily on the mouth—the place where sound is produced and which will serve as the source of taboo sexuality in the text.

After recognizing each other at the Drayton, Irene and Clare remain there talking for an hour, "filling in the gap of twelve years."[158] This encounter continues the foci on Clare's color and her mouth, the dual images that characterize her. She enjoys the reunion, as her response makes clear: "Clare *drank* it all in…she sat motionless, her *bright lips slightly parted*, her whole face lit by the radiance of her happy eyes…for the most part she was *silent*."[159] These references to lips invoke a sexual tone, implying that Clare and Irene fit within Freud's thesis. When Irene announces her departure, Clare implores her to stay, saying, "And now, 'Rene dear, that I've found you, I mean to see lots and lots of you," and she begs Irene to stay with an "ironical smile peeped out on her full red lips."[160] Clare's lips garner the most vivid descriptors, for they are rendered "bright," "red," "full," "slightly parted," and revealing an "ironical smile." Equally important in the qualifiers for her lips are what comes out of them and what does not. Clare initially opts for silence, while Irene informs her of the missing years since their last meeting, quietly internalizing the updates and plotting what to say next. By telling Irene she "found" her and verbalizing her desire to see her often, Clare sounds more like a long-lost lover than a friend. She is excited to see Irene after many years apart, but the tone of her intention raises the question of the source of her

---

[156] Larsen, 9.
[157] Larsen, 9, 12.
[158] Larsen, 15.
[159] Larsen, 15, emphases mine.
[160] Larsen, 16.

excitement: is there a deeper meaning to the physical changes that Clare endures after seeing Irene? Her face reveals her utter happiness too, which the text describes as "lit up" and her eyes "radiant," indicating a fire that burns beneath Clare's surface waiting to spring forth at the right moment. One way to interpret the fire is as a symbol of Clare's desire, especially since the sexual tone of her conversation and behavior makes readers wonder, what precisely is the source of Clare's desire?

Critics have speculated that Clare's desire is for Irene and Brian. In the first sustained analysis of sexuality in the text, Deborah McDowell expounds upon the theory that the novel's ambiguous title refers to sexual passing. She argues that Black women novelists were restricted in how they presented the experience of Black women, due to dominant stereotypes about Black sexuality. As a result, Larsen's *Passing* could finally articulate what previous Black women could only gesture to, namely the latent sexual desire between Clare and Irene.[161] Yet her provocative argument was not without its own set of criticism. Jennifer DeVere Brody, for instance, accuses McDowell of reducing the text to a narrative of "latent sexual passion" at the expense of overlooking the ways in which sexuality intersects with class and race.[162] Similarly, Helena Michie disagrees with the hierarchy of reading racial passing as a cover for sexual passing, particularly because "the hierarchization of the two plots is unnecessary and untrue" to the gendered and racialized ways in which the narrative presents selfhood.[163] She makes a compelling case that racial passing and sexuality cannot be separated, in fact they "are inextricable."[164] By taking this as a starting point, that race and sexuality are informed by and impact each other, we can comprehend the behaviors of the main characters in that racial passing is sexualized and taboo sexuality is racialized.

To claim sexual passing for Clare and Irene fails to take Brian's role into consideration, especially since he serves as "a stock figure, a sign of a conventionally rivalrous plot, a plot that in some sense, for all the pain it causes her,

---

[161] Among the textual evidence McDowell adduces are the sexless marriages that each woman endures and the physical attraction between the two, symbolized by the opening letter which she reads as a "metaphoric vagina" (374). McDowell's explication of the novella is the most well-known; it opens the Rutgers University Press edition of the text, which introduced readers to the text for two decades.

[162] Brody, "Clare Kendry's 'True' Colors," 394, from the Norton Critical Edition of *Passing*.

[163] Michie, *Sororophobia*, 412, from the Norton Critical Edition of *Passing*.

[164] Michie, 412.

Irene seems desperate to enter."[165] Judith Butler reiterates McDowell's homosexual reading by offering a queer reading in which "risk-taking, articulated at once as a racial crossing and sexual infidelity" forms the basis of attraction between Irene and Clare.[166] Boisseron takes both McDowell and Butler to task, arguing that their "repressed homosexuality theory says more about the one who tells about the passing than the one being unveiled."[167] These assertions of "closeted homosexuality...validate the compulsory need to out the passing subject."[168] Asserting that Clare Kendry engages in sexual passing is a myopic endeavor, for it continues a false hierarchy of placing sexuality over race, undermining the influence of intersectionality and inscribing a paranoid reading that reduces Clare's intentions. This argument assumes that sexuality is her prime motivation, though it is merely one reason she acts as she does toward the Redfields. After all, "the iconography McDowell reads as sexual is simultaneously racial."[169] Butler believes that "a certain kind of sexual daring" defines Clare and Irene's relationship, but this fails to completely encapsulate the intersection of race and sexuality that characterizes the two protagonists.[170] Instead, Clare is motivated by layers of what I deem "taboo sexuality": the past miscegenation that yielded Clare's light-skinned complexion (Bob Kendry was born to a White father and Black mother) as well as her flirtations with both Brian and Irene. The attraction to the Redfields is not strictly homosexual since she appears as flirtatious and attracted to both.

This attraction is returned, for Irene pays close attention to Clare too, and goes as far as to assume an affair between Clare and Brian. Irene vows not to see Clare again and avoids her persistent telephone calls throughout the day, yet Clare is persuasive. "What was it about Clare's voice that was so appealing, so very seductive?," Irene ponders.[171] When they meet again, Clare greets Irene "in the hall with a kiss," and her "potent smile" helped Irene's

---

[165] Michie, 415.
[166] Butler, "Passing, Queering," 419, from the Norton Critical Edition of *Passing*.
[167] Boisseron, *Creole Renegades*, 45.
[168] Boisseron, 44.
[169] Brody, "Clare Kendry's 'True' Colors," 394.
[170] Butler, "Passing, Queering," 419.
[171] Larsen, *Passing*, 23.

irritation dissipate.[172] Clare's power over Irene is demonstrated most effectively through her mouth, as it is her "seductive" voice that first convinces Irene to visit, while her kiss and smile both welcome Irene to her home. During this second encounter, Clare's desire initially appears as a romantic one toward Irene. Yet this desire changes during a conversation with Clare's other invited guest, Gertrude. When the latter asks Irene if her husband is "dark too," she is implicitly inquiring if he is light enough to pass, which is their topic of conversation.[173] All three women engage in racial passing, and Gertrude's inquiry is to determine Irene's stance on passing by slyly asking about her husband. When Irene does not answer affirmatively, Clare responds with her characteristic "seductive caressing smile," followed by her "scoffing remark" to change the subject: "Now, please, one of you tell me what ever happened to Claude Jones."[174] The answer she is given is that Claude "was no longer a Negro or a Christian but had become a Jew. 'A Jew!' Clare exclaimed. 'Yes, a Jew. A Black Jew, he calls himself.'"[175] Clare's captivating smile has already been established in the text, but this is the first time it appears in reference to Brian Redfield because knowledge of Brian's inability to pass causes Clare's happiness. Irene later suggests that Clare fetishizes Blackness and may be having an affair with Brian. By smiling when she first learns of Brian's darker complexion (which we later learn is a "deep copper colour"), Clare tethers both assumptions.[176] She desires both Irene and Brian, smiling seductively to both, revealing her ability to transgress boundaries of race, sexuality, and marriage.

If the first part of *Passing* is dominated by the dual images of Clare's mouth and sexuality, the second part focuses on the mouths of others, such as Jack Bellew and Irene. In the case of the latter, Irene's silence contradicts her internal actions.[177] After meeting Clare's virulently racist husband, Jack

---

[172] Larsen, 23.

[173] Larsen, 27.

[174] Larsen, 27.

[175] Larsen, 27. This dialogue serves as another example of Black characters not passing strictly as White, but as Jewish. Claude Jones thus joins Birdie Lee and Coleman Silk in complicating the traditional Black-to-White passing so prevalent in American literature.

[176] Larsen, 37.

[177] Judith Butler agrees with this as well: "the question of what can and cannot be spoken, what can and cannot be publicly exposed, is raised throughout the text,

Bellew, Irene must suffer through his ignorance. She later regrets failing to respond when he addresses his wife as "Nig," asking herself why she "hadn't spoken that day?" and why she "concealed her own origin?" allowing his ideas to pass "undisputed?"[178] Irene supports African-Americans through her racial uplift work, but she questions why her own status as a self-fashioned race woman did not convince her to "take up the defence of the race to which she belonged?"[179] Though she is notorious for her silence, it might indicate her own type of passing: she engages in psychological passing in which she thinks one thing while doing another. For example, after a heated exchange with Brian over their sons' education, Irene forces herself to stop her "trembling lips" as way to stave off "her rising anger."[180] Anytime Irene wants to or is expected to speak up, she chooses silence instead, concealing her thoughts despite knowing that verbalizing her frustrations is the more logical option. Had she rebuffed Bellew's racist remarks, for instance, she would not feel guilty enough to question her own passivity in retrospect. Clare's actions particularly rankle Irene, but she says nothing while acquiescing to her frequent demands. Irene's lips are thus juxtaposed to Clare's in that they do not get the full sensual imagery that Clare's lips garners; whereas Irene's lips are used for silence, Clare's lips indicate sexual and racial transgressions that were largely unspeakable in 1920s America.

Nobody is more averse to these transgressions than Jack Bellew, whose mouth elicits its own memorable descriptors and is the source of the most discomfort for Clare's friends. He is described as having a "soft mouth, somewhat womanish, set in an unhealthy looking dough-coloured face."[181] What angers Irene most and sends her into silence is hearing Jack greet his wife with "Hello Nig," much to the dismay of everyone present except Clare.[182] Their mouths are contrasted with colors, primarily to underscore each character's disgust: Gertrude "caught her lip between her teeth" while "Irene's lips trembled almost uncontrollably" but she "didn't speak."[183] Of all three women

---

and it is linked with the larger question of the dangers of public exposure of both color and desire" (419).

[178] Larsen, *Passing*, 36.
[179] Larsen, 36.
[180] Larsen, 42.
[181] Larsen, 28.
[182] Larsen, 28.
[183] Larsen, 28–29.

there, only Clare appears unbothered, as "her gaze remained level on [her] smiling face," while her "Black eyes fluttered down" before turning into "an expression so dark and deep and unfathomable."[184] She eventually utters "Tell them, dear, why you call me that" as if seeking justification for her husband's ignorance to her audience.[185] Jack, oblivious to the racial background of all the women present, defends himself by noting his observation that Clare is "getting darker and darker," so much so, that he fears she might awaken one day "turned into a nigger."[186] He further notes that he does not just "dislike" African-Americans, instead "I hate them. And so does Nig, for all she's trying to turn into one. She wouldn't have a nigger maid around here for love nor money. Not that I'd want her to. They give me the creeps. The Black scrimy devils."[187] He offers some of the most ironic words in the novella: he is completely unaware that his hatred is unjustified as he sits with light-skinned Black women, including his beloved "Nig."

This scene draws much attention to each character's mouth—Bellew's hateful words from his "soft mouth," Irene's and Gertrude's lack of words, and Clare's awkward words justifying racism. Bellew's words have a physical effect on Clare, as she is described with dark colors for the first time in the narrative, foreshadowing her death at the end. The imagery of mouths and colors again highlights the connection between race and sexuality, for the crossing of one boundary often means crossing another boundary for those who jump the color line. Clare, the racial passer most often associated with color, shows attraction to Irene and Brian, while married to the racist Jack Bellew. Thus, she places herself in a dangerous situation by crossing boundaries of race and sexuality, with her identity precarious enough for her to keep Black maids out of their home. Like Victor and Solaria, she fears that Black housekeepers could recognize her race and disclose it. Irene and Gertrude discuss their own fears for Clare after meeting Jack, with an appalled Gertrude calling it "an awful chance" that Clare is taking by marrying a virulent racist.[188] Gertrude does not think that it is worth the risk, not even "for all the money she's getting out of it, when he finds out. Not with him feeling the

---

[184] Larsen, 29.
[185] Larsen, 29.
[186] Larsen, 29.
[187] Larsen, 30.
[188] Larsen, 32.

way he does."[189] She believes that Bellew's anger could prove deadly for Clare if he discovers her Blackness. Irene eventually breaks her silence when trying to dissuade Clare from attending the Negro Welfare League Dance, pointing to the "possible danger" which her attendance "might incur."[190] Though Irene ultimately fails to reason with her, she reminds Clare that "everything must be paid for. Do, please, be reasonable."[191]

Through this admonition, Irene evokes Bob Kendry's words to appeal to his daughter. The first time Irene and Gertrude meet at Clare's house, they discuss racial passing and the concern that having darker-skinned children would reveal a hidden Black ancestry. Clare defends it by saying "as my inestimable dad used to say, 'Everything must be paid for.'"[192] The logic behind this statement suggests that if one is passing, then "payment" might come in the form of a darker-skinned child, which could undermine the racial secret. When Irene applies Bob Kendry's dictum to Clare, we can infer that Clare herself might be the victim of retribution given the extent to which she has lied about her own identity. It was not enough for her to pretend to be White; she also solidified her Whiteness by marrying someone who fiercely detests African-Americans. Irene's reservations about Clare attending the party are well founded—if anyone sees Clare in proximity with Blacks in Harlem, Jack might find out and can kill her given his deep-seated prejudice. Clare is often depicted with fire imagery, perhaps because she is playing with the proverbial fire by attempting to balance two separate and conflicting lives.

Taking this a step further, Clare's behaviors underscore the impact of the death drive for racial passers. Pioneering female psychoanalyst Sabina Speilrein was the first person to theorize the death drive in her article "Destruction as the Cause of Coming Into Being" in 1912. She argued that "the reproduction of life involved the death of the parent," thus explicitly situating the death drive within sexuality.[193] Freud complicated her work in his 1920 essay "Beyond the Pleasure Principle," observing a division between death and sexuality: Eros (named for the Greek god of love), is the life force for humans and encompasses our desire to be productive, create life, maintain

---

[189] Larsen, 32.
[190] Larsen, 51.
[191] Larsen, 51.
[192] Larsen, 27.
[193] Spielrein, "Destruction as the Cause of Coming Into Being," 160.

harmony, and attain sexual connection. This all contrasts with the opposite ethos invoked by the death drive, which compels humans toward self-destruction, aggression, and reliving trauma. According to Freud, all humans are afflicted with this duality, in that our drives fall into these two categories—Eros (life instinct) or Thanatos (death instinct). He believed that we constantly face the internal battle between these two drives, especially since "the goal of all life is death" yet life instincts often temper this wish. This drive plays out most palpably for passers: imbedded within Eros and Thanatos is a specific racial duality with which they are afflicted. Eros includes the desire not only to survive, but to live specifically as White, while Thanatos defines a desire to die after being discovered as Black. Though Clare does not admit it, she has an internal desire to die as her marriage to a raging racist and her proximity to African-Americans suggest; exposure of her Black heritage could lead to her demise in an instant.

Clare's marriage is built on the falsity of her Whiteness, which is just one manifestation of her death wish. She does not heed her friends' warnings, choosing to attend the ball to enjoy the company of African-Americans in attendance. Her dance partners include Brian Redfield and Ralph Hazelton, who elicits Hugh Wentworth's comment, "Nice study in contrasts, that."[194] "That" refers to Clare's "fair and golden" complexion, which resembles a "sunlit day," contrasting with Ralph's "dark, gleaming eyes, like a moonlit night."[195] Clare and Ralph are literally presented as day and night at the dance, in a scene peppered with references to color. But for Irene, whose contrast with Clare is the starkest, this dance is easily forgettable – it eventually "faded to a blurred memory" with mingling outlines that cannot be distinguished.[196] This dance also augurs the narrative's end, when Clare's death becomes a blur for Irene and all the attendees of that fateful gathering.

"A Nameless Foreboding": Clare Kendry's Thanatos

Though Clare's demise initially appears ambiguous, clues about it appear throughout the narrative. For instance, it is first foreshadowed in the text's second section, when Irene observes a man who faints from the scorching

---

[194] Larsen, *Passing*, 54.
[195] Larsen, 54.
[196] Larsen, 56.

heat. Onlookers gather around his body and ask, "Was the man dead, or only faint?," due to his unexpected passing out.[197] The passersby question the nature of his death in a scene that repeats itself when Clare dies: "What would the others think? That Clare had fallen? That she had deliberately leaned backward? Certainly one or the other. Not—"[198] The party goers who surround Clare's corpse are equally unsure if her unexpected fall from the window was an accident, homicide, or suicide.

Her ambiguous death also recalls the deaths of her parents, who helped to initiate her two deaths: the metaphorical end of her Black self and her physical death in the denouement. This observation of Clare's death places her in line with both Victor and Solaria, in that the death of her parents opened the way for her to transgress racial boundaries. Clare's mother is conspicuously left out of the narrative, with Irene pontificating that she "would have run away if she hadn't died," while the text itself only reveals that her father was a drunk who died in a saloon fight.[199] After his death, Clare went to live with her White aunts, who frequently evoked her "Negro blood" as justification for her hardships—such as when they tasked her with performing difficult manual labor in accordance with the Biblical curse of Ham and when they "forbade" her from mentioning "Negroes to the neighbours."[200] Like Grandmère in "Stones," Clare's aunts prohibited her from verbalizing any association with race; whether it was her biracial father or her youth on the "Black" side of Chicago, Aunt Grace and Aunt Edna made it clear that race was completely unwelcome in their home. As a result, Clare rationalizes that it was easy to begin a relationship with Jack Bellew when they first met, for he was unaware of her biracial ancestry and offered an escape from her oppressive racist environment. The lips that eventually develop into a sexual register with Irene and Brian were forced to remain shut in order to avoid youthful revelations of race.

Clare's escape, however, comes at a cost and reinscribes the racism she sought to avoid. Marrying Jack forces her to straddle the seemingly impermeable boundaries of race and sexuality. Her difficulties in accomplishing these goals contribute to her own death drive, serving as the impetus behind

---

[197] Larsen, 8.
[198] Larsen, 80.
[199] Larsen, 14.
[200] Larsen, 18–19.

the most provocative claim about Clare Kendry and contradicting most critical perspectives on her death: she committed suicide.[201] Freud would have agreed with this, perhaps considering Clare's marriage to Jack and close proximity to African-Americans as the riskiest of behaviors, indicative of her self-destructive leanings. Her death begins with Jack intruding on a party which Clare, Irene, and several of their Black friends attend. Instead of calling her "Nig" as he did when we first encountered him, he utters "So you're a nigger, a damned dirty nigger!"[202] His Whiteness and visible anger differ sharply from the calmness of his wife. The memorable description of Clare's composure invokes color and lips one final time:

> Clare stood at the window, as composed as if everyone were not staring at her in curiosity and wonder, as if the whole structure of her life were not lying in fragments before her. She seemed unaware of any danger or uncaring. There was even a *faint smile* on her *full, red lips*, and in her shining eyes. It was that *smile* that maddened Irene. She ran across the room, her terror tinged with ferocity, and laid a hand on Clare's bare arm. One thought possessed her. She couldn't have Clare Kendry cast aside by Bellew. She couldn't have her free. Before them stood John Bellew, *speechless* now in his hurt and anger. Beyond them the little huddle of other people, and Brian stepping out from among them. One moment Clare had been there, a vital glowing thing, like a flame of red and gold. The next she was gone.[203]

---

[201] Most literary critics, especially those cited in the Norton Critical Edition of the text, concede the ending's ambiguity but adduce evidence that Irene killed Clare. Mary Mabel Youman, for instance, believes that Irene murders Clare to "preserve her ultimate value—security" (340), while Mary Helen Washington agrees that maintaining security is the reason Irene pushes Clare out the window (354–55). Deborah McDowell, Cheryl Wall, and Helen Michie also place blame on Irene for murdering Clare. Fewer critics consider the possibility of other motives for Clare's death: Judith Butler fully explicates the ambiguities in the novel's denouement, showing that Irene, Bellew, and/or Clare can be the reason Clare dies (422–23), while Jennifer DeVere Brody raises the possibility of suicide, but ultimately "points to Irene as the murderer" (408). Claudia Tate comes closest to encouraging readers to consider suicide as the reason for Clare's death, especially since all evidence pointing to Irene is merely circumstantial ("Nella Larsen's *Passing*," 347–49, from the Norton Critical Edition of *Passing*).

[202] Larsen, 79.

[203] Larsen, 79, emphases mine.

In the shock of her public racial unveiling, Clare is at first stoic, so much so, that even her "full red lips" remain unchanging. The same lips that are depicted in sensual language throughout the novel now reveal a smile, masking the deep humiliation she has internalized at realizing that her husband and friends are now fully aware of her identity. Bellew's appearance shocks her into silence, for this is one of the few times in the narrative that Clare is completely speechless. His anger prompts the male attendees to jump to their feet and prepare to stop the raging racist from harming Clare. Irene also appears as though she has her best interest at heart, by placing her hand on Clare to save her from being "cast aside by Bellew."[204] When Brian emerges from the crowd, we can assume that he too hopes to protect Clare from her husband's outrage. In addition, embers of fire die in Clare's death scene when Irene discards her cigarette and "watch[es] the tiny spark" disintegrate to the ground, serving as a precursor to when Clare, "a vital glowing thing, like a flame of red and gold," lands outside the window.[205] A similar image defines an argument with Brian in which he mentions his desire to relocate to Brazil; Irene believes that his "discontent...would surely die, *flicker out*, at last," however it "was still living and still had the power *to flare up* and alarm her."[206]

The image of fire, which the narrative associates with Clare, was used to describe Irene's response to Brian's displeasure, as she equates his desire with a flame needing to die. Fires are not easily put out, such as Brian's longing for Brazil, but Clare's body, "a flame," is easily distinguished when she ends up outside the window. Nevertheless, this similar phraseology of flickering fire underscores the connection that Irene perceives between the two: in questioning the nature of their relationship, she implies that a symbolic romantic fire might be brewing between them that requires extinguishing. After years of cultivating a feigned identity, Clare's death scene forces her to confront reminders of her racial passing and sexual deviancy, in the forms of Bellew's bellowing, Brian's bravery, and Irene's idealism. Yet Irene does not put out either fire; Clare herself does.

Revelers and readers alike question the reason Clare's corpse ends up outside the window. Dave Freeland asserts "she had fainted," Brian informs the police that Jack "[gave] her a shove," while Irene renders it "a terrible

---

[204] Larsen, 79.
[205] Larsen, 79.
[206] Larsen, 41, emphasis mine.

accident," which she justifies to the police as "she just fell."[207] Only Ralph Hazelton comes close to understanding Clare's demise: "I was looking right at her. She just tumbled over and was gone before you could say 'Jack Robinson.' Fainted, I guess. Lord! It was quick. Quickest thing I ever saw in all my life."[208] He qualifies his assertion of her fainting by uttering "I guess," indicating he is not fully certain that she died from blacking out. He is correct though, in his observation that she "tumbled over" quickly, as she committed suicide before anyone could stop her. Clare's death is rendered in colorful romantic terms—"Gone! The soft white face, the bright hair, the disturbing scarlet mouth, the dreaming eyes, the caressing smile, the whole torturing loveliness that had been Clare Kendry."[209] Despite this flowery description, Clare actually dies blackened because Jack Bellew greets her with the vilest epithet used against African-Americans. No longer is it "Hello nig," but the entire epithet is used to dehumanize her as he confirms his suspicions that she is Black. She is thus outed as a Black woman passing as White, which served as the impetus for her death drive. The last group of people she saw were African-Americans, members of a race she belonged to and ran from after reuniting with Irene. When everything goes "dark" at the narrative's end, it represents not only her physical death but also her racial unveiling by a racist in a room of African-Americans. Clare passed as White for her entire adult life, while flirting with Irene and Brian despite her marriage to Bellew. Thus, she wanted to die because she was unable to handle the weight of seeing her racial passing and taboo sexuality on public display at the party. The racial passer did not just "pass out," she actively sought her own death.

One of the characters most affected by Clare's sudden demise is Brian Redfield, whose face "looked aged and altered," and whose lips were purple and trembling."[210] This depiction recalls the first image we have of Irene, as she sits with a seemingly anonymous letter distinguished by its "purple ink."[211] She wants to open it, but delays doing so as she grapples with her memories of Clare's past. We can read Irene's frequent deferrals when interacting with both Brian and Clare as indicative of her overall passive demeanor

---

[207] Larsen, 80–82.
[208] Larsen, 81.
[209] Larsen, 80.
[210] Larsen, 81.
[211] Larsen, 5.

and as another iteration of the two characters/potential lovers being linked through the same color. Irene's repressive behavior throughout the narrative suggests that she would not take the irrational step of pushing Clare to her death. Although she had a motive to murder Clare Kendry, this does not mean that she committed the act, nor does the final scene offer any sign of her guilt. According to Butler, anyone could feel guilty about a friend's death, without being the one ultimately responsible for it.[212] Moreover, despite the crowd at the party, nobody "actually observes Irene push Clare, and Irene never admits whether she is guilty, not even to herself."[213] If Irene, or anyone else in attendance, pushed Clare out the window, somebody would have had to see it, given the amount of party guests present. Yet after being blackened by Jack and chastened by the Redfields in front of their Black friends, Clare chooses suicide instead of further humiliation. *Passing* comes full circle as the concerns that open the novel—death, lips, color, and sexuality—also conclude it. After spending years jumping the color line, Clare jumped out the window to escape the chaos of her "furtive" life. Her disclosed race leaves her unwilling to continue living. In other words, Clare's Thanatos—her desire to die after being discovered as Black—wins out over her Eros.

Suicide As Confession

The conclusion of *Passing* has puzzled readers since its first publication; not only the "finale" of the plot, but the actual words used to end the text. The first two printings of the novel ended with "Centuries after, she heard the strange man saying: 'Death by misadventure, I'm inclined to believe. Let's go up and have another look at that window.'"[214] Knopf's third printing of the novel, however, ends with "Then everything was dark."[215] This latter ending is most familiar to readers, and more aptly dramatizes Clare's end. For a character whose association with several colors defines the narrative, it is appropriate that the concluding words of the text comment on everything being "dark," since Jack renders her Black by calling her a "damned dirty nigger!," and darkness engulfs her as she jumps out the window.[216] Yet the novel's

---

[212] Butler, "Passing, Queering," 422.
[213] Tate, "Nella Larsen's *Passing*," 347.
[214] Larsen, *Passing*, 82.
[215] Larsen, 82.
[216] Larsen, 79.

original ending is a more compelling guide to Clare's downfall: primarily, the "strange man" invites readers to revisit the fateful window with him, to ascertain the precise details of the "death by misadventure."[217] Using Freud's death drive, a deeper analysis of this death scene suggests that Clare, like Victor and Solaria, chose death over Blackness. None of these fictional racial passers die passively through a mere "misadventure" but actively through their decision to die instead of continuing to live with their created identities. In short, their Eros succumbs to their Thanatos.

While everything goes "dark" for Clare Kendry, Victor's lips turn black as does Solaria's body, serving as final reminders that race can still spring forth despite efforts to hide it. Indeed, Gibson argues that

> The association of Black with the more unpleasant things in life is ubiquitous. Evil, mourning, and gloom, among other things are its analogues and no one is more aware of this than the individual whose skin is Black…[as a result]…Blackness becomes the progenitor of inferiority.[218]

With such negative associations with Blackness, the racial passers in these texts viewed passing as White as the end of their problems with race. Though their contrived lives are colored by Whiteness, the deaths of these racial passers are defined by Blackness.

The original ending shows that neither Clare's story nor her relationship with Irene is over despite her suicide. Ending the novel with "Then everything was dark" has a tone of finality to it, as though the story is expected to officially conclude with Clare's death and Irene's falling into oblivion. Most students today are familiar with this ending because it concluded the popular Rutgers University Edition for decades. It stands in sharp contrast to Larsen's original concluding paragraph that begins with "Centuries after," since this ending suggests that the story might continue after Clare's absence. If the strange man is "inclined" to believe that a mere "misadventure" befell Clare, then he is not fully convinced, since "inclined" implies room for doubt. If her death is indeed a "misadventure," it is up to readers to return to "that window" for a closer look at the circumstances, at the strange man's invitation. As Michie asserts, "Clare is not exorcised; neither, significantly, is the entanglement of Irene's body with Clare's," especially since Irene's "swoon into

---

[217] Larsen, 82.
[218] Gibson, "Concerning Color," 413.

unconsciousness" mirrors Clare's own trajectory at the novel's end.[219] The chaos surrounding her life and death continues even after her suicide, when she remains tethered to Irene. With the "Centuries after" ending, Clare and Irene are bound together always, united in their racial passing and the comparable manners of their ends.

The vagueness of this death scene is typical of a suicide, a type of death that is notoriously ambiguous because it can leave one's friends and family without closure as they try to pinpoint the impetus to choose suicide over living. Albert Camus opens his philosophical essay, "The Myth of Sisyphus," by calling suicide the "one truly serious philosophical problem." He believes that "killing yourself amounts to confessing. It is confessing that life is too much for you or that you do not understand it."[220] When Victor, Solaria, and Clare are confronted with their race, none of them say anything to confirm or deny the dangerous allegation, instead they are swallowed up by Blackness and die. Their death drive provides a powerful confession that their words cannot, as if the silence that defined their passing lives prefigured the ultimate silence of death. Although "death is repeatedly seen as a cost of passing," reevaluating the specific nature of the deaths of racial passers points to Freud's influence over passing narratives, vis-à-vis the prominence of the death drive.[221] These texts are prime examples of "active death," in that characters set out to die instead of succumbing passively as their nineteenth-century predecessors did.

Blackness is an internal object for racial passers, and though each protagonist encounters it before dying, they deal with it differently: Victor kills it when he waves away help while he chokes, after it is resurrected at dinner through the image of his Creole grandmother; while Solaria's inorganic Blackness is always close to being revealed through her body, long before her suicide. Her proximity to Black men causes her to blush and become paranoid. She uses suggestive language to assert her fear not just of being called "Black" but of being raced, specifically via her sexuality; this explains why she dies only after she thinks her love interest has discovered her secret. Meanwhile, everything goes black for Clare Kendry after she crosses boundaries of race and sexuality in her flirtations with the Redfields. Her husband calls her

---

[219] Michie, *Sororophobia*, 416.
[220] Camus, "The Myth of Sisyphus," 1.
[221] Stouck, "Identities in Crisis," 288.

out on both, and she commits suicide as a result. Though several important distinctions characterize these novels—such as the fact that Solaria and Clare pass in Chicago and New York, large northern cities that provide greater anonymity from racial and sexual boundaries, and Victor does not have to worry about sexuality as much as Solaria and Clare—all three protagonists decide that it is best to "pass away," a function of their decision to pass as White.

When viewed through a psychoanalytic lens, the texts explored in this chapter conclude that passing is impracticable: the protagonists do not die as White at all. Their Eros motivated them to feign Whiteness to survive, yet Thanatos forced them to accelerate their deaths and they inadvertently die as Black. This is evidenced by enslavement hovering over Victor, Solaria, and Clare, as a reminder of their race and of taboo sexual acts of miscegenation that yielded their light complexions. Slavery endured for thousands of years, yet it became race based for the first time in the United States. Thus, the enslaved who were light enough to pass as White often did so. Once the "separate but equal" doctrine legalized racial discrimination in Jim Crow America, African-Americans continued to jump the color line for safety and socioeconomic privileges. In fact, Larsen described her own foray into the "passing stunt" in 1932. In a letter to Carl Van Vechten, she detailed an incident in which she and a friend "demanded lunch and <u>got</u> it" while travelling through "a rather conservative town called Murfreesborough."[222] She bragged about not only getting lunch in this segregated town, but also about getting the best "service in the world, and an invitation to return."[223] Anecdotes like this one undermine rigid racial customs in the United States: that two African-American women entered a segregated restaurant in the Jim Crow South and received attentive service completely disproves the necessity for racial segregation in the first place.

Larsen's confession to Van Vechten raises a logical question: how much of her life did she infuse into her writings? Just as Larsen passed in this restaurant in Murfreesborough, so too do Clare and Irene in the opening of *Passing*, when they enjoy tea in the Drayton Hotel in Chicago. Larsen's protagonists also ended in oblivion as an eerie prediction of her own story. While we know little of the final three decades of Larsen's life in obscurity, *The New York Times* rectified the absence of her obituary by publishing one as part of

---

[222] Larsen, Letter to Carl Ven Vechten, 170, emphasis in original.
[223] Larsen, 170.

its "Overlooked" series in January 2018. Larsen herself offered the most compelling evidence that she blurred the lines between her life and her fiction when complaining to her friend Dorothy Peterson about her desire to relocate from Harlem: "Right now when I look out into the Harlem streets I feel just like Helga Crane in my novel [Quicksand 1928]. Furious at being cornered with all these niggers."[224] Thadious Davis reads "cornered" as "connected" in her essay on Larsen's "Harlem Aesthetic," due to Larsen's handwriting being difficult to decipher.[225] In Larsen's later years, she relocated to Greenwich Village, when she began "'passing' in the manner developed in her novel of that name," according to curator Jean Blackwell Hutson in 1969.[226] Whether Larsen felt connected to or cornered by African-Americans, her novels reflect elements of her own life as a mixed-race woman in the first half of the twentieth century.

If Nella Larsen purposefully wrote herself into her works, it would be comparable to a long line of writers and theorists who also blurred these lines, including Sigmund Freud and real-life racial passers in the United States. Freud viewed suicide as a wish to escape from the chaos of life. As Danticat reiterates, Freud's version of Thanatos is "what he saw as our longing to self-destruct and return to our pre-existing state through war and other means."[227] For passing characters, this war is one they wage with themselves as they negate Blackness and assume Whiteness in a White-dominated country. Yet as I indicated earlier in this text, Freud also forged identities for himself for personal and professional gain: he was involved in a secret relationship with Wilhelm Fliess and wanted to distance himself from even the mere mention of being a "blackamoor." As Matory puts it, Freud sought to "convince himself and others that he deserved membership in the elite of Europe's emerging global empire."[228] This could have been very challenging if his own "racial and sexual ambiguity" were publicized during his lifetime.[229] Freud did not want anything published about his personal life and wanted most

---

[224] Larsen, Letter to Dorothy Peterson, 164.
[225] Davis, "Nella Larsen's Harlem Aesthetic," 382, from the Norton Critical Edition of *Passing*.
[226] Hutson, "Letter About Nella Larsen to Louise Fox," 152.
[227] Danticat, *The Art of Death*, 129.
[228] Matory, *The Fetish Revisited*, 100.
[229] Matory, 100.

correspondence destroyed about his life in order to become a member of a non-racialized European elite.

Taking Matory's provocative argument a step further, I assert that Freud wanted to pass racially and sexually, and one way to achieve this was to fiercely guard his personal life and prevent aspects of it from reaching the public domain. Like the characters explored in this chapter, he purposely obscured the two areas that could lead to the demise of his career and perhaps even his life: race and sexuality. The other way to achieve the reputation he wanted was by creating the field of psychoanalysis, which allowed him to explore his hidden identities in theoretical form. According to his followers, psychoanalysis provided "a working out of his own demons," which I believe was a way to write about himself from an academic distance.[230] More explicitly, psychoanalysis allowed Freud to write about human race and sexuality without revealing too much of his own race and sexuality, which he sought to obscure. My assumption is supported by the fact that he was "internally divided and deeply ambivalent about himself and his people," which makes me wonder if this internal division was translated as his own personal impetus for invoking Eros and Thanatos, even if he could not articulate it lest it reveal his own struggles.[231]

If so, Eros won out. Freud was afraid of death, and wanted to be remembered for publishing ideas that would garner him "gentile approval."[232] He thus maintained a "lifelong aspiration to worldly wealth, fame, and power, as well as a pharaonic desire to monumentalize himself."[233] Freud accomplished dual goals in his creation of psychoanalysis: he wanted to work out his identity and remain immortal through his theories. He clearly succeeded in the latter, for we are still grappling with his theories a century after they were popularized. It is unclear how much he benefitted personally from his own ideas, as he was interested in creating and sustaining a public persona above all else. What conclusions Freud drew about himself requires further analysis that is beyond the scope of this monograph, especially since he viewed any reference to his "own neuroses as an act of heresy."[234] What is clear though,

---

[230] Matory, 117.
[231] Matory, 118.
[232] Matory, 119.
[233] Matory, 156.
[234] Matory, 123.

is that psychoanalysis is incredibly useful in understanding different types of passing. This theory began as a response to Freud's race and sexuality as a passer, making it even more suitable in comprehending the rationale to transgress lines of race and sexuality since then.

Despite Freud's best efforts, he implicitly wrote about himself throughout his psychoanalytic works, including the essay "Beyond the Pleasure Principle" and his book *Three Contributions to the Theory of Sex*. Other examples of writers serving as their own muses include Larsen, her contemporary Anita Reynolds, and *The New York Times* book critic Anatole Broyard. Neither Reynolds nor Broyard was able to write their life stories; they succeeded in publishing a wide range of creative work, yet their memoirs remained a lifelong elusive goal. As the next chapter contends, fictional racial passers hastened death, whereas real-life passers sought to escape it by writing themselves into their works. Reynolds and Broyard sought the literary immortality that Sigmund Freud aspired to.

CHAPTER 3

PASSING AND LIFE WRITING

"A Thousand Details, Anecdotes, and Stories": Piecing Together the Lives of Racial Passers

If Freud had his way, we would be completely unaware of his personal details. According to Matory:

> While Freud avoided publishing information about his personal life and, indeed, endeavored to destroy the most revealing correspondence about it, his intimate friend, acolyte, and biographer Ernest Jones divined many of the personal motives behind Freud's intellectual and social project, motives more than circumstantially related to the racially ambiguous ranking of Jews within the emerging nation-states and translocal empires of Freud's day.[1]

Yet we are able to glean details of Freud's personal life that he sought to destroy, thanks to Ernest Jones. Freud opted for silence to hide his Jewish identity at a time when Jews faced increasing anti-Semitism, as well as to hide his "then-socially unacceptable homosexual feelings" toward Wilhelm Fliess.[2] Moreover, neither Jewishness nor homosexuality would have helped him sustain the fatherly image he fashioned for himself.

Instead of revealing much about his personal life, Freud wanted to be known primarily through his ideas, which would help him live on in perpetuity. To further advance psychoanalysis, he relied on his disciples; as Matory explains, Freud pursued "immortality through his psychoanalytical sons."[3] He first saw Carl Jung as the heir to Freudian psychoanalysis, yet their relationship ended when Jung promoted the importance of the collective unconscious over sexual development. Their contradictory visions of the unconscious put a permanent end to their relationship. As Freud himself noted "I...find it hard to assimilate alien thoughts that do not quite lie in my path."[4]

---

[1] Matory, *The Fetish Revisited*, 105.
[2] Matory, 106.
[3] Matory, 119.
[4] Jones, *The Life and Work of Sigmund Freud*, 311, 417.

His inflexibility at entertaining dissent caused similar breaks with Alfred Adler, Sándor Ferenczi, and Otto Rank. The latter two in particular rankled Freud, for they did not consider the Oedipus Complex as the impetus for adult neurosis; instead, they believed that the trauma of birth took priority for adults. Jones depicted dissent against Freud as "heresy," yet the division over the birth trauma serves as the starting point for this chapter.

Otto Rank published his pivotal book *The Trauma of Birth* in 1924. As the title attests, birth and parenting are essential to his theorization, as Ahad observes: "Rank understood the role of the mother as the primary source of love and anxiety for the child—an ambivalence that commences at birth."[5] Birth is traumatic because it forces the child to enter the foreign world outside of the womb, which "produces an anxiety that manifests itself in a fixation on the mother's womb or as a desire to return symbolically to the mother."[6] Rank's trauma of birth is also "a theory of anxiety" because of the anxiety inherent in birth. To overcome this anxiety, the child seeks to create an individual personality that is very different from the mother, but he or she still tries to symbolically reenter the womb for safety. The fixation on the womb is also the result of impending death; leaving the security of the former entails the certainty of the latter. To abate this anxiety of death, "the subject performs various symbolic acts that represent the prolonging of life."[7] Rank argues that the people who are best suited for this prolonging of life are artists, for they seek to live forever by creating works "in constantly repeated acts of birth."[8] He theorizes that humans begin fearing death as soon as we exit the womb, resulting in a lifelong quest to extend our lives. Artists, such as writers, are the most successful at living in perpetuity—even though symbolically—because they place themselves in their creative works.

Rank developed his provocative ideas by disputing some of Freud's more established theories. This was the beginning of the personal and professional differences that bred more fissures between them.[9] In a letter to Freud in

---

[5] Ahad, *Freud Upside Down*, 44.

[6] Ahad, 45.

[7] Ahad, 45

[8] Rank, *The Trauma of Birth*, 156.

[9] For instance, Freud's background in medicine informed his vision of psychoanalysis, while Rank drew on his training in psychology and the humanities to put forth his idea of birth trauma and its relationship to creative artists. As a result of his broad background, Rank expanded psychoanalysis from a "narrow medical

which Rank attempted to repair their relationship, he notes that he sees his own work as an extension of Freudian psychoanalysis instead of a deviation from it: "I can boast of a more extensive concordance with your views and an even stronger connection with them….Not only do I find no contradiction, but rather the most perfect harmony with your theory of drives."[10] While Freud believed that the mother is strictly the object of desire, Rank noted that the child's ambivalence toward the mother stemmed from viewing her as the source of love and anxiety. Rank's gesture of reconciliation with Freud proved ineffective, for they saw the role of the mother in fundamentally different terms, leading Freud to renounce the psychoanalyst whom he once taught. Freud considered himself as a father figure to Rank, yet Rank's new theory birthed a fracture in their parental-like relationship.

Whether Freud and Rank interpreted parallels between the theory and their relationship is unclear; what is clear though, is that the ideas put forth in *The Trauma of Birth* are very useful for understanding racial passers, including Freud himself and some of his followers in the United States. Not only did Rank influence Black writers beginning in the Harlem Renaissance through his theory on the ways in which artists seek to live forever through their works, but also his ideas correspond with the anxieties that real-life racial passers deal with—birth, death, and creativity. As Ahad articulates, "Although Rank does not imagine race, or more specifically biracialism, as a feature of the traumatic birth experience, the hostility, alienation, and denigration the mixed-race child would undergo, especially in the early twentieth century, undoubtedly qualifies as a severe experience."[11] Anatole Broyard and Anita Reynolds, two real-life passers born in the first half of the twentieth century, exemplify Rank's theory of birth as well as the tension borne out with creative writing.

Anita Thompson was born in Chicago in 1901 and died in 1980 in the Virgin Islands.[12] Her maternal grandmother was allegedly half White and half Cherokee, while her maternal grandfather was of mixed-race and her father

---

technique" to a "world philosophy" (Kampf, *The Psychology and Psychotherapy of Otto Rank*, 5).

[10] Lieberman, *Acts of Will*, 214.

[11] Ahad, *Freud Upside Down*, 47.

[12] She married Guy Reynolds in the 1950s. Her memoir, *American Cocktail*, was written and published under her married name.

was a Louisiana Creole.[13] She worked as a dancer, actress, educator, writer, and psychologist—all aided by her light complexion, which she used to her advantage by jumping the color line. Anatole Broyard was born in 1920 to French and Caribbean-descended Creoles in New Orleans and died in 1990 in Massachusetts. Through his transgression of the color line, he assumed a White identity in the military and at *The New York Times*, where he became an influential literary critic. Though no evidence exists that their paths crossed, they both spent time in New York City and were transformed by World War II. This war brought Reynolds back to America to be reminded of her Black ancestry again, while it offered Broyard a way out of America where he had the complete freedom to fashion a new identity for himself. Both Reynolds and Broyard also tried to write their memoirs over several years, but they were only published posthumously: Reynolds's autobiography was published as *American Cocktail: A "Colored Girl" in the World* (2014), while Bliss Broyard published her father's biography, *One Drop: My Father's Hidden Life–A Story of Race and Family Secrets* in 2007.

Bliss Broyard cited several of her father's writings to complete his story, including his unfinished autobiography, as well as the fiction and nonfiction he published over four decades. She had to read between the lines of his writing to help paint a compelling and honest portrait of Anatole Broyard, for he was a Creole who hid his Black ancestry to pass as White and took great pains to avoid discussing race in his writings. Anita Reynolds was equally judicious in not writing about her Black past once she began eschewing it, yet she left clues about her Blackness in her works. Broyard and Reynolds attempted to write their life stories for years before posthumously succeeding, believing that writer's block was their primary impediment. However, as this chapter asserts, writer's block was hardly the primary hindrance: they were more productive in other types of creative writing. The issue is not that Broyard and Reynolds wanted to write about themselves, but that they endeavored to write their stories without explicitly addressing their Blackness, a discrepancy which undergirds this chapter. In fact, the mode they were attempting to write in, life writing, was the problem, and not the simple scapegoat of writer's block.

On the surface, the genre of life writing and the theme of racial passing might appear antithetical to one another. The former is predicated on

---

[13] Reynolds, *American Cocktail*, 23.

honesty, while the latter requires stealth and deception to obscure one's race. This dichotomy might explain the reluctance with which scholars apply theories of writing to life narratives of passing subjects.[14] Literary critics hesitate applying theories of writing to the life narratives of passing subjects, lest they miscategorize them for sharing fictionalized lives. Passing subjects who write about themselves often quote from established passing fictions.[15] Real-life passing narratives are inherently literary because their authors are writers themselves who reveal their debts to fictional iterations of racial passing, such as for Anita Reynolds and Anatole Broyard. According to Ian Donaldson, the idea that biography could be a viable area of study is a recent phenomenon, given that English departments shunned this genre for most of the twentieth century.[16] New Critics also rendered biography as unimportant for serious literary study, focusing on texts themselves instead of the lives of authors. Autobiography has fared better as an area of scholarly inquiry because readers are more sympathetic to the intimacy of first-person narratives.[17] This might explain why autobiographies have flooded the literary market while gaining traction as an area of serious critical inquiry over recent years. In the past three decades alone, mixed-race subjects specifically have dominated the genre of life writings.[18] Yet autobiographers face questions about their ability

---

[14] For a thorough literary historiography of passing literature and autobiography, see Werner Sollors, *Neither Black nor White Yet Both*, 246–84; and Juda Bennett, "Black by Popular Demand," 262–75.

[15] For example, Adrian Piper's autobiographical essay "Passing for White, Passing for Black," cites a range of novelists who wrote passing novels, including James Weldon Johnson, Nella Larsen, and Frances Harper, while Martha Sandweiss' *Passing Strange*, a biography of reverse passer Clarence King, opens with a quote from Philip Roth's *The Human Stain*.

[16] Donaldson, "Biographical Uncertainty," 306.

[17] Smith and Watson, "The Trouble with Autobiography," 361.

[18] Beginning in the 1990s, biracial authors have written extensively about their lives navigating race in twentieth-century America, as evidenced in works that include Shirlee Taylor Haizlip's *The Sweeter the Juice: A Family Memoir on Black and White* (1995), Judy Trent-Scales's *Notes of a White Black Woman* (1995), Gregory Howard Williams's *Life on the Color Line: The True Story of a White Boy Who Discovered He Was Black* (1996), Toi Derricotte's *The Black Notebooks: An Interior Journey* (1997), and Wade Hall's *Passing For Black: The Life and Careers of Mae Street Kidd* (1997). Each of these authors, except the last one, is a light-skinned Black person writing about being confused for White and their movement across the color line. In Hall's

to remember specific aspects of their lives, which is best exemplified by Jerome Bruner—one of the founders of narrative construction theory—who believes that a "life as lived" does not exist; a more accurate formulation is "a life created or constructed by the act of autobiography."[19]

Thus, understanding the effect of race on life writing is a novel idea, since critics have paid minimal attention to this literary genre. When it comes to the life narratives written by and about people of color, writers and subjects face an added set of impediments. In writing about postcolonial writers, Spivak originated the term "withheld autobiography" to refer to postcolonial writers who pen fictionalized narratives for subjects who are silent because they lack access to writing.[20] According to her, it is "the genre of the subaltern giving witness to oppression, to a less repressed other."[21] These types of narratives rework the traditional meaning of autobiography by exposing readers to the voices of those who cannot speak directly. This impetus is prevalent in African-American literature as well, since the genre began with narratives of the formerly enslaved, speaking on behalf of their voiceless counterparts who were denied access to literacy.[22] Autobiography and biography thus blur the

---

case, he is the amanuensis for Mae Street Kidd, a Kentucky politician who passed as White during the mid-twentieth century. These texts all refer to passing or at least the potential thereof.

[19] Bruner, "Life as Narrative," 28.

[20] Spivak, "Three Women's Texts and Circumfession," 7.

[21] Spivak, 7.

[22] In *Black Autobiography in America* (1974), Stephen Butterfield notes that Black autobiography is "the unity of the personal and the mass voice," particularly since this field emphasizes "shared life, shared triumph, and communal responsibility" (3). Paul Gilroy argues that the goal of African-American autobiography is twofold: "self-creation and self-emancipation" (*The Black Atlantic*, 69). Taking a sociological approach, Magnus Bassey notes that African-American autobiography is tasked with addressing race relations and critiquing racism ("The Place of Group Consciousness," 216). He reminds readers that the audience for Black autobiography often expects to find insight into "Black life" in these texts, and that the writers deliver by emphasizing group consciousness with the unintended effect of African-American culture becoming pathologized (220). For more on Black autobiography, see William Andrews, *To Tell a Free Story* (1986); JoAnn Braxton, *Black Women Writing Autobiography* (1989); David Dudley, *My Father's Shadow* (1991); V.P. Franklin, *Living Our Stories, Telling Our Truths* (1996); and Sidonie Smith, *Where I'm Bound* (1974).

lines between fact and fiction, complicating the field of life writing as one of scholarly inquiry.

Whether we are reading autobiography or biography, what unites most life writings is an absence, an intangible something that is lost or was never present in the first place. Psychoanalysis provides insight into the source of this lack. As Lacan notes in "The Instance of the Letter in the Unconscious," writing is precisely where one is not: "this reference to the real-life context of my lecture, by showing whom I tailored it for, also marked those to whom it is *not addressed*."[23] Fanon similarly notes that "the white man" knew nothing about him, and thus had "woven me out of a thousand details, anecdotes, and stories."[24] White people pieced together information about Fanon, but nothing was coherent enough to compile a complete history of his life; something was missing, yet we can use psychoanalysis to help close the gap.

This chapter argues that Rank's theory of birth helps to fill this lacuna by explaining the actions of Broyard and Reynolds. Both endured tense relationships with their mothers and tried to write themselves into perpetuity through their life narratives, where they left clues about being Black but could not verbalize race explicitly. While Reynolds's relationship with death was not clear in her writings, Broyard was certainly obsessed with it, as several of his works make clear. This chapter is invested in the divergent ways in which the trauma of birth and the anxiety of death unfold for real-life racial passers. I invoke Rank's expansive application of psychoanalysis in this chapter not as a framework to which their lives strictly adhered, but because he provides critical insight into the questions real-life passers must contend with, including how they can live in eternity while maintaining their passing subjectivity. As well, how can they reconcile their mothers and their Blackness, while passing as White?

Broyard and Reynolds exemplify the difficult dilemma of race versus writing, which other real-life racial passers also endured. They sought relief from the death drive by attempting to immortalize themselves through their life stories. However, they were unable to accurately depict their lives lest they reveal their Black ancestry. As a result, they left behind only fragments of themselves. Broyard and Reynolds were not hindered by writer's block as they presumed; instead, they could not complete their narratives without revealing

---

[23] Lacan, "The Instance of the Letter in the Unconscious," 413, emphasis mine.
[24] Fanon, *Black Skin*, 91.

their Blackness. Today, both live on through their own writings and their depictions in the works of others.

The goals of this chapter are twofold: it continues the distinction from the last chapter between fictional passers who are motivated by the death drive, and real-life passers who run away from it by seeking literary immortality in their publications. Additionally, this chapter elaborates on the racialized scope of psychoanalysis—a topic of which Reynolds and Broyard were well aware. According to her biographer George Hutchinson, Reynolds's education and her parents' connections served her well, for she joined the Hollywood avant-garde at age fifteen and was conversant in "Freud, Adler, and Jung," allowing her to "talk freely about the current political issues" with her artistically minded cohort of friends.[25] As an adult, Reynolds considered "Freud's basic works" among the many books she consumed.[26] Similarly, Anatole Broyard thought critically about psychoanalysis, citing Sigmund Freud throughout his writings. In a piece entitled "Ha Ha," he places Freud on a higher pedestal than Karl Marx, for it was Freud who argued that "the child grows up only to discover that he will always be but a child to mother Nature. Realizing this, he laughs to recover his child's innocuous immunity."[27] In a review of *The Oxford Book of Death*, Broyard praises Freud again, telling his readers that Freud thought it "impossible for us to imagine our own death, that even here we are present, and survive, as spectators."[28] Indeed, as indicated previously, Freud did not like to think about his own death and sought an immortal raceless reputation.

As a result, it might be easier to see the correlations between Freud, Broyard, and Reynolds, for they all sought a reputation after death. Yet it was Rank who hypothesized why this is the case. Broyard and Reynolds were aware of and influenced by the works of Freud's protégé and defiant "son," Otto Rank, who expanded classical psychoanalysis. Rank did not explicitly include race, which is curious since Freud developed his own theories from an anxiety of and preoccupation with race. Yet I join Ahad's reading of Rank's principles by extending them and rendering them particularly apt for racial passers. Though my goal is to continue uncovering the ways in which

---

[25] Hutchinson, "Introduction," 34.
[26] Reynolds, *American Cocktail*, 138.
[27] Broyard, "Ha! Ha!," 12.
[28] Broyard, "Books of the Times," 8.

psychoanalysis helps us to understand those who straddle the color line, exploring the lives of real-life passers is a difficult endeavor because they leave behind so few details to live in stealth. They also represent the challenges in addressing the biographies of anyone, since readers are only afforded a few pertinent anecdotes. bell hooks, for example, believed she did not write a complete account of her autobiography, but one consisting of "those experiences that were deeply imprinted in my consciousness. Significantly, that which was absent, left out, not included also was important."[29] This chapter explores the lived experiences that Broyard and Reynolds attempted to present in their life writings, by focusing on what they conspicuously "left out"—race—in their quest to achieve Whiteness and avoid death.[30]

"My God I'm a Negro": Anita Reynolds's Passive Critique of Racism

The story of Reynolds's life begins with her death. After she died in 1980, her papers were donated to Howard University, where they remained for decades. George Hutchinson, a Cornell University literary scholar, first discovered them at Howard University while conducting research for his biography of Nella Larsen. The similarities between Larsen and Reynolds were too uncanny for him to ignore: they had overlapping life dates and navigated the same social circles in New York City. In fact, their mutual friends included Larsen's best friend Dorothy Peterson, as well as James Weldon Johnson, and Walter and Gladys White. After examining more of their documents, he concluded that the two writers were acquaintances at the very least.[31] These correlations prompted him to carefully read Reynolds's autobiography, which he found "impossible to put down."[32] Indeed, her prose is witty and engaging, and she masterfully employs a range of literary techniques, including figurative language and foreshadowing, in narrating her story. She begins her

---

[29] hooks, *remembered rapture*, 159.

[30] Like hooks, Roland Barthes detested being written about after his death, accusing biographers of paying attention to merely "a few details, a few tastes, [and] a few inflections" that they would surmise from his accomplished life, to assemble a seemingly coherent narrative. He feared that something would be missing when biographers piece his life together. See Stuart Jeffries, "But What Does it Mean?," 14.

[31] Hutchinson, "Introduction," 17.

[32] Hutchinson, 18.

memoir by prefiguring the dual themes that become pivotal throughout her life: race and writing.

Anita Reynolds first began her memoir by recording herself with a tape recorder each day in 1972, before eventually transcribing the recordings. That she employs two ways to record her life—a recorder and a pen—highlights the level of detail and accuracy she desired to ensure that her unique life story lives forever. She opens her written version with an anecdote about race: when tourists visiting St. Croix ask Reynolds how long it took for her to acquire "that wonderful tan," she wittily responds "about four generations."[33] She concludes her preface by hoping that her memoir will serve as a meditation of her life "growing up [as] a 'colored girl' in the United States, Europe and North Africa."[34] This introduction makes it very clear that she is Black, though she tries to obscure her race for most of her life. In between these racial bookends, she refers to her time spent in Paris in the 1930s, where she associated with the likes of James Joyce, Ernest Hemingway, William Carlos Williams, F. Scott Fitzgerald, and Edna St. Vincent Millay. Many of these writers were represented by William Aspenwall Bradley, the renowned literary agent who encouraged Reynolds to write about her family's history, yet she had no interest in writing professionally, choosing instead to pass her time interacting with the American expatriate literati. By foregrounding the themes of race and writing in her introduction, Reynolds shows that she reads people and books the same way, similar to the ways in which the German tourists attempted to "read" her race.

Despite Reynolds's promise to describe memories of being a Black girl, she defers discussing race again for several pages. When she does, she first alludes to it ambiguously, prompting us to read between the lines of her meaning, especially when her critiques of racism are never followed up by actions to combat it. For instance, in reflecting on her formative years before starting school, she expresses concern that her "dark skin might attract unfavorable attention."[35] Once in school, her fear dissipates when her artwork is praised. After her kindergarten teacher gave her some clay to "make anything we like," Anita recreated her favorite teddy bear.[36] The teacher approved it by

---

[33] Reynolds, *American Cocktail*, 55.
[34] Reynolds, 57.
[35] Reynolds, 64.
[36] Reynolds, 65.

parading her around to every class in the building, where she "lifted the clay teddy bear for them to see."[37] Her peers responded by laughing at her, but she enjoyed her "auspicious debut as the only brown-skinned girl at the Washington Street Grammar School."[38]

Conspicuously absent from Reynolds's recollection of school is a discussion of racism. Her concerns about attracting negative attention because of her phenotype are mild, considering this incident occurred at the start of the twentieth century when Jim Crow laws were in full effect. As a Black girl, she could have been the victim of violence resulting from negative perceptions about her race. More importantly, Reynolds does not question her teacher's behavior, though this could be the start of her race-learning. When she boasts about the young Anita, only to elicit laughter from the other students, one must wonder if this entire scenario is racially motivated: did the teacher parade the only Black girl to praise her creativity or to prove that she was some type of racialized novelty? Writing about this incident decades after it first occurred does not prompt Reynolds to acknowledge the racialized tone of the teacher's behavior; instead, she welcomed the attention. When the nameless teacher instructed her to "make anything" out of the clay, she unknowingly foreshadowed Reynolds's racial identity. Just as she took the clay and created a new rendering of her teddy bear in her youth, she takes the confusion over her racial identity to create a new identity for herself in adulthood. In the process, she disassociates from her Black past and considers herself an "American cocktail." This is the primary indication that Reynolds will attempt to avoid addressing race even after calling attention to it in her opening anecdote, lest she reveal herself as a racial passer. However, a closer look at her language indicates that race was never too far removed from her life after all.

For instance, Reynolds's parents' background and distinguished social circle forces her to confront race throughout her youth. Her mother, Beatrice, was born and partly raised in Cambridge, Massachusetts. Though she was able to pass as White—or more accurately, as a "blue-stocking feminist with a Boston Brahmin accent and golden hair"—she chose to identify as African-American instead.[39] Her ancestry placed her at odds with young Anita, whom she frequently chided for not behaving properly. As the author observes,

---

[37] Reynolds, 65.
[38] Reynolds, 65.
[39] Reynolds, 79.

"Mother despaired, however, at my ever becoming a proper lady. I laughed too loudly and too often and danced with far too much enthusiasm."[40] Beatrice rationalized her daughter's liberal ways as the result of her father's lineage: "You are just like your father's Creole sisters…skinny legs, from spending their whole lives with their feet higher than their heads and being slaves to their men and homes."[41] Reynolds characterizes her mother as prudish and overly concerned with the politics of respectability. This continues into her adulthood, when Beatrice's dismissal of Anita's nascent movie career is based on a desire to see her in a more reputable position for Black women. In her memoirs, she is more sympathetic to her mother and confides in her through letters. To use Rank's terminology, Reynolds's ambivalent portrayals of Beatrice reveal the mother as the source of both love and anxiety for the racial passer; as such, she carves out her own individual personality from Beatrice by completely rebelling against her wishes in rejecting her Blackness and becoming an entertainer.

By citing Reynolds's paternal line as the reason for her free spirit, through her references to "Creole sisters" and "slaves," Beatrice forces her daughter to confront race despite her wish to ignore it in her recollections. Her wish is further complicated by her parents' renowned cohort of African-American friends who regularly discussed race. When hotels failed to accommodate Black travelers, Beatrice and Samuel Thompson welcomed them into their home, allowing young Anita to eavesdrop on the conversations of the frequent houseguests, which included A. Philip Randolph, James Weldon Johnson, W. E. B. Du Bois, and Booker T. Washington. Her parents entertained intellectual debates that focused primarily on the ideological differences espoused by Washington and Du Bois on African-American self-improvement; they eventually sided with Du Bois after he took a special interest in their daughter. Reynolds once asked him why Black soldiers returning from World War I were not using their new machine gun skills "making the South safe for democracy."[42] Du Bois mentioned to her mother that she was raising "a little Bolshevik" due to Reynolds's radical ideas.[43] The Bolsheviks seized power from the Russian Social Democratic Party in the October

---

[40] Reynolds, 81.
[41] Reynolds, 81.
[42] Reynolds, 79.
[43] Reynolds, 79.

Revolution in 1917, and the term evolved to refer to a revolutionary with radical or subversive ideas. The irony here is that Reynolds's suggestion that returning soldiers use their weapons to demand equal treatment is her only radical response to racism in her youth. She is far from revolutionary when it comes to her own subjectivity as an adult, as evidenced by her willingness to jump the color line.

Reynolds's rhetorical invocations in her interactions with other African-Americans indicates Du Bois's influence on her early life. For instance, as a bridesmaid for Madame C. J. Walker's adopted granddaughter, Reynolds rendered the ceremony's gaudiness unnecessary in light of the indignities that African-Americans sustained each day. Since the wedding immediately followed the NAACP's annual convention that explored questions about "the Negro problem," it prompted her to contrast the severity of race issues with the frivolity of the ceremony.[44] According to her, this disparity caused "quite a battle within my personality…I, too, was torn by conflicting feels."[45] Invoking Du Bois's tone of duality, Reynolds reflects on her dilemma of wanting to help African-Americans struggling under Jim Crow at the same time she participated in a lavish wedding. Though she enjoyed the ceremony, in retrospect, she believes that "the cost of the wedding would have been usefully applied to civil rights cases and support of the anti-lynching legislation."[46] One might expect her to be more proactive in using her privilege and class position in fighting racism. However, while Reynolds detested racism towards African-Americans, Hutchinson's introduction makes it clear that "she was hardly heroic in her own racial politics."[47] Instead, she chose to act in ways that benefited her at the expense of supporting anti-racist causes.

One of the ways in which she did this was through dance. The famous modern dancer Ruth St. Denis trained Reynolds herself because her "exotic" looks made her appear like an Indian, which eventually helped her to gain admission into the prestigious Norma Gould School of Dancing. However, the school did not have a policy to admit Black or Jewish girls. When Gould introduced Reynolds as Mexican, she obliged, and assumed the pseudonym of "Matelle" to appear less "Black." Looking back, Reynolds considers this

---

[44] Reynolds, 95.
[45] Reynolds, 95.
[46] Reynolds, 95.
[47] Hutchinson, "Introduction," 35.

moment as her first instance of passing as someone else. Instead of using her dance career as a starting point to help undermine racism by questioning the logic of discrimination against Blacks, she passively followed Gould's advice to pass as Mexican. Considering her criticism of the mistreatment of Blacks, the ease with which she accepted the identity someone forced upon her is quite jarring; silence was her response when confronted with personal racism at the dance school. Reynolds herself is complicit in the "problem" of race relations, since she maintained a successful career but with a feigned persona, thus complicating Du Bois's notion that she was radical. Moreover, by relishing the "exotic" roles given to her as an "Egyptian and Spaniard," she foreshadowed her later life in Europe when she passes as "exotic."

As Reynolds's success continued, she viewed race as increasingly irrelevant. Her professional dancing skills brought her to Hollywood, where she attained more roles without questioning why she had to pass to land them. In her most ironic movie role, she acted as though she was not Black. According to her, "the climax of the story came when I had to face the shock of learning who I really was. I had to pull on my face most dramatically and utter with astonishment: 'My God, I'm a Negro!' It was difficult to stifle the giggles."[48] The source of her laughter appears ambiguous at first—because she is an actress this could be read as a character she is paid to portray. Yet a deeper meaning of her laughter stems from the disconnect between her racial background and the passing persona she assumed. Perhaps she "giggled" because her art now imitated life, wherein she was genuinely shocked at being reminded of her Black past considering all the ways in which she passed as other people. When she "giggled" on screen, the joke was truly on her audience: she was acting as someone other than Black, while being content with her phenotype since it yielded access to a wider/Whiter range of roles.

The role that Anita Reynolds performed most frequently was that of a woman passing as different identities while working through her womb separation from her mother. To facilitate this, she moved from city to city to further individuate herself from her mother while seeking racial anonymity. Before leaving the United States altogether, she moved from Los Angeles to New York City, where she became a racially ambiguous social butterfly. In Harlem, she befriended Paul Robeson and Claude McKay, introduced to her by her cousin Langston Hughes. In Greenwich Village, she socialized with

---

[48] Reynolds, *American Cocktail*, 87.

Eugene O'Neill and Edna St. Vincent Millay. After passing to take courses at Columbia University's Teachers College, she moved to Baltimore, then back to New York City, before finally sailing to Paris.

While en route to France, Reynolds recalls her excitement about leaving America: "I felt while crossing the Atlantic a great sense of going home, to a place where I really belonged. Away from the lynchings, away from the Negro problem, away from the polarization, away from all the disagreeable aspects of life in the United States."[49] This curious sentiment underscores her duality when dealing with race: she relocates to Europe despite her initial interest in helping Blacks in America. Her vacillation evolved into a desire to leave African-Americans behind, yet she carefully notes that she was not "running away from American Negroes, [since] Countee Cullen and Yolande Du Bois were coming soon to Paris on their honeymoon."[50] This logic is flawed: if they did not choose Paris for their honeymoon, then Reynolds could have avoided Blacks there, being satisfied that the "Negro problem" is no longer her problem. Given the two themes that open her memoir, race and writing, Reynolds's life in America can be characterized primarily through her relationship to race, even if done so in a distant and roundabout way. Once in Paris however, race emerges as a secondary concern, and writing takes more prominence as she struggles to write herself into perpetuity and further distance herself from her mother. As the next section explains, her disavowal of race in America explains her lack of success with writing.

"My Own Writing Was Not Going Very Well": Writing in Vain as a Passing Subject

As an American expatriate, her identity shifted according to the people with whom she affiliated during her European travels. For instance, after reuniting with a long-lost uncle in Paris, Reynolds introduced her new attire by comparing herself to Gloria Swanson.[51] She was aware of fashionable Black luminaries living in Paris alongside her, as she laments never meeting Florence Mills or Josephine Baker. However, she does not compare herself to either of these African-American women, choosing instead to use a White American actress as the sole basis for comparison. Her invocation of Swanson is

---

[49] Reynolds, 113.
[50] Reynolds, 113.
[51] Reynolds, 115.

indicative of the conscious omission of African-Americans from her new life abroad. Even though her uncle disapproved of this comparison, there was nothing he could have done because she maintained her distance from Blacks while passing as White.

After meeting Dutch surrealist painter Kristians Tonny, Reynolds's identity shifted again. He was fascinated by American Indians and placed Reynolds in this category by comparing her to "Pocahontas or some character out of Fenimore Cooper."[52] Instead of criticizing his assumption, she states, "I never tried to pass myself off as an Indian. Usually, when asked, I was an 'American cocktail,' for among the French that included Indians, Negroes and everything else that made up a different kind of American."[53] Reynolds's defensive tone is based on her presumption that readers might call her a passing subject in light of her interactions with Tonny. However, her defense is weak. If she truly rejected Tonny's characterization of her, then she would have been more forthright in indicating she is not an American Indian but is indeed African-American. However, just as she did when she first began dance school, she allowed someone else to dictate her identity by leaving their assumptions uncorrected. In other words, Reynolds's passivity allowed her to pass.

The moniker she gives herself, "American cocktail," does not ease racial confusion, but further obscures it. George Hutchinson cites this neologism as proof that she never "passed altogether" nor did she ever "hide her Blackness."[54] However, this same term evidences the opposite, in that she actively concealed her race. A "cocktail" is inherently a mixture, and as Reynolds herself notes, adding the qualifier "American" helped her acquaintances to see her as anything—belonging to any racial or ethnic background in the United States, which could include Indian or Black. In Tonny's case it was the former, and her silence about it underscores her willingness to accept, nay, welcome, racial ambiguity. Additionally, Hutchinson notes that Tonny's biographers refer to her as Anita Matelle and never mention her African-American background or her complete legal name. For Reynolds, being "a different

---

[52] Reynolds, 117. In Senna's *Caucasia*, Nick refers to Birdie as Pocahontas as well. These two examples highlight the wide range of identities forced upon lighter-skinned African-Americans.

[53] Reynolds, 118.

[54] Hutchinson, "Introduction," 37.

kind of American" is a pithy euphemism for not openly acknowledging her Black Creole ancestry in Europe.

Despite her wish to hide her Blackness, she did not escape it as easily as she hoped. While living in France, Reynolds socialized with a long list of prominent writers—including Djuna Barnes, William Carlos Williams, Claude McKay, and Ford Madox Ford, as well as the literary agent William Aspenwall Bradley—all of whom encouraged her to write. She obliged, beginning with a "*Gentleman Prefer Blondes* type piece" which she considered as humorous as Anita Loos's original, but she discarded it without revealing it to anyone.[55] Her second piece was a short story about lynching. In describing this latter work, Reynolds states:

> I put my soul into the skin of a girl who was supposed to have been raped by the man who was lynched. Without showing it to my friends in Paris, I sent it off to a literary magazine in London. It was accepted, but the editor wanted me to make it part of a series and asked me to send more immediately. I had no more to say.[56]

The plot of her story centers on the two types of violence that African-Americans, in particular, have been subjected to with alacrity: rapes and lynchings. Her entire writing process was kept a secret, as she did not solicit the feedback of her powerful literary friends, nor did she offer the title or publication information for the story in her memoir. Anita Reynolds, like James Weldon Johnson before her, published her meditations on race anonymously. Rather than expand her nameless piece into a longer series to call attention to racism, she rendered it a stand-alone story written merely on a whim. Several writers, including Ida B. Wells Barnett and Walter White, depicted lynching as a catalyst to their racial identification. In Reynolds's case though, she already had racial identification when she lived in America before penning the narrative, making the timing of its publication intriguing. She does not clarify what prompted her to write this text, but her reaction to it is illuminating. Reynolds wanted to deny its existence by not even referencing the title in her reflections. This is the first indication that she faces the dilemma of wanting her writings to live long after her death but is hindered by the problem of race. Having "no more to say" relates to both her creative output as well as her expatriate life: writing about African-Americans was a

---

[55] Reynolds, *American Cocktail*, 127.
[56] Reynolds, 127.

difficult endeavor because it entailed unearthing a racialized subjectivity which she long denied and left behind in America.

In Reynolds's next writing project, she struggled once again; the topic was race and she did not want her pen to reveal her lost self. Although she argued that her responsibilities in Paris would prevent her from writing about her family's history, Bradley and journalist Louise Bryant convinced her that all she needed was a trip to North Africa for a change of scenery. Before leaving, she received a sobering admonishment from her friend Arthur Wheeler, who said "the sooner I forget the problems of the Negro, the more comfortably I would live."[57] She disagreed with Wheeler, but after spending time in Morocco trying to write in vain, she belatedly realized that her "own writing was not going very well."[58] In retrospect, she cites both her chaotic writing style and lack of documents, which forced her to complete the gaps in her narrative with her own observations instead of scholarly material. Reynolds believed that taking a writing break to read books, which is a common trope in passing narratives, might minimize her writer's block. What escaped her reflections on writing her family history is the role that race played. Travelling to Africa, and ostensibly being around Africans, was *not* sufficient in motivating Reynolds to write her life story, for she had already forgotten "the problems of the Negro" and could not bring herself to write about her racialized family. The real hindrance to her writing process is the conflict between wanting to keep her Black past hidden while being pressured to publish her family's story. If the unconscious is structured like a language, as Lacan articulated in "The Instance of the Letter in the Unconscious," then Reynolds could not find the right words to narrate her unconscious repressed Blackness.

Reynolds remains largely uncritical of the ways in which race impacted her social interactions. This becomes blatantly obvious when she was misread and fetishized but did not acknowledge that her ambiguous phenotype rendered her a mystery to many people. For example, in vivid detail, she describes a train ride from Paris to Marseilles en route to Tangier, sharing a car with a German man who stared at her intently. Though clearly disconcerted by his persistent gaze, she politely engaged him when he sat next to her to inquire about her reading material. She believed that the end of their journey

---

[57] Reynolds, 129.
[58] Reynolds, 138.

would mark the end of their conversation, however, before hailing a cab at Marseilles, he made sexual remarks about two boys. Disgusted by his remarks, she hid in her hotel to prevent him from following her.

Reynolds did not have to worry about the man on the train following her; he was one of countless European men who travelled to Morocco solely to sleep with young Arab boys. She did not consider the ways in which her gender and ambiguous phenotype attracted his unsolicited attention. He might have wanted to speak with her in order to ascertain her racial background, but used the book she was reading as a way to initiate a conversation. This encounter on the train evokes Frantz Fanon's "Look! A Negro!" scene from *Black Skin, White Masks*, in which "the Other fixes me with his gaze" to meditate on the historical and psychical resonances of racial hypervisibility.[59] Fanon and Reynolds stand out to other passengers on the trains they ride in, yet Fanon's commentary after realizing his seemingly exotic status contrasts sharply with Reynolds's lack of reflection. Given the correlations between these two examples of racial hypervisibility, Reynolds's failure to write about race makes her train example even more conspicuous than Fanon's. Due to the long history of Whites gazing upon bodies that are ambiguous or darker-skinned, the passenger may have been intrigued by a desire to categorize her race, even if Reynolds does not explicitly articulate this. Perhaps he too intended to utter some variation of "Look! A Negro!" but chose to sit next to and stare at her instead. His taboo sexual proclivities were with the young Moroccan boys, therefore his interest in her might have started with the "exotic" ways in which he perceived her. For Reynolds to even speculate on his racist intentions would entail invoking the missing Black self that she abandoned in the United States. For her, however, silence is a more feasible and safer option since she has completely removed Blackness from her life as seen by her inability to even write about it.

According to Hutchinson, however, Reynolds's life abroad reflected racial divisions in Europe and North Africa, even if they did not make it into

---

[59] Fanon, *Black Skin*, 89. Among his astute observations, he notes that Blacks are more prone to being the object of the gaze when they are away from their home countries, and they endure a Du Boisian "two systems of reference" in their daily encounters; additionally, they feel "disoriented" when confronting the Other after being reminded of their responsibility to their "race and ancestors."

her writing. This is particularly true in her romantic relationships. In describing her courtship with Charles, a British military captain, Reynolds notes that

> My role in my relationship with Charles was that of the exotic woman. Perhaps he had wanted an East Indian girl and hadn't been able to have one, or perhaps his experience with dull white women had given him the impression that an exotic woman would be the perfect sex partner.[60]

Rendering herself "East Indian" and an "exotic woman" is a provocative claim in light of the colonial history of England and India vis-à-vis the East Indian Company.[61] Whether Reynolds knew about the history of the East Indian Company is unclear, yet she knew that her relationship with Charles in the early 1930s corresponded with British Rule of India. She invokes this colonial context by assuming the identity of "East Indian," while pointing out Charles's British ancestry. This juxtaposition highlights the colonial fetish he evokes by exoticizing his relationship with her, yet she acquiesced by not correcting him at all. She welcomed the identity he imposed on her, especially due to their intense sexual attraction: "Sexually, we enjoyed the same wavelength….I thought he was an elegant English gentleman and he thought I was a pretty East Indian girl."[62] There is no textual evidence that he ever discovered her true racial background. By this point in her life, she could not admit that to continue her relationship with a man who fetishized her entailed maintaining an identity completely unrelated to her own.

---

[60] Reynolds, *American Cocktail*, 160.

[61] Founded in 1600, the East India Company was a British trading company that was initially created to trade items such as silk, cotton, indigo, and opium with Southeast Asia, particularly the Indian subcontinent. Frenise Logan argues that one aspect of their business was also the slave trade, as they "shipped Madagascar slaves to India and the East Indies" ("The British East India Company and African Slavery," 339). According to the British National Archives, their slave trade was not localized in the southeast region of Africa, but the East India Company also "collected slaves from the West Coast of Africa for its settlements in South and East Africa and in India and Asia." In 1858, when Queen Victoria assumed control of the British East India Company, it marked the official beginning of the British Raj—the rule of the Indian subcontinent which lasted until 1947. I am indebted to Dr. Chandrika Kaul for her excellent history of British rule over India, as well as to the National Archives of the United Kingdom for their history of Britain and the Slave Trade.

[62] Reynolds, 169.

Reynolds relocated from Morocco to England to continue their relationship. If she feigned unfamiliarity with colonialism previously, she was confronted with it as soon as she arrived, when a customs agent reminded her that "Africa belongs to us."[63] For the customs agent to remark that Morocco is "in Africa," underscores the long-held stereotype that Africa is a monolithic territory instead of a continent consisting of several unique nations. Looking back, she tersely says that her move to England marked her "return to civilization," raising the question of whether she is being ironic or if she believed her time in Africa meant being "uncivilized" in comparison to her return to England.[64] Considering her fear that writing about race would force her to confront her lost self, it is difficult to ascertain whether Reynolds truly believes that civilization lies in the nation that has been responsible for colonizing many countries populated by darker-skinned people.

Anita Reynolds's passivity about race upon entering England foreshadows her return to America at the end of the memoir when she gets reminded of her status as an African-American. Even though she shared physical space with African-Americans in England, she does not share in their beliefs about racism. For instance, Reynolds is ashamed when she hears Paul Robeson's wife, Eslanda, remarking that the same color prejudice that afflicted America also spread to England. Reynolds's distaste for this comment represented her own desire to avoid hearing about African-Americans lest they remind her that she is Black too. Eslanda Robeson's complaints about racism in both countries highlight Reynolds's privilege to escape such racism with the help of her phenotype, ability to relocate, and disinterest in discussing race.

This last impetus for her aversion to hearing these critiques became obvious within the context of colonialism—a topic that marked the turning point in Reynolds and Charles's relationship. Charles became angry when reading in the newspaper that English engineers were detained in Russia and began comparing the laws of Russia and England. Reynolds, however, was more critical of people from the latter country:

> [Charles]: Those dirty Bolsheviks have no law that compares to English law. English law is the foundation of all civilized codes of law. Englishmen anywhere in the world should be sent home for trial and

---

[63] Reynolds, 162.
[64] Reynolds, 162.

not be subjected to the barbarous so-called laws of countries like Russia!

[Reynolds]: Well, if they don't want to take a chance on being accused or arrested in other countries, or if they don't want to live under the laws of another country, they should stay home.

Charles's rhetoric aligned him with colonialism, especially his use of the epithet "dirty Bolsheviks" and the fact that he viewed English law as superior. In what appears as a belated response to Du Bois's characterization of her as a "little Bolshevik," Reynolds questioned why the colonizing Englishmen were in Russia at all. The difference in perspective prompted Charles's rage: he attacked her by throwing his glass at her face, causing her to have a black eye. Charles quickly apologized and changed his behavior.

After this incident, Reynolds describes him as "anti-imperialist" and "agreeing with the communists," but she is reticent about analyzing her own transformation.[65] Citing global examples, she argues that colonists have the power to improve the lives of those they colonize: the French could teach Arabs advanced medical practices and Indians could learn better plumbing habits from the British. Conspicuously absent from her praise is criticism of the violence that the colonized endure at the hands of their colonizers, and condemnation for the type of education that subjects must attain when colonized. According to Reynolds, colonialism is essentially a benevolent institution, an unsurprising assertion based on her stance on race.

Though Charles renounced the authority of the British Empire in favor of Communism, Reynolds's evolution is far more profound, especially through the lens of Fanonian ideology. According to Fanon, when a colonized person "forgets his place, if he thinks himself the equal of the European, then the European becomes angry and rejects the upstart, who on this occasion and in this 'exceptional instance' pays for his refusal to be dependent with an inferiority complex."[66] Reynolds and Charles map directly onto this theory. He is the Englishman (the colonizer), she is his "East Indian girl" (the colonized), and he has succeeded in colonizing her mind. As the European colonizer, he is outraged that his "East Indian girl" has "stepped out of place" by standing up to his imperialist ideology, prompting the attack. Consequently, Reynolds developed her own version of an inferiority complex, to

---

[65] Reynolds, 177.
[66] Fanon, *Black Skin*, 74.

which her sanguine view of colonialism attests. Not only does she feign the identity of a woman from India, but she also convinces herself that being under British rule is not as detrimental as it initially appears. As a result, Reynolds's dialogue with Charles exposes the pinnacle of her identity as a passing subject living abroad.

Her relationship with Charles is hardly the first time she is associated with an "exotic" identity; she embraced it when she began her career as a dancer and actress, and she continues to do so when she begins her relationship with Guy de Chateaubriant. He views her as "his dream of the island child come true, the creole, the exotic girl of the islands who could live with him in France in a civilized world and yet retain all the charm of the jungle."[67] Instead of commenting on his racialized phraseology, Reynolds is nonchalant, succinctly saying, "I didn't care how he fantasized about me."[68] She confirms that passing ambiguously as "exotic" was now second nature to her after letting others dictate her identity for so long. To Charles, she was "East Indian," but to Guy, she assumed the role of a generic Creole girl from the islands. The specific islands are left ambiguous because they do not matter; what matters is that Reynolds is happy to accept any identity but her own biological one.

As much as she denied her Blackness while in Europe, she was forced to confront it when returning to the United States after World War II begins. On a ship from Spain to the United States, Reynolds was met by a bevy of reporters who took pictures of her, assuming she was a woman of importance. They asked whether she was "Egyptian? Arab? East Indian?" but as soon as she arrived in her homeland, the flashes ceased.[69] The reporters realized that she was "just an Afro-American expatriate of no importance, a common or garden variety of colored women forced 'home.'"[70] Her assumption is correct. The picture of Reynolds on the boat was sent solely to the Black press in Baltimore while her face was not featured in the prominent newspaper that her White shipmates appeared in, *The New York Times*.

Returning to the United States reinstates race for Anita Reynolds, yet she offers minimal commentary on its implication. For one thing, she puts the word "home" in quotation marks, raising skepticism that she really

---

[67] Reynolds, *American Cocktail*, 224.
[68] Reynolds, 224.
[69] Reynolds, 267–68.
[70] Reynolds, 268.

belongs in America at all. Even though she was born here, her beliefs about race developed in Europe. Reflecting in her memoir in the 1970s, she argues that the flag "still looks red, white, and Black" even after integration and the "American Negro revolts" of the 1960s and 1970s.[71] She declares that there are "no tears in my eyes looking at it today," underscoring her pessimism about the American flag's symbolism.[72] In analyzing her concluding remarks, Hutchinson argues that her discussion of the flag suggests that her identity is not representable in America at all. After years vacillating between being an "American cocktail," "exotic," "East Indian," and "Creole," all of these categories were collapsed as soon as she landed on American soil. It is only in the United States, as Hutchinson rightly observes, where "Anita Thompson was once again Black" but she remained unable to reconcile this monolithic category with the ambiguous racial subjectivity she assumed while abroad.[73] In the first version of her manuscript, Reynolds verbalized this explicitly: "I had found it very strange to feel like a 'race' in the presence of Negroes instead of like a person, as I had for so long in France. When I arrived in the U.S. in 1940 it seemed that everything had a racial tone."[74] She omitted these reflections from the final published book and replaced them with the innocuous observation about the reporters and the flag. Reynolds's revision is telling; they reveal her failure to understand that simply because she left behind her African-American self in America while she lived in Europe does not mean that race disappeared during her time away.

For her to write any critique of race is a surprise to readers of *American Cocktail*, since she treads this topic carefully, especially in her creative writing. In her private letters however, some of which are included in the second appendix to *American Cocktail* that Hutchinson edited, Reynolds writes about the two intertwined themes of race and writing that open her text and define her life. On the subject of the former, she complains about racism in America, returning to the "Bolshevik" tones of her youth. For instance, in a letter to her mother where she discusses lynching, she wonders how Americans can remain passive about prejudice, especially since she wishes to "kill barehanded

---

[71] Reynolds, 268.
[72] Reynolds, 268.
[73] Hutchinson, "Introduction," 45.
[74] Hutchinson, 45.

all the vile whites in the world."⁷⁵ This observation is jarring because, with the exception of her adolescent discussion with Du Bois about Black soldiers returning to their racist homeland, she neither promotes violence against Whites in her memoir nor critiques the racialized violence that some White Americans perpetuate. In a letter to her brother, Reynolds advocates for the superiority of mixed-raced people using Fanonian imagery: "despite the inferiority complex which holds them in subjection today," Reynolds argues, "half-breeds have everything in our favor" including physical and moral strength.⁷⁶ She believes that biracial people are "shining examples of superiority" to the "sangs purs" (pure-bloods).⁷⁷ Yet she reserves her harshest criticism for African-Americans: Reynolds does not want Beatrice to tell anyone she's writing a book because "If it falls thru' there'll be no niggers to shut up. You know how it is."⁷⁸ She is concerned that African-Americans would be the most critical of her if they discover she could not complete her book. She sees her Creole status and ability to pass as White as superior to the African-Americans who she assumes will judge her.

When considered in tandem with each other, these letters suggest that she thought about race often, even if her memoir does not betray this fact explicitly. Indeed, she discloses clues about her Blackness while passing, in a memoir that was only published posthumously. This created a tension for her where she sought to hide the fact that she was Black, but still referred to it while living as White. Knowing her autobiography would be for public consumption, she remained guarded about race, whereas she offered more criticism in the private correspondence with her family since she believed nobody else would read them. She views writing as cathartic, promising her brother to "write more often…because I've need to clear my brain."⁷⁹ Consistent throughout her correspondence is the invocation of the humility topos, where she feigns being ignorant of writing skills.⁸⁰ For instance, in a letter in which

---

⁷⁵ Reynolds, *American Cocktail*, 279.
⁷⁶ Reynolds, 286.
⁷⁷ Reynolds, 286.
⁷⁸ Reynolds, 299.
⁷⁹ Reynolds, 289.
⁸⁰ The humility topos, according to the list of literary terms compiled by Carson-Newman University, is "a common rhetorical strategy in which an author or speaker feigns ignorance or pretends to be less clever or less intelligent than he or she really is. Often donning such a *persona* allows a writer, poet, or playwright to create

she responds to her godchild's request for short stories, Reynolds complains that she is "not very ingenious in narrative."[81] Similarly, she complains to her mother that "I've been writing a long time, haven't I? And it all doesn't mean much," which implies that even though she has extensive drafts written, she feels as though she really has nothing since the story lacks fundamental elements such as plot and setting.[82] In yet another letter, she suggests that a "change of environment" would help to reinvigorate her and ease her writer's block, citing a friend who told her she's "surrounded by people who do not encourage" her to write.[83] This letter, dated on New Year's Day, 1931, contradicts another letter she sent on August 2, 1930, where Reynolds confesses "I had absolutely no idea of race in my mind as I've almost forgotten it exists, being always with *real artists*."[84]

---

humorous, self-deprecating effects, or in the case of an argument, may cause the opponent to underestimate the opposition. One of the first examples of the humility *topos* in action includes Socrates and his Socratic method of argument, in which Socrates pleads his own ignorance so he can ask particularly difficult questions to those who disagree with his philosophy, eventually forcing them to make self-contradictory assertions." The humility topos appears in African-American literature as well. Most critics point to the Middle Ages as the point when this strategy was most prevalent, particularly in the works of Geoffrey Chaucer. However, the humility topos has always been present in African-American literature for a few centuries. For instance, in John Marrant's *Narrative of the Lord's Wonderful Dealings* (1785), he is "at a loss to find the words to praise [God]" (75); in Harriet E. Wilson's novel *Our Nig* (1859), she claims to be in a "humble position" which explains why her narrative is full "of errors" (209); in Harriet Jacobs's *Incidents in the Life of a Slave Girl* (1861), Linda Brent hopes to be "more competent" as she lets northern women know of the conditions that Black enslaved women had to endure, and closes her preface wishing for "abler pens" (2). In the twentieth century, Booker T. Washington uses his preface to *Up From Slavery* to admit that he is telling an "imperfect story" (1), while W. E. B. Du Bois's Forethought to *The Souls of Black Folk* (1903) expresses his wish for his "little book" to be well received (2). In self-consciously calling attention to her seeming lack of writing skills, Reynolds joins this lineage of Black writers who express humility about their texts, but she is the only passing subject to do so, making her all the more fascinating as a figure to study in light of this chapter's dual foci of writing and race.

[81] Reynolds, *American Cocktail*, 275.
[82] Reynolds, 296.
[83] Reynolds, 293.
[84] Reynolds, 288, emphasis mine.

Through this observation, she creates a false hierarchy where "real artists" are in a class of their own and do not have to think about race—a topic that non artists must deal with, according to her logic. Her goal is to publish her family's history, but she has a difficult time doing this because it entails dealing with their racial history as well. After submitting an incomplete draft of her manuscript "MOCKING-BIRD" to the editor William A. Bradley, she secluded herself in France to write each day. She then wrote to her mother that she hoped to receive more information "about Grandma; she is the heroine of the story and I don't want to go on making up stuff."[85] Reynolds implies that her writing stalled due to the minimal amount of information she had about her grandmother, however lack of information is not the primary issue: Reynolds's grandmother was Black and inscribing this onto paper would be tantamount to admitting her own renounced Blackness. As long as she has a missing Black self that she left behind in America, she would have been unable to write about anything related to African-Americans because it would force her to confront her denied truth: she is of Indian, African-American, Creole, and White ancestry, but she passed generically as White. Indeed, her acquaintances included several artists, but the problem with Anita Reynolds's writing project is not who is around her, but what she promises to discuss: race—a topic she is unable to confront.

Whether or not Reynolds is surrounded by other artists is irrelevant for her own family story; after all, she can "succeed with the pen in criticisms and reviews and impressions," but the story of her family's Black ancestry proves much more difficult.[86] However, her artistic friends helped her to understand the importance of living on through creative works. Otto Rank's theories appealed to artists like Reynolds and members of her inner circle because "he thought the artistic mind mastered anxiety by inserting the self into a creative product that would long outlive the subject. In this way, the subject's wish for perpetuity is met through the ability to transcend the self through artistic production."[87] Reynolds's anxiety about race and writing made their way into her works, yet she has lived on through the publication of her autobiography, *American Cocktail*, and by appearing in the works of others. For example, she is a character in Eric d'Haulleville's surrealist novel *Le voyage aux Iles*

---

[85] Reynolds, 298.
[86] Reynolds, 293.
[87] Ahad, *Freud Upside Down*, 46.

Galapagos (1934) and appears in the poetry of Jacques Baron. Reynolds must have been proud of these literary representations of her, for she "sent copies of all these books to Mother," as a way to correct her mother's image of her.[88] Beatrice was easily "influenced by what she saw in the newspaper" and Reynolds relished bragging to her mother that, at least in her literary depictions, her "feet never touched the ground."[89] If she feared death when she left Beatrice's womb, according to Rank's theory, sending copies of work she appears in highlights her desire to reunite with her mother, her difference from her mother, as well as her wish to live in perpetuity. When it comes to Reynolds's own work though, all she can do is promise her godchild that the narrative on which she has been diligently working will have a "history that's stranger than fiction"—a resonant phrase that categorizes her entire life.[90]

Anita Reynolds traversed the United States, Europe, and North Africa, a transgressive feat for a Black woman in the first half of the twentieth century. In the process, she emerged as the protagonist of her own narrative, with a plot predicated on equivocating about her ambiguous background in her personal and professional lives and a cast of characters that included an eclectic variety of notable writers. This helped her life story live on after her death, which occurred long after she tried to individuate herself from her mother. One such notable writer with whom she was affiliated was F. Scott Fitzgerald. After he published his short story collection *Tales of the Jazz Age* in 1922, Reynolds wrote an award-winning review of it in *Flash*, an African-American magazine in the 1920s.[91] The book review includes diction that foreshadows Reynolds's later life in Europe: "'May Day,' the best story in the book, is nevertheless a bitter modern cocktail in which ex-soldiers, Socialists, college failures, flappers and alcohol are shaken together and mixed like oil and water."[92] This is where the title of her memoir is derived from, since Reynolds renders herself a "cocktail" and encounters people who are as diverse as the characters she observed in Fitzgerald's collection. The original titles for her drafted memoir referred to color in some form: "The False Spring Violet," "The Tan Experience," and "Caramel: Autobiography of a Drop of Burned

---

[88] Reynolds, *American Cocktail*, 198.
[89] Reynolds, 198.
[90] Reynolds, 278.
[91] Reynolds, 274.
[92] Reynolds, 272.

Sugar."[93] Reynolds's final choice calls attention to her race explicitly, but only as a secondary concern, as her subtitle makes clear: *American Cocktail: A 'Colored Girl' In the World.*

Readers can only speculate what Reynolds thought about Fitzgerald's second novel, *The Great Gatsby*, which is "a novel about American self-invention" according to Bliss Broyard.[94] In Fitzgerald's most canonized text, Jay Gatsby reinvents himself, not unlike Reynolds's own reinvention when travelling to Europe. Both Fitzgerald and his magnum opus appear in *One Drop* (2007), Bliss Broyard's biography about her father. Like Reynolds, Anatole Broyard maintained several excuses for his writer's block, never admitting that his left-behind self was the primary impediment. Yet as the next section reveals, Broyard's trajectory diverged from Reynolds; his relationship with his parents, his preoccupations with death, and his need for a prolonged reputation are more sustained and pronounced, thus impeding his ability to write his life story.

"This Gentleman's Color is White":
Anatole Broyard's Omission of Race

Similar to *American Cocktail*, Bliss Broyard's *One Drop* tethers the dual themes of race and writing. *One Drop* is her biography of her father, who was born Creole but who passed as a White man in his adulthood, particularly during his time as *The New York Times* book critic. Anatole Broyard was born to Paul (whom everyone called Nat) and Edna, French-descended Creoles in New Orleans, in July 1920. He was the middle child and only son, as Lorraine was born before Anatole and Shirley came two years after. Of the three children, Anatole had the lightest complexion, thus explaining why Bliss never saw her darker-skinned aunts; he shunned them when he decided to pass.[95] Through passing, he created a fictional life that Bliss tried to reconstruct by exploring his documents, including legal papers, journal entries, book reviews, his published creative writing, as well as incomplete drafts of fiction and memoirs that he worked on continuously but never published. Undertaking this task after his death from prostate cancer, Bliss discovers that he wanted to live on forever through his work. However, he could not write

---

[93] Reynolds, 51.
[94] Broyard, *One Drop*, 34.
[95] Broyard, 308.

honestly because he hid his true race for most of his life and never addressed it directly, though a few clues are peppered throughout his oeuvre. Like Anita Reynolds, the fact that his Black self is also his left-behind self-made writing about African-Americans a challenging endeavor. Writing about this topic would have entailed admitting the truth of his Blackness and undermining the fiction he wanted to live.

Discovering Anatole Broyard proved to be a Herculean task, since Bliss's research raised more ambiguities than conclusions. Indeed, she struggled to determine when her father first began passing because he was not candid about it in his journals; instead, she discovers other important details about his origins. For instance, the Broyards relocated to Brooklyn in the winter of 1927. During this train ride, crossing the Mason-Dixon Line was tantamount to the end of Jim Crow service and marked the freedom to move and sit alongside White travelers. He entered the train as a Black boy but departed seeing the better treatment afforded to White passengers. As a result, Bliss surmises that this train ride was her father's introduction into realizing the privileges he can enjoy with his lighter complexion: "the journey from South to North was my father's first trip from Black to white. He saw that crossing the color line could be as simple as walking a few steps down the platform of Washington's Union Station."[96]

This might explain the second area in which she struggled: determining his Creole status through legal paperwork. As Bénédicte Boisseron argues in *Creole Renegades*, Broyard's "birth certificate identified his race as Black, but when he died in 1990 from prostate cancer, his death certificate identified him as white."[97] Within those seven decades, he vacillated in his response when asked about his race. Growing up in Brooklyn, he purposely told his acquaintances he was Creole because of its elusive meaning. In doing so, Broyard "clearly took advantage" of the indefinable nature of the word "Creole," in part because the term "can be either Black or white, and not necessarily Black and white."[98] By rendering himself Creole during his early years, Broyard circumvented the Black versus White binary, allowing everyone to draw their own conclusions about his racial background. Citing this background, Boisseron argues that "Creoleness is fundamentally unpredictable"

---

[96] Broyard, 312.
[97] Boisseron, *Creole Renegades*, 29–30.
[98] Boisseron, 31.

in that "the Creole subject [is] a natural-born noncommittal subject."[99] As a result, Boisseron believes that Broyard lived out the inherent slipperiness of his Creole identity instead of passing. However, this argument would be stronger if he persisted in calling himself "Creole" as an adult. Instead, he fashioned a new White persona for himself in adulthood. Broyard's passive passing in his youth laid the foundation for when he began actively passing, by representing himself not as Creole but as White.

Life in New York City was challenging for the transplanted Broyards, due to unfamiliar racial tension they never encountered in New Orleans. In the French Quarter, Nat Broyard only interacted with Creole friends and family within walking distance of his home, particularly since he viewed his Creole background as an "intermediary position in the racial order."[100] He went out of his way to avoid confronting the realities of racial conflict, which did not pervade his Creole enclave even when racism defined Jim Crow America. As Anatole's sister Shirley Broyard recalls, "there wasn't much conversation in her family about racial identity" and certainly her parents never disclosed their true racial background to anyone, going so far as to tell census workers in 1930 that they were Mexican and Portuguese.[101] In their new home though, the Black-and-White racial boundary was harder to ignore, despite their best efforts. Indeed, realizing that Whiteness is tantamount to privileges, Nat and Edna passed as White to gain employment—he did it to join the carpenters' union, and she did it to attain a job ironing clothes at a commercial laundry.[102]

These biographical details contextualize Anatole Broyard's own racial development. After starting elementary school in Brooklyn, both the Black and the White children harassed him: "the Black kids picked on him because he looked white and the white kids picked on him because they knew his family was Black."[103] He developed his running skills after being chased by the neighborhood children. This running from childhood bullying prefigured his return from the Second World War, when he wanted to run away from the racial distinctions of Black and White. When Anatole returned home

---

[99] Boisseron, 29.
[100] Broyard, *One Drop*, 311.
[101] Broyard, 312.
[102] Broyard, 328–31.
[103] Broyard, 17.

from school with a torn jacket, Nat Broyard never questioned his son; questioning him would be tacit acknowledgment of his own culpability in Anatole's problems. Nat appeared racially conservative and subscribed to colorism; his distaste for African-Americans contributed to his son's racial confusion. For the Broyards, racial passing was an intergenerational response to racism, leaving the young Anatole to feel uncertain about his place within the American racial spectrum.

As a student then, Anatole followed a trajectory that parallels John Warwick, the Ex-Colored Man, and Victor Grabért, as a sheltered child contending with racial confusion for the first time in school. Bliss argues that her father first began passing at Brooklyn College, based on the fact that "he certainly seemed to change around the time" of his matriculation.[104] He was already conspicuous on campus because he began college at sixteen after skipping two grades in his youth, and he donned an oversized coat that resembled the "kind of cape someone might have worn to a nineteenth-century duel."[105] This cape allowed him to hide part of himself, symbolizing the concealment that racial passing inherently entails. Coupled with his youth and atypical attire, Broyard also stood out racially, causing his classmates to guess his race when he tried to sit with White students at lunch. Shirley concedes that since he was the first in their family to attend college, Anatole entered Brooklyn College unaware how to act, and created a new identity as a result. Bliss is more speculative, arguing that it is very difficult to know when her father first passed as White. She believes he merely failed to identify as Black while in college, by avoiding the Black students in the cafeteria and neglecting to reveal that he resided in Bedford-Stuyvesant, a predominantly Black neighborhood.

Some of the ambiguity about Broyard's first instance of passing can be attributed to the documents Bliss cites, which suggest that he could have officially started jumping the color line at any point in his young adult life. For instance, in March 1938, seventeen-year-old Anatole applied for a social security card for the first time. A microfilmed copy of his application appears in *One Drop* and has two check marks for the question about his race, one for "White" and the other for "Negro."[106] The check mark for "Negro" had been

---

[104] Broyard, 345.
[105] Broyard, 341.
[106] Broyard, 354.

scratched out, while the one for "White" remained, thus raising the question of who made this change and under what circumstances. On one hand, it could have been Anatole himself, who first admitted his Blackness then decided, before submitting the form, that he would be better off claiming White status, or the change could have been made by an office clerk who collected the forms. Bliss creates a fictionalized narrative of the event, in which the clerk's supervisor takes one look at Anatole and proclaims "this gentleman's color is white," therefore making the final decision of his race even if it had already been determined on the application.[107] Since Broyard's original application has long been lost, we will never know whether the application had two different inks or one—two inks would mean two different pens marked the paperwork. While the dual answers to the question of color highlight confusion or vacillation of Broyard's background, they do not reveal who contributed to the source of this change, which is precisely the point. Regardless of who made the decision to render him White, the fact remains that it was the first time his race was reaffirmed on a legal document. Writing and race became inextricably linked for Broyard upon his visit to this office, and he subsequently began adulthood as a White man. Not only was this possible based on his light complexion and racial silence, but it was now legally verifiable based on his government application.

Over the next several years, legal documents continued to classify Broyard as White. After dropping out of Brooklyn College in 1939, he began dating Aida Sanchez, a Puerto Rican woman. When they decided to marry, their marriage license listed them both as White.[108] Similarly, his military application to fight in World War II also listed him as White. Just as with the aforementioned social security application, Bliss is uncertain whether he checked off the "White" box himself, or if the military intake administrator assigned this classification to him because of his phenotype. Broyard would not have corrected this anyway since he endeavored to avoid Blackness. One of the ironies of his time in the military was that he led an all-Black company in the army, due to his ambiguous race, which the officers interpreted as "non-white." This experience could have contributed to his reticence about

---

[107] Broyard, 353.

[108] Sanchez was his first wife, with whom he had a daughter. Sandy, Bliss's mother, was his second wife.

discussing the military, and his ending affiliations with African-Americans altogether.

By all accounts, Broyard was a lackluster commander of the 167th Port Company because he did not enforce the orders directed by his superiors. Being chased by African-American boys in his youth traumatized him so deeply that he was not able to assert himself with Black men as an adult, thereby rendering him an ineffective leader. Bliss raises another possibility of his wartime experiences with race by assuming that her father would have "heard the kinds of remarks that whites felt free to make when Blacks weren't around" and that he would have witnessed the inferior treatment that Black soldiers endured.[109] The most compelling evidence that the war changed Broyard's racial outlook came from the only wartime story he shared, about having to chase a deranged Black soldier who stabbed another serviceman. Bliss wonders if the shouts of "catch that crazy nigger" from other officers made him fear for his own life while he was in pursuit of the stabber; her father began questioning if he was really the "crazy nigger" being chased.[110] These assumptions suggest that Anatole Broyard's experiences interacting with African-American men in the army altered his view of race after his return. Keeping his war stories silent implies that race is an unspeakable topic for a person pretending to be White.

Bliss puts his transformation gently: "my father's service in the army probably made him feel more distanced from Blacks than ever."[111] Her use of the tentative adverb "probably" coupled with her euphemistic "feel more distanced from Blacks" points to uncertainty with her own assertions, even though the evidence is clear that the Second World War forced him to be around Blacks for a sustained amount of time and he was transformed as a result. Bliss situates her father's life story in the tradition of passing fictions, which "often feature a pivotal scene where the light-skinned protagonist witnesses some mistreatment of Blacks that convinces him or her to cross to the other side."[112] Invoking *The Autobiography of an Ex-Colored Man* as a prime example, she refers to the lynching scene as pivotal in convincing the protagonist to abandon his Blackness and live completely as a White man. Reading

---

[109] Broyard, *One Drop*, 374.
[110] Broyard, 374.
[111] Broyard, 375.
[112] Broyard, 374.

the Ex-Colored Man's life as an analogue for Broyard's, Bliss argues that a similar racial catalyst occurred when her father was stationed in New Caledonia: "he saw something during his time with the 167th that helped him make up his mind about how he would live his life when he returned to New York."[113] This is a vague way of saying that he would "live his life" without any reference to his Black past. Despite the ambiguities of his overseas encounters, Anatole Broyard left his Blackness behind long before returning to New York City after World War II.

Broyard's quest to begin a new life for himself and eschew racial boundaries is further evidenced by his desire to open a bookstore in Greenwich Village. After returning to the United States, he vowed to "live outside a world where roles were predicated on race."[114] This is similar to his father's ideas about race, since Nat Broyard actively avoided the Black/White binary by referring to himself simply as Creole. The senior Broyard did not appreciate the value of different types of writing, but he encouraged his son to always appreciate literature. During his summers off from school, Nat encouraged Anatole to devour Tarzan books and the works of Alexandre Dumas, specifically because Dumas's Black and French ancestry paralleled the Broyards' own racial background.

Young Anatole enjoyed Tarzan to such a great extent that he conceived of a creation myth that would put Tarzan's story to shame: he claimed that his grandfather was walking one day when he "saw a pretty girl sitting in a coconut tree. He coaxed her down and made her his wife."[115] This fictional tale of his beginnings paradoxically acknowledges his great-grandmother's Caribbean roots, while "dismissing his bit of Blackness as just another accident of lust."[116] He told this Tarzan-esque story as a joke to his close friends and to his second wife, Sandy. To the majority of people with whom he interacted after World War II, he was a White man without a Black heritage. The Tarzan-inspired narrative encapsulated his relationship to books, wherein he was drawn to the fantasy lives that his favorite authors created. Books convinced him that he had the freedom to choose his life in the same manner that his favorite literary characters choose theirs. He devoted the

---

[113] Broyard, 374.
[114] Broyard, 375.
[115] Broyard, 142.
[116] Broyard, 143.

remainder of his new life to literature, through the bookstore, his friends in the New York literati, and eventually through his position as the influential New York Times book critic.

Despite Broyard's immersion in books as an adult, his own creative writing stalled and he was unable to write all the narratives he wanted to, especially the ones based on his life. Like Anita Reynolds, Broyard struggled to write creatively because it would have brought him too close to the racial truth that he renounced after World War II. The dual themes of race and writing defined Broyard's life as much as it did Reynolds's life: he progressed from circumventing race by rendering himself Creole to living completely as White, a trajectory that corresponded with his increasing inability to write about himself. Creative writing proved to be a futile endeavor for Anatole Broyard, because it would have forced him to remember that he is actually Black.

"A Wonderful and Important Story": Broyard's Lost Self and His Failed Writing Projects

Anatole Broyard's life in books continued after World War II through his small used bookstore. However, it did not survive because it was not generating enough money. After closing it, his immersion in literature caused him to blur the lines between fiction and his own life. According to Bliss's biography, which has been the basis for my assertions thus far, her father's "favorite writers became his adopted family."[117] Anatole says this more bluntly in his posthumously published autobiography, *Kafka Was the Rage*: "I could trade in my embarrassingly ordinary history for a choice of fictions. I could lead a hypothetical life, unencumbered by memory, loyalties, or resentments."[118] As both his autobiography and biography make clear, being engrossed in fiction permitted his refashioning without the limitations of racial identity.

In tethering the real and the fictional, Broyard devoted his adult life to weaving his own narrative, beginning with nebulous histories about his origins. One example of his fictional history appeared in his invocation of the Tarzan narrative, rendering himself "exotic" to the people who heard this story. Sandy Broyard believed this for years after her husband's death, as she

---

[117] Broyard, 384.
[118] Broyard, *Kafka Was the Rage*, 136.

states in her own autobiography that she "married an exotic man."[119] The use of "exotic" raises the question of whether Anatole relished this description just as Anita Reynolds did. She passed as an "exotic" character while living in Europe and Africa, and Anatole may have also been pleased to escape racial characterization by rendering himself "exotic." In yet another narrative of a creation myth, he also declared that he "sprung from [his] own brow, spontaneously generated the way flies were once thought to have originated."[120] This vision is preposterous because he is far from having been developed in a vacuum, as Bliss's research makes clear. Yet it was his way of saying "he'd come from nothing."[121] Broyard was not alone in holding this sentiment in 1950s Greenwich Village, since post-War Lower Manhattan was a place for everyone to recreate their identities according to their own standards.[122]

A deeper level to this second invented narrative is apparent in Bliss Broyard's biography. In trying to understand her father, she quotes from Fitzgerald's novel *The Great Gatsby*: "The truth was that Jay Gatsby, of West Egg, Long Island, sprang from his Platonic conception of himself…so he invented just the sort of Jay Gatsby that a seventeen-year-old boy would be likely to invent."[123] Both Jay Gatsby and Anatole Broyard portrayed themselves with variations of the verb "spring" to express their subjectivities without families or histories, thereby explaining why the latter "greatly admired Fitzgerald's novel about American self-invention."[124] Fitzgerald showed up in the lives of both Anita Reynolds and Anatole Broyard, which points to a generative matrix of references. Reynolds knew him and reviewed his short stories; Broyard did not know Fitzgerald but saw his most famous character, Jay Gatsby, as a fictional reflection of himself. Bliss understands the connection after remembering that her father often "admired the view from the porch" just as "Jay Gatsby stands in front of his mansion and stares at the green light of Daisy Buchanan's dock across the bay."[125] The green light represents a close yet unrealized goal for Gatsby—Daisy Buchanan. According to Brett Kaplan, Broyard's goal was not just to attain many women but to write the "Great

---

[119] Sandy Broyard, *Standby*, 142, emphasis mine.
[120] Broyard, *One Drop*, 23.
[121] Broyard, 23.
[122] Kaplan, "Anatole Broyard's Human Stain," 135.
[123] Fitzgerald, *The Great Gatsby*, 105.
[124] Broyard, *One Drop*, 34.
[125] Broyard, 34.

American Novel," in the same vein as his literary heroes, including F. Scott Fitzgerald.[126] He sought to abate his own anxieties and prolong life by creating fiction in which he can insert himself. However, he was unable to do so.

Instead of a novel, Broyard published an impressive collection of writing over his lengthy literary career, which included books, short stories, and book reviews. His personal archives served as Bliss Broyard's primary source for her research, the "many drafts of stories that he wasn't able to publish and the journals and notes he kept for the novel he could never finish."[127] Interspersed through these early writings are hidden clues about Broyard's racial identity, as if he figuratively took a page out of Anita Reynolds's book. His first published essay was "Portrait of the Inauthentic Negro" from *Commentary* in July 1950, which was a play on Sartre's essay "Portrait of an Inauthentic Jew" from a May 1948 issue of the magazine. Broyard's version referenced "various avenues of flight" for African-Americans.[128] He asserted that Blacks should maintain a "stubborn adherence" to their own identities, despite all of the "distorting pressures of one's situation."[129] They should remember their "innate qualities and developed characteristics as individuals, distinguished from preponderantly defensive reactions as members of an embattled minority."[130] He also wrote that "thousands of Negroes with 'typical' features are accepted as whites merely because of light complexion."[131]

In her biography, Bliss Broyard interprets this article as proof that her father did not see any fundamental differences between Blacks and Whites, because each person had the freedom to create his or her own identity. However, the theme of "Portrait of an Inauthentic Negro"—as well as the provocative title—evidences the exact opposite and alludes to Anatole's justification for passing. Even though he argued that Blacks should remember their essential selves, it is not enough to prevent others from categorizing light-skinned African-Americans as White. In his own case, he passed not only because others imprinted their beliefs on his skin, but also because he enjoyed all the benefits of a fictional identity, with the first one being ensconced in the

---

[126] Kaplan, "Anatole Broyard's Human Stain," 128.
[127] Broyard, *One Drop*, 316.
[128] Anatole Broyard, "Portrait of an Inauthentic Negro," 60.
[129] Broyard, *One Drop*, 394.
[130] Broyard, 394.
[131] Broyard, 395.

Greenwich Village literati. In light of his racial duplicity, we can interpret this essay as an admission of passing, though he embedded it in diction that made him appear sympathetic to the problems that plagued African-Americans. If he truly believed that racial differences between Blacks and Whites were non-existent, why did he choose to ward off the former in favor of the latter?

His next essay for *Commentary* was "Keep Cool, Man," about Jazz music. In situating his early publications in tandem with each other, Bliss Broyard concludes that "the majority of what my father had published [in his early years as a writer] did concern Black people and Black culture."[132] We must qualify this statement to avoid overstating the case of his relationship to Black Americans. While the two essays for *Commentary* were indeed directed towards African-Americans, this focus changed when he began writing personal short stories a few years later. The first one he published was "What the Cystoscope Said" (1954), which fictionalizes his father's death. Shortly after this story appeared, Anatole published his second autobiographical story, "Sunday Dinner in Brooklyn" (1954), about a man residing in Greenwich Village who feels estranged from his parents in Brooklyn when he visits for weekly Sunday dinners.

When viewed from the perspective of Broyard's racial passing, the characters exemplify his attempts to resolve his Black past with his White present. In the first story, the protagonist (Paul) tries to return to the past to mend his relationship with his distant yet ailing father. In the second text, the protagonist's parents are unable to read him, and are unsure how he conducts his life when he is away from them during the week. Without these obligatory dinners serving as a lifeline, Paul would completely divorce his family. These autobiographical short stories focus on parents, suggesting that Anatole Broyard used his pen to work out the problem of how to address his own Creole parents after starting a new life as a White man. In the second text especially, the narrator from Greenwich Village disdains his parents in Brooklyn, raising the major themes of intergenerational conflict and the difficult choice of separating from family. The less obvious theme that he could not overtly articulate was race. If Paul is a passing subject like his literary creator is, then it would provide him with another reason to avoid the parents who represent a racial past he has renounced.

---

[132] Broyard, 399.

At times, Bliss appears surprised that her father's fiction "was mostly autobiographical," assuming that a racial passer would avoid writing about family.[133] Yet according to Otto Rank's theorization, writing about this topic would be inevitable if his goal is to create works that would outlast him. In Anatole's stories, he does not reference his mother very often, perhaps because she was the source of both love and anxiety for him. Moreover, he is well aware of death, as the first story is a fictional account of Nat's death four years prior. In working out his own apprehension with death, Broyard wrote himself into these works to promote his own immortality. In fact, he inserts himself into these stories in multiple ways—the narrator's name is Paul (Anatole's middle name), and his nickname is Bud (a truncated version of Anatole's own nickname, "Buddy"). Missing from these narratives is race, explaining their resonance: readers read the racelessness of the characters as generically White. Since the audience who read his stories in 1954 were unaware of Anatole's background, the added layer of race for the characters was lost on them. This was a purposeful choice, as he was both racially passing and adamantly opposed to the potential pigeonholing of his writing.

Broyard's first two autobiographical short stories, "What the Cystoscope Said" and "Sunday Dinner in Brooklyn," established him as a serious writer. As a result, he received "a contract for a novel expanding the story of his father's death against the backdrop of leaving his childhood home of Brooklyn for Greenwich Village."[134] He received this offer by the end of 1954, which entailed combining the two pieces into a longer work. Anatole faced pressure from the likes of Norman Mailer and John Updike, who were both anticipating his novel. Although he sincerely hoped to complete his fictionalized life story about "a young man's journey from a provincial Brooklyn boyhood to sophisticated Greenwich Village alienation," it was never published, and he did not actualize the literary fame he felt he deserved. The problem is that he would have had to confront race in order to continue, which was untenable because his left-behind self would have sprung to the surface.[135]

Many of Broyard's contemporaries attempted to diagnose the impediment to his writing. Bliss surmises that her father "became paralyzed under

---

[133] Broyard, 144.
[134] Broyard, 316.
[135] Broyard, 401.

the weight of everyone's expectations" and set the standards too high for himself.[136] Some of his closest acquaintances suggested that he spent "all his creative energies on seducing women" when he should have been writing instead.[137] The reading public did not learn of his status as a racial passer until Henry Louis Gates published an article in a 1996 issue of *The New Yorker* and again in his book *Thirteen Ways of Looking at a Black Man* (1997). In both instances, he is heavy handed in critiquing Broyard, rendering him a "guilt-ridden fugitive" who was "racked by his inability to write his own Magnum Opus" largely because his writer's block was an extension of his refusal to admit his racial identity.[138] Gates in particular uses gossip, inuendo, and speculation to depict Broyard as overly enamored with women; so much so, that it dominated his life and diverted his attention away from writing. Maureen Perkins questions whether Broyard was hindered by the typical "mixed race person's inability to speak of whiteness."[139] Gates and Perkins overlook the fact that Blackness, *not* Whiteness, contributed to Broyard's inability to write a narrative based on his life.

One Drop includes an effective image which helps to explain Broyard's writing troubles: "For my father, trying to write honestly about his childhood without being honest about all its particulars was rather like trying to write one of those lipogram novels that never use the letter e".[140] Knowing of his racial background makes this analogy an apt one. For Broyard to pen a tale about his life, without addressing how it was mediated by race, would be a particularly arduous endeavor. By leaving his Black past officially behind during World War II, he precluded the possibility that he could ever write about himself honestly. Writing an autobiography means that "everything must be told, that secrets are the equivalent of a betrayal of the autobiographical pact, and that the author should hold nothing back."[141] However, as a passing subject, Broyard was certainly holding back—or more accurately, keeping back—his Black past, thereby preventing him from writing a complete and honest narrative about his life that transcended mere "writer's block."

---

[136] Broyard, 401.
[137] Broyard, 407.
[138] Gates, *Thirteen Ways of Looking at a Black Man*, xix, 198.
[139] Perkins, "Resisting the Autobiographical Imperative," 275.
[140] Broyard, *One Drop*, 400.
[141] Perkins, "Resisting," 271.

Once he began working as a New York Times book critic, however, his publisher canceled the contract. Broyard tenaciously held on to the notion that he would complete the book despite this loss. With this goal in mind, he spent much of his free time throughout the 1970s writing and revising the chapter on his mother, Edna, hoping to at least publish it as a stand-alone section from the incomplete manuscript. He wanted to reconcile with the woman who caused his birth trauma, using his craft as a writer to speak to her and for her. He completely disowned her once he became a father himself, but neither "his mother's mortality" nor "his guilt about their relationship" remained abstract anymore.[142] Broyard's constant revisions coincided with Edna's deteriorating health, and each draft made her look "slightly different from the last," thus hindering his efforts at a coherent conclusion.[143] He was mortified when he visited Edna in the nursing home and she could not recognize him at all, translating this experience into print by portraying the mother in the narrative as "devolving into vagueness" until she could not recognize Broyard's fictional doppelganger, Buddy.[144] Both Paul and Anatole failed to see the irony of the situation, that if a son can forget his mother, his mother can just as easily forget her son.

After Edna's death, Broyard abandoned the chapter altogether and turned to revising other sections of the manuscript, realizing that writing about his mother would not bring her back into existence nor would it help him to reconcile his life as a White man with his past as a Black one. He turned his attention to the sections that focused on him, as though Edna's demise motivated him to perfect the image he wanted to leave after death. As will be discussed later in this chapter, Broyard's fascination with death brought about creative ways in which he would live forever in print. Like a true racial passer, he disavowed his parents once he began crossing the color line. As such, Edna Broyard endured three deaths: one when her son symbolically killed her to live with his White family in bucolic New England, her second, biological, death, and her third death when he abandoned the notion of publishing the excerpt memorializing her.

In Sandy Broyard's autobiography, *Standby* (2005), she is as cryptic about her husband's Creole status as he was. She alludes to his "struggles with

---

[142] Broyard, *One Drop*, 437.
[143] Broyard, 439.
[144] Broyard, 439.

his roots" and "unresolved issues of his own childhood."[145] In addition to rendering him "exotic," she admits to remaining silent, since "there are some things that as his wife of thirty years only I know."[146] One can only imagine that the purpose of her enigmatic rhetoric is to obscure Anatole Broyard's Black ancestry. Her silence is conspicuous because *Standby* first appeared in 2005 at a time when Americans had a greater tolerance for mixed-race status. She focuses much of her memoir on Broyard's illness and death, but his race is absent, as are her reactions to knowing of his secret for three decades, and her Sisyphean task of forcing him to confess to their children. Bliss acquiesces to discussing his racial passing to Henry Louis Gates for his work on Broyard but stops short of inscribing it onto paper herself. This silence implies that his racial transgression must always be protected in print, even if everyone was already privy to it.

Based on the lack of race in the Broyards' respective autobiographies, we can infer that neither passing subjects nor their relatives can rewrite the societal-imprinted racial codes. Perhaps they did not need to, since his reputation as a White man of letters was long solidified. By the late 1960s, he "produced more writing than he had in years," including short stories for *Playboy* and *The New Yorker*.[147] The two books he published were collections of his book reviews, *Aroused by Books* (1974) and *Men, Women and Other Anticlimaxes* (1980). The sexual imagery of these titles—"Aroused" and "Anticlimaxes"—further solidified his other reputation, as a frequent seducer of women. In commenting on Gates's exposé on Broyard, Boisseron argues that Gates "skillfully stages a sexual subplot to stage the outing of Anatole Broyard, thereby suggesting that a narrative on passing infallibly carries a sexual subplot to be deciphered."[148] Her reading of Gates also raises the pivotal question, "what precisely was the story" given his history as a womanizer?[149] Just as Broyard considered himself an expert at navigating his Blackness, he also believed he navigated discreet relationships with women successfully. His later writing projects did not present any problems for him because race was not a topic at all; his pen only failed him when writing his autobiography

---

[145] Sandy Broyard, *Standby*, 133, 205.
[146] Broyard, 142, 166.
[147] Broyard, *One Drop*, 430.
[148] Boisseron, *Creole Renegades*, 48.
[149] Boisseron, 48.

since his Creole family's Blackness was a Rubicon he could not cross. Broyard actively sought to immortalize himself through his body of work, which had the unintended consequences of tethering his racial passing with his sexual deviance. As a result, he literalizes Gubar's observation about the tethering of race and sexuality when it comes to racechanging: hardly just "sexual iconography," as a racial passer whose sexual deviance elicited posthumous exposure, Anatole Broyard himself is the "provocative connection" between these two subject positions.[150]

When race did appear in his book reviews, it was often to critique the category of authors of whom he was most critical: Black writers. He disliked writers who sacrificed "aesthetic concerns for a political agenda."[151] For example, even though Toni Morrison's novel *Tar Baby* was generally well received, he quipped that it was a "protest novel, but the reader might have a few protests too."[152] He refused to use his position at *The New York Times* to help Black writers, angering his contemporaries who knew he was passing. Their anger stems from the notion of African-American solidarity, assuming that powerful Black writers should help those who were trying to succeed. Toni Morrison, for instance, helped to edit and publish the works of Toni Cade Bambara, Gayl Jones, and Angela Davis when she edited books at Random House. In Broyard's case, his approval or disapproval could impact an author's career, and if he had his way, many Black writers would not have had writing careers at all. In being angry with Broyard for his racial passing and ignoring African-American writers, his detractors realized that his lack of support was less about them and more about his own inclination to ward off his past and prevent being labelled as a Black writer; he wanted a reputation simply as a writer, without the burden of race as a topic on which he was expected to write. In 1950, he was open to addressing race in his writing, as proven by his essays in *Commentary*, but by the time he was writing

---

[150] Gubar, *Racechanges*, 11. Sex was a theme that appeared throughout Broyard's writings, just as often as race did, but in more subtle ways. For instance, in his writings for *Neurotica* in 1950, Broyard focused on the then popular dance of mambo. In particular, he observed the sexual connotations of the dance and noted that as it spread across the United States, American dancers emphasized a less submissive role for women. For more on his thoughts on dancing/sexuality, see "American Sexual Imperialism."

[151] Broyard, *One Drop*, 436.
[152] Quoted in Broyard, 436.

autobiographical works in the late 1970s, he grew averse to supporting Black writers and writing about Black culture/subjects. This reversal represents his transformation into a passing subject: he did not just assume Whiteness, he actively sought to avoid race at all costs even if it meant condemning Black authors.

Despite this inclination to avoid reminders of his Creole status, Blackness periodically appeared for Broyard in his affable demeanor with the few African-Americans he regularly encountered. Brent Staples relayed a story to Henry Louis Gates about their time at *The New York Times*: "when Anatole came anywhere near me…his whole style, demeanor, and tone would change….I took that as him conveying to me, 'Yes, I am like you'."[153] Bliss shares a similar story in *One Drop* with the example of Leroy, the man in charge of the crew who cleaned their home during her youth. She recalls that her father spoke to Leroy "in a familiar way, saying *Hey man!* and *What's happening?*, which made it seem as if they knew each other from somewhere."[154] She goes on to note her shock that her father spoke in "Leroy's particular way of speaking."[155] Sandy Broyard supports this claim by making gestures to demonstrate the ways in which Leroy and Anatole related to each other, which Bliss interpreted as "they used to be Black together."[156] Yet Broyard only felt comfortable around the African-Americans he felt superior to: Staples was a junior staff member at the *Times* when Broyard was senior, and Leroy was the Broyards' house cleaner, yet he stopped visiting their home after one of his men "broke a decorative plate and hid the remains rather than confessing the accident."[157] Perhaps Broyard fired Leroy for emphasizing an apt analogy for himself: he too "hid the remains" of his past instead of admitting his true racial heritage. Encountering Black men like Leroy and Staples reminded him that he maintained the secret of his race, yet his diction and gestures signaled that he was indeed one of them. This was his own furtive way of "confessing the accident" of his racial deception.

Broyard was less willing to interact with most other African-Americans, choosing instead to espouse prejudiced ideas. For instance, 1963 was the year

---

[153] Gates, "White Like Me," 77.
[154] Broyard, *One Drop*, 42, emphasis in original.
[155] Broyard, 43.
[156] Broyard, 44.
[157] Broyard, 43.

in which the Broyards relocated from New York City to suburban Connecticut and also the year when the Civil Rights movement reached its apex. Images of the March on Washington, the bombing of the 16th Street Baptist Church, and the protests of segregated lunch counters made their way into most American households. The Broyard home was not one of them. Bliss admits to growing up sheltered not just from her race but from the racism African-Americans fought against in the 1960s. Just as Nat Broyard kept his children away from race talk, Anatole continued the same regime for his own children by not welcoming any talk about race or racism in their home. According to Bliss, her father loathed the movement that Dr. King fought so hard for:

> He was opposed to turning race into a movement that collapsed affiliation and identity, requiring adherence to a group platform rather than to one's 'essential spirit'…my dad only saw the ways that such collective action could become an avenue of flight, distorting a person's sense of self.[158]

Coupled with this belief was his friend Michael Vincent Miller's observation that Broyard's attitude about race radically changed during the 1960s. According to him, Broyard's lexicon now included words like "spade" and "jigaboo," while he also began "making derogatory comments about Black people."[159] Unbeknownst to his friends, Broyard's new vocabulary and stance on civil rights was an extension of his racial passing, creating two ways in which to read his behavior. On one hand, he could have shared the same concern raised by his fellow Creole Victor Grabért, that openly supporting equal treatment for Blacks could be misinterpreted as a tacit admission of Blackness. Broyard tried to convince himself and his peers that he was racist, thereby preventing the slightest suspicion of his true racial origins from being raised.

On the other hand, it was possible that he began internalizing some of the racism that he endured before deciding to pass. Perhaps he really did believe that Blacks were wasting their time fighting for equality, especially since he always said that "Blacks were and should be different and separate from whites."[160] If this Fanonian reading is true, then it would mean his

---

[158] Broyard, 428.
[159] Broyard, 428.
[160] Broyard, 429.

internalized racism is much stronger than Anita Reynolds's: while she internalized colonial ideas about Indians, Broyard adopted America's long-standing racist ideology. Miller's defense of his friend was that he genuinely did not see segregation as a problem and was not prejudiced. This assertion is difficult to believe in light of his angry comments about his neighbors. When selling his home, Anatole became angry with the "Black kids playing outside down the street…these people aren't going to want to buy this house when they see that!" "That" referred to nearby low-income housing, to which Bliss responded with "Jesus Christ Dad, you sound like a goddamned racist."[161] As the literary connoisseur, he might have considered the irony that he could not be considered racist because he was part Black, or he might have also recalled his youth in Brooklyn, when he was bullied and humiliated by Black children not much older than the ones he now wanted to keep at a distance.

More likely the case though, he adopted the racist mentality of his wealthy White neighbors, who also complained about their Black neighbors. Fanon expounded on internalized racism throughout *Black Skin, White Masks*, of which Anatole seems to be a prime example. This self-hatred emerged as a function of his racial passing. He took it one step further by wanting to sell their home altogether and move to a racially homogenous location, thereby enacting his version of White flight. Anatole Broyard "loved children indiscriminately," but he disliked that they were specifically African-American children whose mere presence could have alarmed potential buyers.[162] Seeing these Black children suggested that race was encroaching too close for him to handle. After decades living as White, he knew that his death loomed as cancer ravished his body. He thus wanted to die away from Blackness, where Black kids would not have to remind him of the past from which distanced himself.

His efforts to run from his Black past proved futile, since it kept appearing in the area he was most accustomed to finding solace and where he wanted to have a long-term future: the written word. Whereas Anita Reynolds appreciated being the inspiration for some of her friends' creative writing, seeing it as a way for her to enjoy life after death—at least on the page—Broyard found certain depictions insulting, especially since he wanted to control his immortal image, just as Freud once did. For instance, he was a model for Max, the

---

[161] Broyard, 50.
[162] Broyard, 50.

writer and critic in William Gaddis's novel *The Recognitions* (1952). He did not take issue with what appeared to be an accurate representation in this text, yet he disliked Anais Nin's overt reference to him in *The Diary of Anais Nin* (1971). Nin describes "three striking figures: Anatole Broyard, New Orleans-French, handsome, sensual, ironic; Vincent, tall and dark like a Spaniard; and Arthur, with mixed Negro and Jewish blood."[163] Broyard disapproved of this observation on the grounds that he was "falsely accused of being someone else," which is an unfair assessment.[164] Nin does not mention his race in her text, but by grouping the three men together—two of whom are described explicitly in racialized terms—Broyard was displeased with the list for merely implying that he too is "racially different from white."[165] Fearing that readers would discover his race based on this fleeting reference, he sought to carefully control his image in print, especially since he most desired to be preserved there.[166]

He leveled his harshest vitriol toward Chandler Brossard for publishing the novel *Who Walk in Darkness* (1952). Broyard was flattered to be Brossard's best man at his wedding, and equally flattered to serve as the inspiration for his best friend's protagonist, Henry Porter. Yet this friendship

---

[163] Nin, *The Diary of Anais Nin*, 4:180.

[164] Quoted in Kaplan, "Anatole Broyard's Human Stain," 131.

[165] Kaplan, 131.

[166] Years before Nin described these men in racialized terms, she escorted Otto Rank to Harlem for the first time in 1934 to gaze upon African-Americans. He was her therapist and lover, and as Ahad reminds us, Nin believed that traveling to Harlem was the ideal break Rank needed from work. They both enjoyed Harlem, believing that "negroes are natural and possess the secret of joy. That is why they can endure the suffering inflicted upon them. The world maltreats them, but among themselves they are deeply alive, physically and emotionally" (Nin, *The Diary of Anais Nin, 1934–1939*, 2:37). Nin fetishized men of color, as evident in her diary description from 1934 and her commentary on Broyard, Vincent, and Arthur over three decades later. According to Ahad, Rank himself "was apparently oblivious to the Harlem scene in the 1920s and 1930s" but appealed to Harlem Renaissance writers (*Freud Upside Down*, 39). One must wonder how much influence Harlem had on Rank's work, since he loved fetishizing African-Americans to such a great extent that he proclaimed to Nin "I am tempted to prescribe it to my patients. Go to Harlem!" (Nin, *The Diary of Anais Nin, 1934–1939*, 6). Perhaps Harlem (and the African-Americans who lived there) influenced Rank's formulations, just as mixed-race subjectivities and racial anxieties influenced Freud's.

ended once Broyard read a draft of the novel's introduction: "People said Henry Porter was a 'passed' Negro. But nobody knew for sure. I think the rumor was started by someone who had grown up with Porter in San Francisco. He did not look part Negro to me."[167] Broyard felt that his race was revealed through this introduction. In response, he refused to sign the release, thereby compelling Brossard to remove his identifying information. The published American version describes Henry as illegitimate instead of Black, but the change was not enough to salvage their friendship, nor does it clarify his race any further. Due to slavery and its aftereffects, especially slave masters raping enslaved women and producing mixed-race children who were often not recognized, to be rendered "illegitimate" still maintains the overtone of Blackness, which also reiterates the intertwined history that racial passing has with sexual deviance.[168] Bliss believes that her father's resentment was caused by Brossard's undermining the "[East] Village credo that they were all free to discover themselves without being encumbered by familial or ancestral histories."[169] The real justification for his response, which Bliss does not articulate, is that Brossard excavated Broyard's Black past and put it into print. Broyard was not amenable to seeing his passing revealed in a book, even under a fictional guise, after using books as an escape from his Blackness in the first place.

As a result, Anatole Broyard used his own pen to retaliate against Brossard two decades later. In his very first book review for *The New York Times* after taking over as book critic, he argued that Brossard's new novel *Wake Up. We're Almost There* (1971) was "so transcendently bad it makes us fear not only for the condition of the novel in this country, but for the country itself."[170] His words outraged Brossard and many readers, causing enough controversy that the *Times* editors contemplated his dismissal, rendering him "too blinded by his desire for revenge to think through the possible consequences."[171] Though *Wake Up. We're Almost There* is not a roman à clef, Broyard still resented the racial revelation of Brossard's first novel and

---

[167] Brossard, *Who Walk in Darkness*, 1

[168] Both the French and British versions have maintained their original introductions calling out the protagonist's passing subjectivity, however the American version does not.

[169] Broyard, *One Drop*, 398.

[170] Quoted in Broyard, 434.

[171] Broyard, 435.

couched it in the disparaging review of this second text. As he rehashed the feud with Brossard in print, Bliss notes the absence of "one crucial detail: exactly what my father had found so offensive about Brossard's characterization of him."[172] Broyard's peers speculated about his race in hushed tones but did not dare to put anything onto paper. Perhaps they feared speaking up as well, lest they encountered his wrath as Brossard did. Another rationale for their silence is that, in order to protect Broyard from exposure, they decided against writing anything that could lead to even remote speculation. In doing so, they anticipated Sandy Broyard's actions, when she spoke about his race but could not write about it, even after his death.

For six years after Broyard's death, his race was an open secret among many of his contemporaries. Gates first revealed it to the public in the sensational *New Yorker* article "White Like Me," in 1996. In preparing the story, he told Bliss it was imperative she write about her father's "racial identity, that it would make a wonderful and important story."[173] Hyperbole aside, Broyard's biography is a curious one, since his wish to live in perpetuity conflicted with the secrecy mandated by his racial passing. He navigated the two by being a prolific writer of all things but his life story, which was published posthumously. Only in death were the frictions partially worked out: his legacy as a powerful book critic (not novelist or memoirist) is sustained, while he is finally allowed to be Black instead of White.

"Exposing and Concealing": Passing, Dying, and Writing

When Anatole Broyard died from cancer in 1990, it was the second death he endured; his first was the Creole ancestry he killed when he decided to pass. He also endured the deaths of his parents, particularly Nat, who was diagnosed with cancer just as Anatole later would be. Passing subjects have a long history of enduring multiple deaths, with the first one being the symbolic loss of their Black past. Passing and writing are inextricably linked, just as the themes of passing and death are equally tethered to each other, which explains the morbid fascination Broyard maintained with death throughout his life. His first published short story was "What the Cystoscope Said" (1954) about his father's death, and his first posthumous publication was *Intoxicated by My*

---

[172] Broyard, 435.
[173] Broyard, 107.

Illness and Other Writings on Life and Death (1992), about his incurable cancer. According to critic Maureen Perkins, "he was determined to observe and chronicle his body's decline" at the end of his life.[174] Broyard tried to keep death away as vehemently as he tried to keep Blackness away: he did not want the cancer to disfigure him because, as he observed in his journal, "at the end, you're posing for eternity" and "dying should be like a birthday party to end all birthday parties."[175] Though Broyard sought literary immortality, he did not achieve it with his autobiography, which was published as *Kafka Was the Rage: A Greenwich Village Memoir* in 1993. Three years after his death and almost forty years after he began drafting it, Sandy edited this work and published it. Literary reviewers praised it for its candor. As Greg Carter writes, the narrator is "forthcoming about his working-class background and his recent enrollment as a part-time student at the New School for Social Research"[176] while Maureen Perkins argues that he "made no attempt to be coy about his sexual adventures."[177] These remarks encapsulate all that Broyard reveals about himself, especially his class status, educational aspirations, and sexual proclivities. Noticeably absent from his life story, however, is race, just as Broyard originally intended, rendering it far from a complete personal narrative. As a result, most of my analysis has been drawn from Bliss Broyard's *One Drop*, which is a far more honest and compelling exploration of Anatole Broyard than the limited scope of his autobiography.

In justifying the ease with which one can write about deceased subjects, Ian Donaldson notes that "they can't answer back, they can't prove you wrong, they're unlikely suddenly to change their habits and most importantly, they can't be hurt."[178] Considering Broyard's curiosity in understanding death and his desire "to live everything…[even] be alive at his death and remain conscious and writing for as long as he could," he would be the one to want to change in his dying days, to make sure that he gets the final story right.[179] Anita Reynolds, however, was full of life and enjoyed every minute of it. In a letter to her friend Jean, she admitted to feeling "a little

---

[174] Perkins, "Resisting the Autobiographical Imperative," 272.
[175] Broyard, *One Drop*, 20, 34.
[176] Carter, "Anatole Broyard's *Kafka Was the Rage*," 98.
[177] Perkins, "Resisting the Autobiographical Imperative," 272.
[178] Donaldson, "Biographical Uncertainty," 311.
[179] Perkins, "Resisting the Autobiographical Imperative," 276.

guilty saying how much fun I have had being a colored girl in the twentieth century."[180] Her autobiography includes several references to all the "fun" she had, and death was the last thing she considered—at least openly. Reynolds was able to have "fun" because of her light complexion, which she used to pass as White. Yet death implicitly hovered over her life too, since she had to kill her Creole past to ensure she could pass.

Other differences define these two real-life racial passers. For one, Reynolds makes it clear that her first willful act of passing occurred when she enrolled in dance classes, while Broyard's first act of jumping the color line is more ambiguous due to his lost government documents. Secondly, *One Drop* encompasses Broyard's entire life, while *American Cocktail* ends prematurely with the start of the Second World War, though Reynolds lived another four decades. Settling in St. Croix, she continued passing until her death in 1980. The most palpable difference is how they are remembered today through the written word. Though Reynolds called literature "beyond my wildest dreams," she maintained friendships with writers and an interest in publishing her memoirs—which only occurred posthumously.[181] Broyard, on the other hand, maintained a lifelong obsession with it, spending decades working on a life story that was also published after death. He was tortured by this, especially because he published other types of literature, just not the one that would define him as the true literary man he saw of himself. If Reynolds and Broyard were truly honest about their Blackness, they might have achieved their stated goals. Yet real-life racial passers struggled to actualize the fiction of their assumed White identity, with their goal of publishing nonfiction—their memoirs. As such, they were unable to have their life writings published while alive, yet they live on in perpetuity because of the Blackness they killed off.

Though we are unsure if Otto Rank explicitly considered race at all when he developed his ideas, his theory of birth trauma is apropos for understanding racial passers, beginning with Reynolds and Broyard. Specifically, Rank's foci of birth, death, and creativity are all concerns that dominate passers' lives. According to him, "the removal from the mother's womb thus signals the certainty of death. The subject performs various symbolic acts that represent the prolonging of life, hence the artist's superior ability to confront

---

[180] Reynolds, *American Cocktail*, 50.
[181] Reynolds, 50.

the death drive."[182] This explains why Reynolds and Broyard write to and about their mothers: returning to the protection of Beatrice's womb and Edna's womb, respectively, is untenable and impossible, thus forcing these two passers to reach their mothers by depicting them on the page. Reynolds would much rather have a Puritanical mother than none at all, just as Broyard would much rather have a sickly mother than a deceased one. Yet both mothers are relics of their Black past with whom the passers struggle to reconnect. Rank's ideas also explain why Reynolds and Broyard engage in a lifelong quest to ward off death, with as much energy and focus as they ward off their Creole history: their impending deaths make these writers anxious about inserting themselves in their published works in an attempt to "live" forever, albeit symbolically.

As such, one must wonder what Reynolds and Broyard would have thought about their literary reputations today, which they were both occupied by. Indeed, elements of both writers appear as characters in various other works, in addition to their own. The most canonical example for Reynolds is *Quicksand*. George Hutchinson questions whether Audrey Denney is a fictionalized version of Reynolds, given Larsen's reputation of constructing characters based on people she actually knew.[183] For Anatole Broyard, literary critics interpreted his representation in a more recent text, as Coleman Silk in Philip Roth's passing narrative *The Human Stain* (2000). The obvious correlations include the fact that Coleman and his friend Nathan Zuckerman (the novel's narrator) are neighbors in New England, just as Broyard and Roth lived near each other in New England. Moreover, Zuckerman writes a story of his friend's racial passing, not unlike Roth himself who wrote the story of his literary acquaintance Broyard's racial duplicity. According to Kaplan, Broyard and Silk led lives that were "strikingly similar": both fought in World War II before spending the postwar years in the East Village, both sought love in the New York City subways, both were content that their children were born with lighter skin that could not betray their Black ancestry, and both were circumspect about race while passing.[184]

Despite these correspondences between the two racial passers, Philip Roth himself asserted that Coleman Silk was not modeled on Broyard, as

---

[182] Ahad, *Freud Upside Down*, 45.
[183] Hutchinson, "Introduction," 18.
[184] Kaplan, "Anatole Broyard's Human Stain," 127.

discussed in the next chapter. More germane to this chapter is the shared trope of writing. Broyard lauded Roth for his willingness to listen to critics and revise his writing accordingly. On a narrative level, elements of Coleman Silk's life appear as a fictionalized version of Anatole Broyard's story. Silk struggles to write about his life, before eventually asking his friend Nathan Zuckerman to take over his pen. He is agonized by writing about his own life as he wonders if he will ever be able to "maneuver the creative remove," and belatedly realizes that "every page of it makes [him] sick."[185] After completing the first draft of his manuscript, he wonders if it can truly compete with "what the pros do," which sounds as though he is questioning the value of his own prose.[186] Adding to Coleman's dissatisfaction is the fact that he is a professor who has been publishing throughout his academic career. While Broyard was not as hard on himself as Silk is, he also struggled for a long time to narrativize his life story, while Nathan Zuckerman justifies Silk's writer's block by saying that he could not write the book because it had already been written: "the book was your life. Writing personally is exposing and concealing at the same time but with you it could only be concealment and so it would never work."[187] The same logic applies to Anatole Broyard, who devoted his adult life to "concealment" because writing his life story caused much anxiety about the repressed truth of his Blackness. Fearing that their pens would betray their racial duplicity, both Silk and Broyard died leaving behind partially written reflections of their lives.

Coleman Silk dies under mysterious circumstances, yet Broyard's demise is from prostate cancer. Broyard's story begins with his death, as Bliss opens her biography with the image of her dying father. With the family all gathered around, his wife Sandy Broyard prompted him to finally confess the secret to his children although he equivocated each time. He doubted whether his children were interested in him at all: "if we did, he wondered, why didn't we read more of his writing?" Sandy persisted in prodding him, noting "this secret is more painful than the cancer."[188] She was concerned about the possibility that he would die without finally admitting that he descended from mixed-race Creoles. Indeed, if the secret was "more painful

---

[185] Roth, *The Human Stain*, 19.
[186] Roth, 19.
[187] Roth, 345.
[188] Broyard, *One Drop*, 10.

than the cancer," he did not reveal it, opting for one final effort to pretend that his racialized past never existed, as his inability to admit his Creole ancestry evidences. In response to this, his son Todd quipped "I'm supposed to understand my father by knowing his opinion on the latest Philip Roth novel."[189] Broyard might have appreciated this sarcastic comment since he consistently "looked at himself through the scrupulous lens of a literary critic."[190] Ultimately, Sandy is compelled to reveal his Creole status and racial passing to their children. In this strange irony, both Philip Roth and racial passing appear at the end of Broyard's life, implying that the two themes that dominated his life—race and writing—also conclude it. The next chapter continues Todd Broyard's line of thinking, by exploring parallels between Broyard and a Roth novel he never had the opportunity to review, *The Human Stain* (2000).

---

[189] Broyard, 11.
[190] Boisseron, *Creole Renegades*, 50.

CHAPTER 4

HE "COLORED HIMSELF JUST AS HE CHOSE": A CASE STUDY OF COLEMAN SILK

Todd Broyard's assumption that his father is only legible through reading a review of Philip Roth's work is a particularly apt one; book reviews were the first printed works speculating that Anatole Broyard was the inspiration for Coleman Silk. Lorrie Moore, for instance, suggested in *The New York Times* that "many readers will feel, correctly or not, [that Coleman Silk is] partly inspired by the late Anatole Broyard."[1] Similarly, Michiko Kakutani believes *The Human Stain* "seems to have been inspired by the life story of Anatole Broyard."[2] These critics employ tentative terms, highlighting their hesitation in forcing a one-to-one, mechanical reading of Broyard's life onto Roth's creation. However, as Clarence Page reminds his readers in the *Chicago Tribune*, Coleman Silk's life "seems to be largely based" on Anatole Broyard's.[3] Broyard died a decade before Roth published his novel, but the correlations between him and Silk that these book reviewers note are too uncanny to overlook.

Philip Roth's *The Human Stain* (2000) is the story of Coleman Silk, a racial passer who enjoys an illustrious career as a professor and dean before it unceremoniously ends when he refers to absent students as "spooks." His use of this racially charged epithet is ironic of course: though Silk looks White and passes as Jewish, he is truly African-American, uttering the term in reference to their absence and not their presence as Black subjects. He renounced his Black identity long before beginning his career as an academician, but not before his extended race-learning and his inclination towards death. Since Coleman Silk, like Anatole Broyard, is unable to complete a draft of his own life story, he relies on his neighbor and confidante, Nathan Zuckerman, to write it for him. Though Broyard's career did not end over a controversial accusation of racism, similarities between his life and Silk's life abound, as

---

[1] Moore, "The Wrath of Athena."
[2] Kakutani, "Confronting the Failures of a Professor Who Passes."
[3] Page, "America's Peculiar 'Passing' Fancy."

enumerated in reviews and scholarly critiques of the novel.[4] This chapter is less interested in the specific correlations between Broyard and Silk and more invested in the broader ways in which Coleman Silk's story invokes psychoanalysis and other passing narratives.

This chapter reads through the theories developed in this monograph, to assert that Philip Roth revised upon several passing narratives to create his own. He highlights the importance of psychoanalysis in understanding the color line by referencing a range of texts. Indeed, like the other characters in this study, Coleman endures race-learning, suffers anxieties with writing his own life story, and is inclined toward death for much of the novel. Undergirding his actions is his racial anxiety, which afflicted him just as it did Sigmund Freud, as evidenced by his decision to pass specifically as Jewish and not generically as White. The intertextual references throughout *The Human Stain* underscore Roth's indebtedness to psychoanalytic theories as well as real and fictional passing narratives, including Anatole Broyard's story. Even though *The Human Stain* predates *One Drop*, Broyard's racial passing was common knowledge within the northeast literati for decades—a circle that included Philip Roth. This chapter explores *The Human Stain* as a case study in further comprehending the psychoanalytic motivations for jumping the color line.

The Race-Learning of Coleman "Silky" Silk

Like other passing protagonists, the seeds for Coleman's racial passing began in his youth, through dual relationships with his Blackness and with his family. This latter one began as a complicated relationship with his distant yet demanding father, Mr. Silk, who is a dominating presence in the Silk household. He remains out of the home for extended stretches at a time, working long hours for the Pennsylvania Railroad. While at home, he compels his family to discuss literature instead of addressing race. Mr. Silk's own father

---

[4] The influence of Broyard on Coleman Silk first appeared in book reviews by Gail Caldwell, "Philip Roth's Latest Hero is a Man Undone by Freedom and Identity"; and John Leonard, "A Child of the Age". For scholarly discussions of this Broyard-Silk connection, see Elaine B. Safer, "Tragedy and Farce in Roth's *The Human Stain*"; William G. Tierney, "Interpreting Academic Identities: Reality and Fiction on Campus"; and Brett Kaplan, "Anatole Broyard's Human Stain: Performing Postracial Consciousness."

was a saloon owner who consistently pushed him to take his studies seriously. He thus follows in his father's footsteps by placing his family's erudition and love of literature above all other demands, and encouraged Coleman's study of Latin and Greek as part of the "old-fashioned curriculum."[5] Mr. Silk thoroughly enjoyed canonical literature; so much so, that each of his children are given middle names from Shakespeare's play Julius Caesar: "the eldest Silk son was Walter Antony, the second son, Coleman Brutus; Ernestine Calpurnia, their younger sister, took her middle name from Caesar's loyal wife."[6] As his children developed, so did Mr. Silk's fascination with the English language, as evidenced by his manner of discipline: he never "lost his temper…[but] had another way of beating you down. With words. With speech. With what he called 'the language of Chaucer, Shakespeare, and Dickens'."[7]

Mr. Silk's focus on classical education compelled the Silk family to attend museum exhibits, and to employ precise classifications instead of using vague descriptors for what they see. This well-rounded curriculum motivates Coleman to become a formidable classics professor. Yet Mr. Silk's idealized quest to have his children love the English language as much as he does also smothers them and prevents their growth in other crucial areas. The narrator, Nathan Zuckerman, describes it, saying, "even in ordinary conversation [the elder Silk sounds as if] he were reciting Marc Antony's speech over the body of Caesar."[8] Absent from interactions with his children are notions of what it means to be Black in a highly racialized society. Even when Coleman inquired about his father's encounters with racism when he worked for the Pennsylvania Railroad, it was "beneath" the senior Silk to respond.[9] Indeed, Mr. Silk actively avoided racial topics of conversation, and after enduring racism himself, Coleman Silk regrets that his father stood as "the enormous barrier against the great American menace" of racism.[10] Further reflecting on his youth, he knows that he benefited from his parents' "conscientious kindness and care" and "got just about anything he wanted."[11] However, what he failed to "get" is a racially conscious education, a statement that also describes the

---

[5] Roth, *The Human Stain*, 22.
[6] Roth, 93.
[7] Roth, 92.
[8] Roth, 92.
[9] Roth, 103.
[10] Roth, 105–6.
[11] Roth, 95.

Ex-Colored Man and John Warwick; just as their parents were silent about race—leaving their sons incapable of fully dealing with racism—so was Mr. Silk in his interactions with his children.

These interactions leave Coleman unprepared to verbalize the subtle racism he encounters in East Orange High School. Looking back, he recalls the less pernicious form of racism there:

> There were teachers from whom Coleman sensed an unevenness of acceptance, an unevenness of endorsement compared to what they lavished on the smart white kids, but never to the degree that the unevenness was able to block his aims. No matter what the slight or the obstacle, he took it the way he took the low hurdles.[12]

Coleman lacks the critical terminology to call out the type of racism exhibited towards him, but modern-day readers would render this "passive racism" because it is not the overt form of exclusion exhibited towards Black pupils.[13] I see this term as expanding the list of terms psychologist Derald Wing Sue began to investigate in his research on racial microaggressions. He defined instances of "microassaults," "microinsults," and "microinvalidations," as well as their psychological effects on people of color.[14] Psychiatrist Chester Pierce first defined microaggressions in the 1970s, yet this concept has received renewed interest in the twenty-first century. As this research suggests, Coleman's educators did not explicitly highlight his Blackness, but their behavior toward him made him feel that his Blackness was strange and out of place at school. He further contrasts with his equally high achieving brother Walter Silk, who was told "I couldn't believe your grades were as high as they were" after having to contest a low grade he knew was unfair.[15] Mr. Silk's silence on race, coupled with the different treatment Coleman intuits despite consistently earning high grades at East Orange High School, teaches him that race is a topic to be endured, avoided, and perhaps escaped. Thus begins Coleman Silk's race-learning, which structures the rest of his life.

Coleman's race-learning is further contextualized during his extracurricular activities in high school. His first act of narrative secrecy comes in the

---

[12] Roth, 104.

[13] For more on the key terms to call out prejudice, see Beverly Tatum's *Why Are All the Black Kids Sitting Together in the Cafeteria?*.

[14] Sue, *Microaggressions in Everyday Life*.

[15] Roth, *The Human Stain*, 104.

form of boxing training, which he hides from his father because it contradicts Mr. Silk's strict focus on academics. As Zuckerman puts it, Coleman "had been sneaking down to the Newark Boys Club, below High Street in the Newark slums to Morton Street, and secretly training to be a fighter."[16] When Mr. Silk discovers this, he encourages young Coleman to take boxing lessons from Doc Chizner, a Jewish dentist and boxing coach. What he does not predict is that Chizner will emerge as a father figure for Coleman. In a tense dinnertime exchange between father and son, the elder Silk questions his son's extracurricular activity by suggesting that Coleman disregards him as a father. The scene ends with Mr. Silk rhetorically asking Coleman if he is really his father, to which Coleman responds:

> "No!" Coleman shouted. "No, you're not!" And here, at the very start of Sunday dinner, he ran out of the house and for nearly an hour he did his roadwork, up Central Avenue and over the Orange line, and then through Orange all the way to the West Orange line, and then crossing over on Watchung Avenue.[17]

By questioning his status as father, Mr. Silk implies that someone else is Coleman's parent—an assumption that is well-founded considering Doc Chizner becomes a surrogate father to the promising athlete, teaching him the rules of the social order. He and Mr. Silk are foils for each other: the former enjoys everything but literature while the latter is obstinate in his strict focus on literary endeavors. When Coleman sprints out of the house at the end of the conversation and runs through New Jersey neighborhoods, this is his physical act of renouncing his father. He eventually returns home, but not before "throwing punches" as his substitute father Doc taught him to do.[18] As Coleman escapes his biological father, he mimics his symbolic one in the process. Moreover, by physically running from his biological father, his race-learning teaches him to run from his Blackness, foreshadowing the rest of the narrative.

Part of the impetus for his constant running stems from the lessons he gleans through his race-learning as he prepares to graduate high school and begin college. Dr. Fensterman, described as "the Jewish doctor, the big surgeon from Mom's hospital down in Newark," visits Coleman's parents to

---

[16] Roth, 89.
[17] Roth, 92.
[18] Roth, 92.

convince them to let Coleman graduate as salutatorian instead of valedictorian of East Orange High School.[19] This visit is prompted by young Bert Fensterman, who aspires to be a doctor like his father, but who believes the only way to achieve it is to graduate at the very top of his class. In exchange, the elder Fensterman offers to promote Mrs. Silk and pay three thousand dollars towards Coleman's college education.[20] The only stipulation is that Coleman must earn Bs on two of his final exams instead of As, thereby ensuring secondary status and the expectation that he would be the "highest-ranking *colored* student ever to graduate E.O [East Orange High School]."[21] Despite the compelling immediate financial benefit, Mr. and Mrs. Silk refuse to be bribed into forcing their high achieving son to accept secondary status. Dr. Fensterman's request is highly unethical because it compromises his career as a medical professional as well as Coleman's hard-earned position as the valedictorian. Not until years later does Coleman realize the full scope of Dr. Fensterman's blatant racism that inspired his visit, for he assumes that Fensterman could not bear to see a Black student graduate at the top of the class over his own son, even though being salutatorian is not tantamount to exclusion from the highest echelons of academic excellence. Coleman also realizes the ways in which Fensterman is situated on a continuum of men whose racial beliefs on his achievement are seen, retroactively, as aiding his race-learning.

One such example is Doc Chizner, who believes that Coleman's boxing skills can impress the visiting University of Pittsburgh coach: "if nothing [about race] comes up, you don't bring it up. You're neither one thing or the other. You're Silky Silk. That's enough. That's the deal."[22] According to his logic, when anyone sees the light-skinned Coleman Silk alongside Doc, they would assume he is "one of Doc's boys," which is a euphemism to indicate that he's "Jewish."[23] To be one of Doc's "boys" means that Coleman is under his tutelage and that he officially recognizes him as an adopted son. This latter category is made possible by the lack of parental bonds as evidenced in the fiery dinnertime exchange explicated above. In filling the void that the rigid

---

[19] Roth, 85.
[20] Roth, 85.
[21] Roth, 87, emphasis mine.
[22] Roth, 98–99.
[23] Roth, 99.

Mr. Silk cannot, Doc Chizner provides Coleman with the real-world education into race, about which Mr. Silk is perpetually silent.

This education inevitably includes race, and it presents itself in Coleman's promising boxing career. For instance, when Doc Chizner promotes him to a boxing instructor, the other students were "repelled" by his sweat and protest his desire to donate blood to an injured teammate. These fears criticize the irrationality of eugenics and recall the prominence of blood that is so prevalent throughout passing narratives. Coleman slowly realizes that he cannot escape racist beliefs that are deeply imbedded in society, regardless of his stature as a boxer and his ability to serve as fighter and instructor. Coleman's race-learning now transcends the two arenas in which he excels, the classroom and the boxing ring. Both are sites that exhibit his growth and exceptional talent, while also underscoring his confinement, as represented by the walls of the classroom and the ropes surrounding a boxing ring. The classroom and the boxing ring also complicate the ease of passing. Even though he admits to "laugh[ing] loudly" at Doc's suggestion to remain silent about being Black, passing represents multiple levels of freedom for Coleman: freedom from the raced confines of the boxing ring, freedom from the dismissive treatment he tolerates from his teachers, and freedom from the discrimination he would face as a Black man in mid-twentieth century America.

Thus, he seriously considers Doc's insinuation. In one of his boxing matches, he notes that he "love[s] secrets. The secret of nobody's knowing what was going on in your head…that's why he liked shadowboxing and hitting the heavy bag: for *the secrecy* in it."[24] He relishes in the ability to lie and keep everyone guessing, which is a step towards jumping the color line. The rapidity with which he vacillates shows the effect that the possibility of passing has on him, as well as his developing race-learning. Much like Judge Straight offers a legal and racial apprenticeship to John Warwick, and much like the Ex-Colored Man realizes the weight of his race when travelling throughout Europe with his nameless benefactor, Coleman Silk's race-learning is helped by Dr. Chizner's suggestion that passing will afford him the privilege of being welcomed in predominantly White spaces, beginning with the University of Pittsburgh.

Because of this, Coleman's tenacity in wanting to attend Howard University is unexpected, since it is a Historically Black college and the school

---

[24] Roth, 100, emphasis mine.

that Mr. Silk has long decided would be the one his son would attend. The ultimate act of defying his dominating and intellectual father would be to matriculate at a school other than the one that Mr. Silk desired "for as long as Coleman could remember."[25] Placed in tandem with each other, these reasons raise the question of Coleman's sincerity in studying at Howard. Is he genuinely interested in studying with African-Americans, contrasting with the predominantly Jewish influences from his youth in which he feels most comfortable, or does his behavior parallel that of the Ex-Colored Man, who embarks on a reverse migration south to criticize and categorize African-Americans?

This question remains unanswered because his time at Howard University ends almost as soon as it begins. He is not on campus long enough to fully embrace it: he is rendered a "nigger" at a nearby Woolworth's in his first week there.[26] Coleman realizes how hastily he goes from graduating at the top of his class to being called the vilest epithet for African-Americans: "At East Orange High the class valedictorian, in the segregated South just another nigger."[27] This level of racial conspicuity is too much for Coleman; he disavows Howard altogether and matriculates at New York University instead. In the meantime, he decides to "play his skin color however he wanted, color himself just as he chose," while his heart begins "banging away like the heart of someone on the brink of committing his first great crime."[28] The "color" Coleman chooses is White, and there is minimal chance that the "crime" to which he refers will warrant legal repercussions, yet the threat of being outed as Black and sanctioned by public opinion is far more damaging for racial passers. The diction here is very provocative, in that he wants to return to being the subject of the gaze instead of the object. In short, being rendered a "nigger" is a major step in his race-learning and he again runs—this time from Black Howard University to predominantly White New York University.

Relocating to liberal New York City is a conventional move for real and fictional passers who want to create new identities for themselves. Coleman takes it a step further by not passing generically as White, but instead passes as Jewish—a specific ethnic group that has resurfaced in contemporary novels

---

[25] Roth, 99.
[26] Roth, 102.
[27] Roth, 102.
[28] Roth, 109.

of racial passing.[29] Ross Posnock believes that passing as Jewish is a strategic move for Coleman: "Seeking to be neither Black nor white, Coleman shrewdly elects a third possibility—the equivocal form of whiteness that is postwar American Jewishness."[30] Matthew Wilson puts this explicitly, in his theory that Coleman's ultimate desire is to be "unraced" since he does not want to be either "Black or white" but maintain an "oblique angle to the American racial binary and the color line" by pretending to be Jewish.[31] In justifying Coleman's new identity, Roth himself said:

> Coleman's choice has nothing to do with the ethical, spiritual, theological or historical aspects of Judaism. It has nothing to do with wanting to belong to another "we." It's a cunning choice that successfully furnishes him with a disguise in the flight from his own "we." The choice is strictly utilitarian—as so much is for this man.

This description recalls Fanon's views of Jewishness:

> The Jewishness of the Jew, however, can go unnoticed. He is not integrally what he is. We can but hope and wait. His acts and behavior are the determining factor. He is a white man, and apart from some debatable features, *he can pass undetected.*[32]

Though Fanon's *Black Skin, White Masks* was published a half century before Roth's novel, Fanon's prescient position on passing as Jewish seems to open the way for Roth and contemporary critics who explore the image of Jews in contemporary literature. If a Jewish man can "pass undetected," it helps to explain the allure of Coleman's feigned Jewish identity. Like Birdie Lee, adherence to Judaism is the last thing he considers when realizing that being a race shifter is more logical than being Black. He wants to remain

---

[29] As Lori Harrison-Kahan and Dean J. Franco argue, Jewishness is used as a way to complicate the American racial binary, thus highlighting the nuances of monolithic Whiteness while challenging the ways in which the Black and White dichotomy can be construed (Harrison-Kahan, "Passing for White, Passing for Jewish"; Franco, "Being Black, Being Jewish, and Knowing the Difference." For critical discussions of African-Americans and Jews in a historical context, see Hasia Diner, *In the Almost Promised Land*; Ethan Goffman, *Imagining Each Other*; and Jeffrey Melnick, *A Right to Sing the Blues*.

[30] Posnock, "Purity and Danger," 94.

[31] Wilson, "Reading *The Human Stain* Through Charles W. Chesnutt," 144.

[32] Fanon, *Black Skin, White Masks*, 95, emphasis mine.

inconspicuous and avoid being boxed into monolithic Whiteness. In writing about Roth's *The Plot Against America*, Walter Benn Michaels puts it another way, by asserting that "Jewish success in America today is less an effect of the triumph over racism than it is an effect of the triumph of racism."[33] Passing as a Jew underscores Coleman's intention to imitate the Jews of his youth, which completes his transition to the adopted son of Doc Chizner. More specifically, he enacts Doc's advice to proceed passively by being "neither one thing or the other" but to accept an assumed identity as "Silky Silk."[34] This type of passing allows Coleman to not only revise the traditional passing-as-White narrative trajectory, but he also highlights the interrelatedness of race and ethnicity that have characterized Black-Jewish relations in America.

One of the aftereffects of his trauma and of his newfound assumed identity is his fluctuation between Black and White—exhibited most tangibly through juxtaposed romantic relationships with African-American and White women. He claims to love Steena, a White woman, but sabotages their relationship when he invites her to have dinner with his family before telling her they are Black. He then dates Ellie, a Black woman, and confides in her that he is a passing Black man. Even though life with Ellie was "fun, but some dimension is missing" he again damages their relationship because he yearns "to be secretive again."[35] Romantic relationships do not fulfill him; only a life of concealment motivates Coleman Silk. He thus runs again, this time to Iris Gittelman, a Jewish woman, from whom he keeps the secret of his true racial heritage and gains the thrill of duplicity that he lost with Ellie and Steena.

Like Anatole Broyard, Coleman's passing is incomplete without testing relationships with women who run the gamut of race. His choice of Iris is a curious one, considering he speaks about their courtship not in traditional romantic terms as we might expect, but in language reminiscent of Du Bois's notion of "double consciousness." Indeed, dating Iris allows him "to be two men instead of one....To be two colors instead of one....To be possessed of a double or a triple or a quadruple personality."[36] Coleman revises upon Du Bois's "two souls, two thoughts, two unreconciled strivings and two warring ideals" when rationalizing his marriage to Iris. He informs his wife that he is

---

[33] Michaels, "Plots Against America: Neoliberalism and Antiracism," 290.
[34] Roth, *The Human Stain*, 98.
[35] Roth, 135.
[36] Roth, 130.

not the Coleman Silk of East Orange, New Jersey, but a Jewish man whose original pre-Ellis Island surname was Silberzweig—a lie he maintains throughout his life.[37] Iris and Coleman's marriage is based on a racial falsehood, or as Moynihan cogently observes, their relationship is formed by "superficial affinities" instead of love.[38]

Coleman's silence about his Blackness might be immoral for his marriage, but it serves him well for his career. Internalizing his father's teachings, he eventually becomes a professor of classics and then dean. However, his career ends prematurely when he wonders aloud if two students who never attended class are really people "or are they spooks?"[39] When the Black students hear about this remark, they accuse him of racism, despite his attempt at evading culpability: "I was using the word in its customary and primary meaning: 'spook' as a specter or a ghost. I had no idea what color these two students might be."[40] This same statement could be said of Coleman, since the new dean of faculty—who must disclose the charges to Coleman—has no idea that the distinguished scholar is a Black man passing as White. Had his Blackness been known, Coleman's claims that being rendered a racist are "spurious" and "preposterous" would be more convincing. As a result, he is forced to assume a diminished role at the university but chooses to resign from the school entirely.

In fighting the allegations, Coleman seeks support from another Athena professor, Herb Keble, who tersely withholds his support, saying, "I can't be with you on this, Coleman. I'm going to have to be with them," which Coleman repeats in a mocking way.[41] He assumes that since he went out of his way to hire Herb to be the first Black faculty at Athena, Herb would return the favor and support him while the university investigates this racial incident. Yet Coleman Silk himself was the first Black professor at Athena, not Herb; he does not want Herb or any of his other colleagues to know about his Blackness. More to the point, he looks to Herb because the support of Black faculty can help to abate the widespread criticism he endured for rendering Black students "spooks," yet he fails to realize that after presenting

---

[37] Roth, 130.
[38] Moynihan, *Passing into the Present*, 121.
[39] Roth, 6.
[40] Roth, 6.
[41] Roth, 16.

himself as Jewish at Athena for decades, belatedly refuting racist allegations against him is a moot point.

Coleman's association between "spooks" and "specters" demonstrates the relevancy of psychoanalysis in narratives of racial passing. His utterance of "spooks" is a Freudian slip, which clearly articulates the reality of his own hidden Blackness after spending his adulthood as a Jewish man. Another way to read "spooks" is as an extension of the mirror image, which relates to the psychoanalytic concept of imagos. According to Lacan, imagos are "those veiled faces we analysts see emerge in our daily experience and in the penumbra of symbolic effectiveness—the specular image seems to be the threshold of the visual world, if we take into account the mirrored disposition of the image of one's own body in hallucinations and dreams."[42] An imago refers to the image that an infant sees in the mirror and with which he identifies. However, it is a fragmented image, with an illusion of wholeness instead of a unified one. Lacan believes that a disavowed, left-behind self occurs at this point. In *The Human Stain*, this disavowed self is Coleman's lifelong shunning of his African-American ancestry. Though he runs from it, his Blackness perpetually hovers over his daily interactions as he toes the line between hiding it and living out his Jewish persona. This Black shadow could have presented itself at any point, but it becomes most noticeable in the racialized encounter when he says "spooks"—epitomized as the specter of Blackness in the classroom. As someone who is conscientious about using precise diction, he could have chosen any number of more accurate terms to refer to the absent students, but he chooses "spooks" because the term summons the Black past that he himself expected would remain hidden but is always at the surface.

In what sounds like his own eulogy, Coleman reflects on the triumphs of his life, remembering that he "had pursued the most demanding curriculum" in his youth, but his entire educational prowess proves futile as he becomes increasingly bitter, irrational, and vindictive, with a distinguished career that does not end on his terms.[43] The true "curriculum" that he engages in has nothing to do with "Chaucer, Shakespeare, or Dickens" or other classic writers from his youth; he instead spends his life engaging in race-learning—transgressing boundaries of race to grant him opportunities that Blacks rarely

---

[42] Lacan, "The Mirror Stage as Formative of the *I* Function as Revealed in Psychoanalytic Experience," 77.

[43] Roth, *The Human Stain*, 59.

had access to. This "curriculum" begins as a boy when he was not supposed to graduate at the top of his class, and it unfolds as he matures and understands his racialized subjectivity. Coleman's amateur boxing career and educational attainment stem from his complexion gaining admittance into the White world. This formal and informal education structure his life as a Black man turned Jewish, whose academic career ends with an unshakeable charge of racism. The final "lesson" for him is that running away from his race is hardly tantamount to it being completely behind him: the lingering specter of "spooks" is responsible for the demise of his career, the demise of his family, as well as his own demise. In short, Coleman Silk's decades-long race-learning is now complete, thanks to his Freudian slip in uttering "spooks."

A Disease Called Passing: Silk's Death Drive

After Coleman's career abruptly ends, the controversy engulfing his small college town strains his family, to the extent that he even blames the school for his wife's sudden death.[44] Iris Silk's death is the first of many deaths narrated in the text, though it is not the first chronologically. In the opening pages of Roth's work, Nathan informs readers that Iris "suffered a stroke and died overnight while he [Coleman] was in the midst of battling with the college over a charge of racism brought against him by two students in one of his classes."[45] Coleman agrees, claiming that "his enemies at Athena, in striking out at him, had instead felled her."[46] After once again hearing Coleman's irate proclamation, "these people *murdered* Iris!"[47] Nathan notes that his neighbor's face has become "dented and lopsided," resembling a "piece of fruit that's been knocked from its stall in the marketplace and kicked to and fro along the ground by the passing shoppers."[48] In trying to persuade Nathan to write a story about their ordeal, Coleman twice renders her death a "murder" and thinks "they meant to kill me and they got her instead."[49]

---

[44] Roth, 12.
[45] Roth, 4.
[46] Roth, 11.
[47] Roth, 12, emphasis in original.
[48] Roth, 12.
[49] Roth, 12.

The narrative conjoins the themes of passing and death, as evidenced by these opening descriptions. It is not mere coincidence that as a classics professor, Coleman views Iris's death as being "felled," similar to the way Homer writes about the Trojan War in the *Iliad*. Homer's epic is Coleman's favorite literary work, and just as Athena (through Achilles) slaughters Hector, Coleman believes Athena College slaughters him by ruining his career. Coleman's main battle, however, is with his former colleagues, whom he persistently bullied as dean. After news of his alleged racism develops, they happily rejoiced to see the powerful Dean Silk desperate to save his career. According to Coleman's logic, his former colleagues "murdered" Iris as the ultimate form of retaliation. Moreover, the reference to passing in this description explicitly refers to patrons who would not notice a discarded piece of fruit, which Coleman's face now resembles. However, "passing" is also the endeavor that the protagonist engages in and is the initial reason for his wife's demise—for if he had been forthcoming with his Blackness all along, there is minimal chance that the question of his racism would have been raised and he would not have had to suffer the loss of his career and wife. Coleman is quick to blame others for Iris's demise, which transforms him to such an extent that his face loses its youthfulness to become "strangely repellent" and "distorted."[50]

While Iris's death has a physical effect on Coleman, his father's death has an emotional effect on him. Mr. Silk dies while "serving dinner on the Pennsylvania Railroad dining car that was pulling out of 30th Street Station in Philadelphia."[51] He never understood how his father endured racism each day, especially since "in one form or another," it happens every day in the dining car."[52] Yet Mr. Silk's demise affords Coleman autonomy since he was no longer "circumscribed and defined by his father"—a man who thrived at "making up Coleman's story for him."[53] The only detail revealed is that the elder Silk died while serving dinner on a train departing from Philadelphia, but there are no other facts about the circumstances. Two possibilities arise from this glaring ambiguity. Primarily, Roth implies that prolonged exposure to racism can result in death for African-Americans, as seen by the fact that

---

[50] Roth, 12.
[51] Roth, 106.
[52] Roth, 105.
[53] Roth, 107.

Mr. Silk collapses in a Jim Crow train car while serving passengers. In other words, how African-Americans die is less important than that they die, because racism will inevitably lead to death either through physical violence such as lynch mobs, or through the cumulative effects of having to navigate a raced society. Secondly, Mr. Silk's nebulous death foreshadows Coleman's own seemingly ambiguous death at the end of the narrative, when it appears that he dies in a car crash, yet rumors circulate about the specific cause. For Mr. Silk, he also dies in a mode of transportation, but whether it is a stroke, heart attack, aneurysm, or some other ailment is omitted from the narrative.[54]

Though Mr. Silk suffers an actual, albeit mysterious, death, the rest of his family dies symbolically, which Coleman uses to his advantage as a racial passer. He cuts ties with his widowed mother and his siblings, envisioning an easier life for himself because they represent a Black past that he detests. This symbolic death begins early in his adulthood: when visiting his mother to announce his engagement to Iris, a Jewish woman, Coleman admits that he told Iris that his entire family is dead.[55] After his father's actual death, Coleman is free to live his own life without the added pressure of his father's approval. It is not enough for him to say that he has deceased parents, making it seem as though he "sprung up"; he takes it a step further and kills off his siblings too. This leads Mrs. Silk to intuit that she is "never going to see" her grandchildren as a result of the new life Coleman wants to create for himself, unencumbered by race.[56]

---

[54] There is a very long history of interracial settings on trains constraining African-Americans. For instance, Lutie Johnson, in Ann Petry's novel *The Street*, knows that she can speak to her employer, Mrs. Chandler, while they travel on the train from Queens to Manhattan. However, the minute "the train pulled into Grand Central, the wall was suddenly there" (51). In James Baldwin's novel *Another Country*, the narrator notes that the train Rufus travels on—leading to his own suicide—moves in a way to "protest the proximity of white buttock to Black knee" (86). Amiri Baraka's play *Dutchman*, takes place entirely on the New York City subway, where Lula, a White woman, attacks Clay, a Black man, after making sexual advances and racist comments to him. As previously articulated, Fanon also uses the train for his meditations on the daily experiences of being Black, in his famous "Look! A Negro!" encounter from *Black Skin, White Masks*. This representative list suggests that Mr. Silk's death on a train car serves as a powerful protest against forced and degrading encounters he endured while serving the Jim Crow car.

[55] Roth, *The Human Stain*, 137.

[56] Roth, 137.

Mrs. Silk's initial composure gives way to anger, which is powerfully evident when she admonishes his multiple levels of deception:

> You've been giving fair warning almost from the day you got here. You were seriously disinclined even to take the breast. Yes, you were. Now I see why. Even that might delay your escape. There was something about our family, and I don't mean color—there was always something about us that impeded you. You think like a prisoner. You do, Coleman Brutus. You're as white as snow and you think like a slave.[57]

Mrs. Silk interprets her son's rejection of her breast milk as the initial act of foreshadowing that suggests he never wanted to be Black in the first place. Her exasperation evokes psychoanalyst Melanie Klein's theorization. Klein argues that the primary experiences of an infant are divided into two opposing states, good objects and bad objects, which are manifested in their mothers' breasts. The "good breast" provides nourishment and is the most desired one, whereas the "bad breast" is the one that does not feed the infant, leading to hunger. The "bad breast" then becomes the object of malevolence for the child, who fears abandonment because of the lack of food.[58] Klein may not have had passing subjects in mind when formulating this theory, yet her profession—psychoanalysis—was founded by a man whose interest in passing inspired the field. The "good breast/bad breast" theory is an accurate lens through which to view Coleman Silk. If the "good breast" and the "bad breast" represent split, opposing entities, then applying her theory to Coleman raises the issue of whether his psychological splitting is race-based, in that the breasts represent his internal racialized duality. If Mrs. Silk's assumption is accurate, the newborn Coleman felt "disinclined to even take the breast" because he equated the "bad breast" with the Blackness he eventually shuns.

Since his family has "impeded" his lifelong aspirations to pass as White, Coleman takes the liberty to create an entirely new genealogy for himself, but not before his mother lectures him about the family he decided to ward off. Mrs. Silk reminds him about their family history, which included enslavement. In her first reference to slavery, she uses hyperbole to call him "white

---

[57] Roth, 139.
[58] Mitchell and Black, *Freud and Beyond*, 92.

as snow" while simultaneously holding an enslaved man's mentality.[59] She believes his Blackness is strictly in his mind. Unlike Victor Grabért and Solaria Cox, who both refer to slavery as they pass, Coleman stands out because his mother renders him a slave first, before anyone else does, by implying that he is afflicted with a Fanonian inferiority complex that makes him want to be White despite being born Black. She believes he was running from his Blackness beginning in infancy, which is an affront to their family history: Mrs. Silk's lineage includes runaway slaves who escaped via the Underground Railroad to settle in Lawnside, New Jersey, and a slave whose owner was killed in the French and Indian War.[60] By providing these specific details of her family's enslaved past, she hopes to convince Coleman of the dilemma with his decision, since he comes from a long line of African-Americans who refused to be hindered by slavery and Jim Crow because of the pride in their Blackness. Mrs. Silk finds it insulting that, considering her ancestors' escape from racial hatred, her son runs away from his race to create an entirely new identity for himself. In doing so, she calls attention to two of the areas that occupy the racial passing imagination: enslavement and psychoanalysis.[61]

To complete his new identity sans a biological Black family, Coleman not only verbalizes his family's symbolic demise, but he also wishes for his mother's physical death.[62] During Mrs. Silk's diatribe, he silently envisions her death, particularly "the disease that would kill her, the funeral they would give her, the tributes that would be read and the prayers offered up at the side of her grave."[63] These related images of family, enslavement and death at this juncture imply that Mrs. Silk's metaphorical death is hardly sufficient for

---

[59] Roth, *The Human Stain*, 139.

[60] Roth, 141. Lawnside, New Jersey was a station on the Underground Railroad and developed into an all-Black town. It was also the birthplace of Jessie Fauset, author of *Plum Bun*.

[61] The language of slavery is also echoed in the scholarly discourse on Coleman Silk. For instance, linguist Marcia Alesan Dawkins believes that "even without a master, Coleman is enslaved by the future he imagines for himself" (*Clearly Invisible*, 117). According to Ronald Emerick, Roth's protagonist is motivated by "total freedom to live his life on a grand scale, and passing for white appears to be the best way to gain such freedom" ("Archetypal Silk," 74).

[62] Michele Elam accurately notes that he "consciously decides he must metaphorically 'murder' his mother" (*The Souls of Mixed Folk*, 111).

[63] Roth, *The Human Stain*, 140–41.

Coleman; for him to truly pass as something else, he can only imagine her physically dead at the hands of a hypothetical ailment. In fact, her imaginary physical demise is as nebulous as her husband's real one, revealing that death by any means will allow Coleman to further fashion a new identity for himself. In doing so, he simultaneously renders his mother's Blackness and bad breast as inorganic. When Walter, his brother, discovers that Coleman has cut ties with their family, he becomes more vocal in critiquing the race-shifter than Mrs. Silk: "Don't you even try *to* see her. No contact. No calls. Nothing. Never. Hear Me? *Never.* Don't you dare ever show your lily-white face around that house again."[64] Casting aspersion to Coleman's Whiteness just as Mrs. Silk does, Walter intends to make his brother suffer through a symbolic death in the same way he made their mother endure one. The Silk family is dead to Coleman and he is now dead to them, thereby granting him his long-desired freedom to pass without any of his relatives impeding him.

These metaphorical deaths all proceed Coleman's physical one, which occupies the most narrative space in *The Human Stain*. After a horrific car accident, rumors circulate about the specific details of his demise. The speculation begins almost immediately after his nemesis and successor at Athena, Delphine Roux, first hears the details of the crash, which she reports as: "Dean Silk...is dead! A terrible crash. It's too horrible...[he died] in the river. With a woman. In his car. A crash."[65] The "woman" turns out to be his mistress, Faunia, and he indeed drove his car into the river, which Nathan confirms. Everything else about Coleman's death is hearsay from the gullible residents of the town, in their hasty quest to determine what caused the once powerful dean of faculty to meet such an abrupt and horrific end.

The first rumor is that Faunia performed oral sex on Coleman as he drove, causing him to lose control of his vehicle. Police officers supposedly deduce this detail from the position of their corpses after his car is pulled from the river. However, Nathan's conversation with a state police trooper contradicts this notion. The officer explicitly refutes the "oral sex" theory with the terse statement "none of that's true, sir."[66] Instead, he tells Nathan that while speeding, Coleman took a sharp turn that even "[professional race

---

[64] Roth, 145, emphasis in original.
[65] Roth, 280.
[66] Roth, 295.

car driver] Jeff Gordon couldn't have taken" and thus lost control of his car.[67] Moreover, before getting behind the wheel, Coleman consumed wine and Viagra. These details raise the question of whether he wanted to die, especially since he mixed alcohol with prescribed medicine before driving and was too incapacitated to approach the sharp turn with caution. Was this Coleman Silk's active death as a result of his multiple levels of passing—his relationship with race coupled with his affair with a younger woman?

In search of some semblance of the truth, Nathan Zuckerman questions the officer to corroborate his own theory that Faunia's ex-husband, Lester Farley, chased Coleman off the road in his car. He calls his friend's death a "freak accident" motivated by "the presence somewhere nearby of Les Farley and his pickup truck," because Farley threatened the protagonist for sleeping with his ex-wife.[68] Though Nathan sees Farley's continuous harassment as enough reason to blame him, it does not entirely hold up: Farley knows of his ex-wife's every move, and if he intended to chase Coleman off the road and into oblivion, he could have done so without her in the car. Thus, if Farley wanted to be truly vindictive, he could have killed Coleman while he traveled alone, keeping his ex-wife out of any danger. The narrator is stubborn in his persistence, telling Faunia's family at her funeral that Coleman "was forced off the road" at the hands of "her ex-husband."[69] They are unwilling to entertain his speculation though, preferring to distance themselves from this ordeal while rumors about the deaths persist.

After Faunia's family ignores him, Nathan is intent to reach them via the written word. He drafts a letter in which he confidently proclaims to be "absolutely sure" that Farley and not Coleman deserves the blame for the car crash.[70] Despite Nathan's attempts to serve as an amateur investigator, his actions undermine his own notions of certainty. For one thing, he claims to know "who murdered them," but in the next sentence he concedes that he "did not witness the murder but [knows] it took place."[71] He also does not completely end the letter, but instead says "My telephone and address are as

---

[67] Roth, 295.
[68] Roth, 294.
[69] Roth, 300.
[70] Roth, 303.
[71] Roth, 303.

follows—" before it abruptly ends.⁷² Concluding with the rhetorical device of an aposiopesis shows Nathan's inability to continue writing, realizing that he too is speculating on the impetus behind his friend's ambiguous demise. After pondering this situation, Nathan decides it would be best to "[tear] up what I'd written."⁷³ He does not just end the letter in the middle of a sentence, he takes it an extra step by completely discarding it; he realizes that Faunia's family will not do anything about the letter, which makes him lose confidence in his own theory that Farley bears sole responsibility. If he were as confident as he proclaimed to be, then he should not have any problem with sending it and placing the blame on Farley.

With insufficient evidence to incriminate the Farleys—Faunia was not performing oral sex nor was Lester in close pursuit—the culpability of the crash turns back to the driver, who sped in his car while under the influence. In a post on the Athena College listserv, Nathan provides a cryptic rejoinder to the faculty who speculated on the causes of the car crash: he twice says that the "car accident was no accident" because the protagonist "*yearned* to do it with all his might."⁷⁴ Nathan highlights Freud's rhetoric of desire in his post, and asserts that Coleman's death drive was the main impetus for driving his car into the river, believing "it was to prevent Faunia from exposing him for what he was that Coleman Silk took her with him to the bottom of the river. One is left to imagine just how heinous were the crimes that he was determined to hide."⁷⁵ This rhetoric calls attention to Coleman's layers of secrecy. Though they remain reticent about it, everyone in town has already discovered Coleman's exploitative relationship with Faunia, an illiterate housekeeper who is half his age. This dalliance is viewed as taboo, but it is not the aspect of his life that he is most "determined" to obscure. What his neighbors and former colleagues are not privy to is that he spent his adult life as a Jewish man despite his African-American heritage. Knowledge of his racial passing could have done far more damage to his reputation than any "heinous crimes" he could have committed, after decades of tricking his colleagues into believing that he was Jewish and not Black. In pointing to Coleman's "history" and "what he was," Nathan's vague diction highlights the protagonist's desire to

---

[72] Roth, 303.
[73] Roth, 304.
[74] Roth, 293, emphasis mine.
[75] Roth, 293.

ensure that nobody discovered his Blackness or his affair. Two types of passing are thus revealed through Coleman's death, supporting Boisseron's claim about the existence of a "sexual undertone" to all racial passing narratives. Indeed, that the first chapter of *The Human Stain* is entitled "Everyone Knows" is a "double-entendre, [since] the narrative builds on a metonymical shift from racial passing to dirty sexual secret."[76] What "Everyone Knows" can refer to Coleman's racial duplicity and/or his taboo sexual relationship with an illiterate woman who is half his age. Like other narratives explored in this book, *The Human Stain* encapsulates race and sexuality through passing, leaving it up to readers to excavate the sexual secret obscured by the racial secret.

In continuing the digging, Nathan Zuckerman speaks with Coleman's sister, Ernestine. She shares details about Coleman's biography, providing more fodder for Nathan's book based on Coleman's life, *The Human Stain*. Through their discussion, Nathan discovers that Coleman did not completely turn his back on his Black family: Ernestine called her late brother at his office every year on his birthday. They used these annual conversations to update each other about promotions, births, deaths, and other milestones that could not be shared publicly since he now assumed a Jewish identity. Ernestine reveals that, like Victor and Solaria, Coleman was very concerned about fatherhood: each birth "was always a great trial for him" because he feared seeing visible markers of race in his progeny.[77] He never told them anything about it and failed to see the implications of his actions. One of the implications of his new life is his complete disavowal of their mother. According to Ernestine, Mrs. Silk often examined "his photos, his report cards, his track medals, his yearbook" as well as his valedictorian's certificate and the toys he played with as a child, in hopes of figuring out what exactly caused Coleman to pass as White and disavow their family.[78] Perhaps she assumed that her son's racial passing was due to his race-learning, since she examined his school-related documents in search of elusive clues to explain why he jumped the color line. When Mrs. Silk's own health declined, she began to see her son's racial transgression as a sickness. On her deathbed, she repeatedly asked her nurse to get her to a train because "I got a sick baby at home," whom both Ernestine and

---

[76] Boisseron, *Creole Renegades*, 47.

[77] Roth, *The Human Stain*, 320.

[78] Roth, 325.

Walter surmised was her favorite child, Coleman.[79] Considering his disinterest in taking her breast milk, it is quite revealing that she sees him specifically as a sick baby. She never accepted that even as an infant, he used his lips to reject her Blackness, yet she now seeks to prevent her son from dying of the disease called passing. This inclination is too late: by the time she dies, the disease has consumed Coleman to such an extent that his sole interaction with his Black past is through annual conversations with Ernestine held in stealth. Mrs. Silk sees her son as still stuck in childhood, when he was still Black and a time frame that psychoanalysts use to make projections about the ways in which children will live as adults. Neither Mrs. Silk's nascent psychoanalytic endeavors nor her training as a nurse could prevent her "sick baby's" death drive from motivating him to thwart the repercussions of passing.

Coleman's death drive led him into a sexual relationship with someone like Faunia Farley, which further led him to kill them both to prevent his secrets from reaching the public eye. The Freudian slip of "spooks" is his first implicit admission of Blackness, and the death drive motivated him to remain perpetually silent about his race and deviant sexuality. Coleman was so adamant about his decision to pass, that he had to "even be buried as a Jew," referring to the Kaddish that Coleman's son read at his grave.[80] The Kaddish is a hymn of praises delivered at the funeral services for Jewish people, or as Nathan succinctly notes, it reflects "the sobering message they bring: a Jew is dead. Another Jew is dead."[81] Ernestine views this moment with some hilarity because it completes Coleman's lifelong resolve to pretend to be someone that he was not. Nathan's reading of the morbid observation is simpler: his friend was "buried as a Jew, I thought, and, if I was speculating correctly, killed as a Jew."[82] To be clear, this is the Jewish Coleman Silk who is buried; the Black Coleman Silk has been long gone. Nathan tries to resurrect him though, in his wish to speak with Walter as he completes the book about Coleman. For the Silks though, their brother's death could have been a suicide, an accident, a murder, or the result of natural causes; the specific nature of his departure will not bring him back to life as the African-American brother they lost decades before.

---

[79] Roth, 321.
[80] Roth, 325.
[81] Roth, 314.
[82] Roth, 325.

With Coleman's death still haunting Nathan and the narrative, he confronts Lester Farley to confirm his suspicion of Farley's culpability in murdering Coleman. The discussion yields no new details about Coleman's demise, since Farley utters nary an incriminating word in what Nathan hopes would be a revelatory exchange. Assuming that Farley is merely an astute liar, the narrator remains unconvinced, yet to disabuse him of Farley's guilt, Nathan can look no further than the story he once overheard Faunia telling Coleman about someone else's active death. In foreshadowing Coleman's own end, Faunia recalled having to clean up after another man's suicide—a man who had a happy family and who outwardly appeared content with life. However, he drank too much and shot himself in the head, and it was Faunia's responsibility to hide the blood that would not disappear since it was "on the walls everywhere."[83] This act of violence initiated her interest in the subject of death and specifically in suicide, a morbid phenomenon which she renders "fascinating."[84] At first, it was difficult for her to understand why this nameless person resorted to suicide, but then it became explicitly clear:

> I got to the medicine cabinet. The drugs. The bottles. No happiness there. His own little pharmacy. I figure psychiatric drugs. Stuff that should have been taken and hadn't. It was clear that he was trying to get help, but he couldn't do it. He couldn't take the medication.[85]

With the exception of the gunshot, this story reads as Coleman's. To everyone outside the Silk home, he appeared happy with his family, yet he and Iris slept apart for several years before their deaths. Like the suicide victim, Coleman also mixed drinking with medication—particularly the Viagra pills that he needed to satisfy Faunia sexually. The dual references to pills and sexuality recall Solaria Cox: she feared that Blackness would come alive through her sexuality, but Coleman's Blackness is not specifically linked to it. Instead, using Viagra for his erections proves that he is sexually dead, just as having the Kaddish recited at his service proves that his Jewish identity (and not his biological Black one) is dead.

Moreover, medical examiners found wine in his blood during the autopsy. This image of blood further connects the two men with each other and with the lineage of passing narratives: whereas Faunia tried to cover up the

---

[83] Roth, 339.
[84] Roth, 339.
[85] Roth, 339.

man's blood, Coleman hid his African-American ancestry, lest it revealed him as a racial passer. This anecdote appears in a chapter aptly entitled "The Purifying Ritual," which explicitly refers to the bodily fluids that must be cleaned according to the tenets of many religions. It would be difficult for Coleman's blood to be made "pure" though, since he denied his Black heritage in favor of a manufactured Jewish one. Nathan does not see the generative juxtaposition of the two suicides. If he did, then the impetus behind Coleman's death drive might appear to him. The late scholar was not chased into the river, nor was his vehicle forced off the road by Farley. Though Coleman's actual death is not narrated—we get numerous details leading up to it, the gruesome aftermath and the range of rumors—the conspicuous narrative gap raises the question of whether Coleman wanted to kill himself by driving into the river after ingesting Viagra and wine. This option is more appealing to him than revealing his African-American background. Just as his affair and purported racism were exposed and tethered in his furtiveness, his racial background could have endured a similar fate if his former colleagues continued prying into his life. If this happened, then both his blood and reputation would have had to endure a "purifying ritual"—which entails explaining why he built his life on a racial charade without admitting to being Black when students accused him of racism, and also refers to his initial unwillingness to consume Blackness in the form of his mother's milk. As this narrative arc implies, Coleman's entire life is spent attempting to purify himself of Blackness, beginning with Mrs. Silk's nourishment and ending with his Jewish burial. Despite his constant running though, best symbolized during his teenage boxing career, the "stain" of his race is one he cannot fully escape or wipe out: the utterance of "spooks" initiates a domino effect in the disclosure of his sexual passing and racial passing.

The trend among literary critics is to focus almost exclusively on Coleman's demise in *The Human Stain*, as they agree that his death is simply the result of being a tragic mulatto. In making this assertion, they overlook the agency that Coleman has in hastening his own death.[86] Coleman Silk is not

---

[86] Marcia Dawkins's monograph *Clearly Invisible*, 114; Ronald Emerick's article "Archetypal Silk," 73–80; and Matthew Wilson's article "Reading *The Human Stain* Through Charles W. Chesnutt," 138–50, all blame Coleman Silk's death on Lester Farley's virulent anti-Semitism. These critics overstate the case by placing the blame

simply a tragic mulatto who died at the hands of Farley's anti-Semitism; by assuming this, many critics situate him within the rigid and narrow lens of this specific literary trope. The only scholar who comes close to blaming Coleman for his own demise is Marcia Alesan Dawkins, who sees the protagonist's "symbolic suicide" as an extension of his matricide. Her accurate observation of a continuum between Mrs. Silk's death and Coleman's is reiterated by Matthew Wilson's argument that characters who cross the color line kill off their families and are unable to return home.[87] By default, Coleman Silk must metaphorically kill his mother, beginning with his rejection of her breast milk. Derek Parker Royal argues that the trope of mortality is further evidenced by "the death of Faunia's children, Les Farley's social 'impotence,'…Faunia's invalid father, [and] Silk's dying relationship with his children."[88] Added to this list are Iris Silk's stroke, Mr. Silk's death in a Jim Crow train car, and the purposeful distance Coleman places between himself and the rest of the Silks. Coleman's family all die either physically or symbolically before he does, foreshadowing his own death. The main difference is that he is the sole character in the text who passes racially and sexually; dying as Jewish in an illicit relationship is an easier choice than dying as African-American with the "stain" of Blackness.

Royal argues that death is "a dominant theme in the novel," similar to other passing narratives which unite passing and death.[89] Indeed, dead bodies and dead body parts pepper Roth's text, placing it in a long lineage of death in twentieth-century passing narratives. In doing so, *The Human Stain* encapsulates psychoanalytical endeavors. The death drive is propelled, at least in part, by the way every organism seeks to die in its own idiosyncratic terms, which is supported by the characters in this study. Victor Grabért, Solaria Cox, Clare Kendry, and Coleman Silk accelerate their deaths since they can no longer maintain the safe façade of their White identities. More importantly, the loss of their Black pasts renders them unable to handle its resurrection during their lives as non-Black. Hence, Coleman's passing indirectly leads to his death, as the direct cause is having to encounter Blackness

---

solely on Farley, thus overlooking the role Coleman played in his own death by driving drunk into a river.

[87] Wilson, "Reading *The Human Stain* Through Charles W. Chesnutt," 141.

[88] Royal, "Plotting the Frames of Subjectivity," 129.

[89] Royal, 127.

when defending himself from the charge of racism, leading him into a downward spiral that is literalized by his driving his car into the bottom of the river. Of course, "passing away" is a polite euphemism for death, a semantic connection that further connects dying with racial passing. The relationship between passing and death is most palpable in passing narratives where literal and figurative deaths foreshadow the impending death of each protagonist. When light-skinned African Americans decide to pass, they also inadvertently decide to die, with Coleman Silk being a prime example.

Despite these correlations, Roth himself denied the influences on his novel that I am uncovering. Due to the intertextual connections between *The Human Stain*, other passing narratives, and psychoanalysis that critics have meditated on, he penned a powerful rejoinder to literary critics in 2000. In an interview with *The New York Times Book Review*, Roth admitted that his knowledge of passing came from his time as a graduate student in the 1950s, when he dated a light-skinned African-American woman who passed as White. Back then, he did not envision that the woman's story of "self-transformation [and] self-invention" would motivate him to publish a passing narrative decades later.[90] However, it left a "lasting impression" on him and provided the impetus for *The Human Stain*. What he describes in this interview is his own tangential relationship to race and to passing specifically.

However, a dozen years later, *The New Yorker* published Roth's "An Open Letter to Wikipedia," where he implores Wikipedia to remove the entry that *The Human Stain* was "allegedly inspired by the life of the writer Anatole Broyard." Instead, he argues in the 2012 letter that the inspiration for this novel was the late Mel Tumin, a sociology professor at Princeton University for three decades. One day during a class session, Tumin referred to absent students as "spooks":

> Having finished taking the roll, Mel queried the class about these two students whom he had never met. "Does anyone know these people? Do they exist or are they spooks?"—unfortunately, the very words that Coleman Silk, the protagonist of "The Human Stain," asks of his classics class at Athena College in Massachusetts.[91]

---

[90] McGrath, "Zuckerman's Alter Brain," 8.
[91] Roth, "An Open Letter to Wikipedia."

Princeton University then investigated him, but he emerged unscathed "of the charge of hate speech."[92] As with Coleman Silk, this charge of racism is one of many ironies, since Tumin built his career as a White man who first gained prominence as a liberal-leaning scholar of desegregation in the 1950s. *The New York Times* encapsulated his legacy by calling him a "Specialist in Race Relations" in its obituary for him in 1994. As such, Roth argues that Tumin's story specifically "inspired me to write '*The Human Stain*': not something that may or may not have happened in the Manhattan life of the cosmopolitan literary figure Anatole Broyard but what actually did happen in the life of Professor Melvin Tumin."[93] In adducing evidence to support his claims, he points to precise distinctions between Coleman Silk and Anatole Broyard, the latter of whom is described as a man he barely knew and whom he ran into only a few times over three decades. Yet he knew Tumin closely and heard of hushed insinuations that Tumin's complexion, lips, hair, and his area of study, suggested he was a Black man passing as Jewish.

These interviews reveal Roth's own conflicting observations, which raise, rather than clarify, an important question about the source material for *The Human Stain*: was he inspired by his graduate school girlfriend from decades ago, whose relatives "could physically pull it off, had given up identifying themselves as Negro, had moved away and had joined the white world, never to return,"[94] or was it the 1985 incident of Tumin's poor word choice that led to Princeton's investigation? Or could it be the combination of the two, since his ex-girlfriend and Tumin were both accused of passing—a phenomenon that has interested writers for well over a century? This wavering points to a contradiction in Roth's inspiration to write *The Human Stain*, which indicates that it could be either of these reasons or neither of them. There are one-to-one correlations between Tumin's and Coleman's lives—as Roth tells it—but they do not exclude other areas of influence that he did not publicly admit to. Since Roth did not have firsthand knowledge of racial passing, he based his novel on something, but he shifted on what that something was over the span of twelve years. I believe he read passing narratives to supplement his knowledge and to make his own narrative more convincing. Hence, references to blood, death, physical and symbolic running, lost family,

---

[92] Roth.
[93] Roth.
[94] McGrath, "Zuckerman's Alter Brain," 8.

relocating to New York, taboo sexuality, and education not only define Coleman Silk's life but also the tradition of passing narratives, as a way for Roth to give credence to his own contemporary tale of jumping the color line. In other words, Broyard's story was one of many passing narratives Roth could have referred to; he probably knew about Broyard's history of passing, yet Tumin's story was the real-life inspiration for Coleman Silk. Though Broyard was long gone, it is possible Roth remembered the manner in which he eviscerated Chandler Brossard for publishing a novel whose passing protagonist loosely resembled Broyard. Not wanting to contribute to the posthumous speculation about Broyard's race or possibly face the rebuke of his family, Roth penned a lengthy letter discrediting Wikipedia's entry that lists Broyard as his muse.

Completing Coleman Silk's story not only required passing narratives, but also a range of psychoanalytical elements. Though David Gooblar and Maren Scheurer believe that Roth's early writings antagonized psychoanalysis, he reconciled with it by the time he wrote *The Human Stain*, as evidenced by characterizing Coleman in ways that support theories by Freud, Klein, and Fanon.[95] They come from different stands of psychoanalysis, yet the field itself began with Freud's anxiety over sexuality and race, as his own references to mixed-race and Blackness make clear. Thus, for Roth to pen a passing narrative, he simultaneously had to evoke canonical passing narratives and psychoanalysis, since the two are directly correlated.

Toward the end of his letter to *The New Yorker*, Roth reminds readers that the word "pass" does not "appear in *The Human Stain*" at all, which he

---

[95] According to David Gooblar, Roth specifically used Sigmund Freud's theories in his fiction, beginning with *Portnoy's Complaint* (1969) and ending with *The Prague Orgy* (1985). Gooblar notes that "an understanding of psychoanalysis becomes almost essential to an understanding of [Roth's] fiction" ("Oh Freud! Do I Know!," 67). Maren Scheurer situates the psychoanalytic influence later in Roth's career, as she reads the "playful interaction with psychoanalysis" vis-à-vis "therapeutic moments" in elements of his later works: *Deception* (1990), *Patrimony* (1991) *and Sabbath's Theater* (1995) ("'What It Adds Up To, Honey, Is *Homo Ludens*!',"35). According to Scheurer, this psychoanalytic move is also apparent in *Portnoy's Complaint*. Clearly then, Roth has been interested in Freudian psychoanalysis for most of his writing career, whether he is critical of it in his early works or needs it to critique racism, as in *The Human Stain* (2000). Though he did not explicitly state his use of psychoanalysis for this later novel, I extend Gooblar and Scheurer's time frame by observing the psychoanalytic elements of his only passing novel.

hopes would further differentiate Broyard's real-life passing from Silk's fictional one.[96] Though the word is absent from the novel, the concept was very much present during these men's lives in the first half of the twentieth century, as it was hardly just a fictional endeavor. Roth offers a compelling argument for why many African-Americans felt obliged to pass: they "imagined that they would not have to share in the deprivations, humiliations, insults, injuries, and injustices that would be more than likely to come their way should they leave their identities exactly as they'd found them."[97] Even though some of the beginnings of passing appear nebulous, each racial passer in this book realized that jumping the color line was tantamount to avoiding racism.[98] Historically, discovering that someone has passed initiated shock and scorn for passers, as though they deceived everyone simply out of malice or selfishness. Yet racial passing is hardly a selfish endeavor; it is also a matter of safety and social mobility, often instilled in African-Americans through traumatic youthful encounters. Coupled with this is the history of African-Americans, who were forcefully removed from Africa and brought to the United States to work as free labor for generations, before they gained Emancipation in theory only. After the end of enslavement, overt racism kept African-Americans in segregation; today overt racism and implicit systematic racism combine to show African-Americans that they still face an uphill battle towards acceptance and equality. As a result, passing will continue to persist, both in writers' imagination and in real life, as long as race continues to be used as a marker of classification.

---

[96] Roth, "An Open Letter to Wikipedia."
[97] Roth, "An Open Letter to Wikipedia."
[98] For instance, Birdie Lee, who assumes a Jewish identity at her mother's request, grows to understand that pretending to be non-Black entails freedom from racism. Angela Murray also understands that passing as White means less social stigma and better access to privilege.

CONCLUSION

THE PASSING HUSTLE AND THE FAILED LANGUAGE OF RACE

It is difficult to accurately address racial passing in the twenty-first century, in part because the language used to discuss race in this era of alleged "postracialism" is often vague and inaccurate. According to Werner Sollors, passing is "an Americanism" which refers "to the crossing of any line that divides social groups."[1] The word "passing" first appeared in slave ads in the 1830s, when slaveowners were anxious that their runaway slaves might attempt to pass for White to aid their escape.[2] Juda Bennett also argues that the American usage of the term began in slavery, but locates it in another form of paperwork:

> [The] pass given to slaves so that they might travel without being mistaken for runaways. The 'pass' is a slip of paper that allows for free movement, but white skin is itself a 'pass' that allowed for some light-skinned slaves to escape their masters.[3]

Marcia Alesan Dawkins renders passing a "phenomenon in which a person gains acceptance as a member of social groups other than his or her own, usually in terms of race, ethnicity, class, gender, sexuality, religion, citizenship, or disability status."[4] In order for passing to occur, it relies on "a series of rhetorical intersections," which she pithily calls "passing passwords."[5] Exploring contemporary writers, Moynihan argues that "racial passing and writing emerge as analogous pursuits."[6] At the heart of the definitions of passing as put forth by Sollors, Bennett, Dawkins, and Moynihan are both the literariness of passing and the Americanness of it: passing is as much about

---

[1] Sollors, *Neither Black Nor White Yet Both*, 247.
[2] Sollors, 255.
[3] Bennett, "Black by Popular Demand," 36.
[4] Dawkins, *Clearly Invisible*, xii.
[5] Dawkins, xi.
[6] Moynihan, *Passing into the Present*, 22.

communication, both verbal and written, as it is about transgressing racial boundaries, specifically within the United States.

The literariness and Americanness of passing are well reflected in antebellum American literature. In the first two novels published by African-Americans—William Wells Brown's *Clotel; or, The President's Daughter* (1853) and Frank J. Webb's *The Garies and Their Friends* (1857)—passing is dramatized and used as an important plot device. Harriet Jacobs's *Incidents in the Life of a Slave Girl* (1861) also features scenes of both racial and gender passing. As I previously noted, the preponderance of passing in these seminal Black-authored texts "reaffirms its appeal in antebellum America as a route to liberation as well as its importance for the African-American literary imagination."[7] White writers employed racial passing in their works as well. For instance, in James Fenimore Cooper's *Last of the Mohicans* (1826), Cora passes for White, while Harriet Beecher Stowe's *Uncle Tom's Cabin* (1852) includes a scene of George Harris darkening his skin to pass as a Spanish gentleman to escape slavery. His "Spanish masquerade" occurred at a time when the popular entertainment in the United States was Blackface minstrelsy. After the Civil War, writers of both races published passing narratives in a variety of genres, with each person nuancing the definition of passing. One of the more recent examples is Brooke Kroeger's book *Passing: When People Can't Be Who They Are* (2003), which offers a collection of narratives about people who are passing in the twenty-first century. She notes that passing occurs "when people effectively present themselves as other than who they understand themselves to be."[8] This expansive definition lays the groundwork for the different types of passing in her work, of which race is just one category.

"Passing" is also the name of a road in Central Point, Virginia, and according to local legend, it is named after the generations of "Black residents white enough to pass."[9] It intersects with another road sign, "Hustle," and we can imagine that "the intersection of Passing and Hustle makes for the most intriguing road sign."[10] It provides an effective image and fitting metaphor for racial passing. One definition of the term "hustle" in contemporary urban

---

[7] Ramon, "'The Times, Alas, The Times!,'" 16.
[8] Kroeger, *Passing: When People Can't Be Who They Are*, 7.
[9] Kroeger, 51.
[10] Kroeger, 47.

vernacular implies obtaining items through deceitful or illicit means. Racial passers engage in a type of hustle as they maintain dual identities. "Passing and Hustle" is more than an obscure rural intersection; it epitomizes many of the ways in which passing subjects are forced to "hustle" to avoid having their true racial backgrounds revealed.

One twenty-first-century example of the passing hustle occurred with Rachel Dolezal, who created a firestorm in 2015 when her parents disclosed to media outlets that she was born as a White woman. This revelation complicated her assumed Black identity. Leading up to that point, she spent several years pretending to be Black, as evidenced by her chairing the local chapter of the NAACP, protesting against the systematic mistreatment of Blacks, marrying an African-American man, and teaching Black Studies, while stylizing her hair and phenotype to appear "Black"—as she construed it. Her atypical behavior raised questions about whether she engaged in cultural appropriation or passing, especially since, according to Robin DiAngelo in her acclaimed book *White Fragility*, "passing" has conventionally meant Black passing for White. She defines it as referring "to the ability to blend in as a white person, [yet] there is no corresponding term for the ability to pass as a person of color. This highlights the fact that in a racist society, the desired direction is always toward Whiteness and away from being perceived as a person of color."[11] Understanding passing also means exploring race, which is complicated by terminology that has remained conspicuously inconsistent and woefully incomplete. This is due to the rigid racial boundary between Black and White that defines racial categorizations in the United States.

It remains difficult to accurately encapsulate Dolezal's behavior, leaving room for critics to create the neologism "transracial" to accommodate her. The original definition of the term was used to describe parents who adopt children of a different race, but it has now been co-opted to define people who engage in unconventional iterations of passing, such as Dolezal. The term "transracial" now refers to people who maintain a racial identity for themselves that differs from their birth identity. Implicit in this revised definition is that the term "passing" is insufficient in accommodating those who pass in unconventional ways, especially since it connotes a specific historical necessity for African-Americans which Dolezal could not tap into given her biological Whiteness. Long before Dolezal was outed for feigning a Black

---

[11] DiAngelo, *White Fragility*, 20.

identity, scholars have theorized the notion of passing as Black. For instance, in researching biracial individuals, sociologists Nikki Khanna and Cathryn Johnson uncovered several reasons why biracial individuals choose to pass specifically as Black: "to fit in," "to avoid a stigmatized identity," and "for advantage."[12] They conclude that this version of passing implies "the changing terrain of race relations and racial politics in the United States. The practice of passing as Black, rather than White, suggests that Blackness is arguably less stigmatized today than in earlier eras of American history" as well as the fact that the definitions of race are "undergoing revision."[13] Whereas these sociologists use the term "passing as Black," Susan Gubar's term is "race-change," which she defines as "the traversing of race boundaries, racial imitation or impersonation, cross-racial mimicry or mutability, white posing as Black or Black passing as white, [a] pan-racial mutuality."[14] In adducing support for this idea, she points to the disfigurement African-Americans have endured when Whites employ various means in attempting to be Black.

Other recent examples of White to Black passing include the cases of Jessica Krug and CV Vitolo-Haddad—two scholars who were racially outed within weeks of each other in fall 2020. These cases are particularly egregious because they both benefited from research on and proximity to people of color. Krug in particular wrote extensively about race in her research on Africa and the African Diaspora, and as an undergraduate, benefited from the McNair Scholars Program. The McNair Program, much like the Mellon Mays Fellowship that prepared me for doctoral study, is geared toward preparing undergraduate students of color for graduate work. Krug, however, is a Jewish woman from outside Kansas City. Like Vitolo-Haddad, Krug did not settle on being a White ally, which would have been an even more powerful role during the Black Lives Matter movement; instead, they both opted for racial fraudulence. Additionally, both Krug and Vitolo-Haddad were affiliated with University of Wisconsin-Madison: the former is an alum, and the latter was a student until their racial outing as Black. These correlations make it clear that the critical lack of people of color at prestigious schools allows for greater racial deceptions, as well as that academia quietly fosters an

---

[12] Khanna and Johnson, "Passing as Black," 390–92.
[13] Khanna and Johnson, 394.
[14] Gubar, *Racechanges*, 5.

environment for jumping the color line in the name of misguided liberalism and colorblindness.

Academia has produced a range of scholars who research White to Black racial passing, yet they cannot agree on accurate terminology for this phenomenon. This is because racial boundaries are more fluid now than ever since race is not a stable category. Their scholarship also highlights the incongruity of the phenomenon, considering that passing as White has transpired for most of American history. Indeed, Gubar argues that passing as White is "the most morally acceptable representation of racechange," as evidenced by the narratives explored in this monograph.[15] She cites her fellow literary critic Leslie Fiedler, who writes in *Waiting for the End*, "Born theoretically white, we are permitted to pass our childhood as imaginary Indians, our adolescence as imaginary Negroes, and only then are expected to settle down to being what we really are: white once more."[16] His claim here is a provocative one, for if we apply this theory to Dolezal, she was still stuck in the adolescent stage of being an "imaginary Negro." Even after her passing charade came to an end, she rejected the idea of being "white once more"—she kept her box braids, changed her name to Nkechi Diallo, became a single mother, and committed welfare fraud. Americans have long used these categories as markers of Blackness, particularly the single-mother-welfare-recipient trope that provided the impetus for social and economic stereotypes about Black Americans for the past several decades. Nevertheless, if Dolezal is still trapped in adolescence with her longing to be Black, we can locate her behaviors within psychoanalysis. Although Fiedler published his theories decades before Dolezal came into the national consciousness, his writings often applied psychological criticism—especially Freudian psychoanalysis—to American literature. He was well aware of the primacy that psychoanalysts placed on the role of childhood/adolescence in human development. Dolezal herself noted that she changed her perspective on race as a teenager, after her White parents adopted four Black children. Her parents were in fact practicing transracialism before it was used to (mis)categorize their daughter's racial charade.

For the purpose of this study, childhood is crucial not just for human development, but specifically for racial development. Sigmund Freud and Frantz Fanon situate their theories in childhood as they argue that trauma

---

[15] Gubar, 11.
[16] Fiedler, *Waiting for the End*, 134.

begins there. Fanon notes the trauma of racism and colonialism afflicts Black children in particular. Otto Rank and Melanie Klein, however, root their psychoanalytic perspectives in infancy. For the former, removal from the mother's womb is the initial trauma, while the latter asserts that the differentiation between the good breast and bad breast paradigm causes malevolent feelings in babies. These psychoanalytic perspectives are all borne out in the lives of real and fictional passers. Doreen St. Félix argues that the Netflix documentary "The Rachel Divide" uncovers Dolezal's "real story" as a "primitive power game between mother and child, one that forecasts calamity."[17] Similarly, most of the subjects explored in this text endured traumatic experiences in their youth, which was the first step to their racial passing. As young boys, John Warwick, the Ex-Colored Man, and Victor Grabért were beaten and called "nigger," while Birdie Lee and Angela Murray learned about passing in adolescence from their mothers. In most passing narratives, protagonists have difficult relationships with their parents, and metaphorically seek their death in order to jump the color line. The demise of families is just one category of deaths that ensues with racial passers: they kill off their Black selves before succumbing to what Freud deemed the "death drive," as Coleman Silk, Solaria Cox, Clare Kendry and Victor Grabért all make clear when they hasten their deaths to prevent exposure for their racial and sexual deviance.

Real-life passers Anatole Broyard and Anita Reynolds kill off their former selves as well, but not before leaving clues about their race in their writing. According to Rank, creative writing is one way to combat the trauma of birth because artists' publications provide them with an afterlife long after their physical lives cease. Both Broyard's and Reynolds's life stories were published posthumously, which ensures that critics will continue to pour over their writings to glean what they thought about race and racial passing, among other topics. All the racial passers in this book, including White to Black passers, demonstrate that the passing hustle has occurred in countless ways since the era of Jim Crow. Several recently uncovered examples would attest to this as well. For instance, writing for National Public Radio, Tanvi Misra argued that in the mid-twentieth century, some people of color, including African-Americans and people visiting America, donned turbans to pass. Misra names several examples to support her claim—beginning with

---

[17] St. Félix, "'The Rachel Divide' Review."

Chandra Dharma Sena Gooneratne. As a Sri Lankan-born graduate student at the University of Chicago in the 1920s, he was shocked when faced with the anti-Black discrimination he encountered while travelling in America. To circumvent harassment, he wore a turban, believing that it can "make anyone Indian."[18] A turban is not only used by Indians, but he was tapping into America's historical consciousness of being more welcoming to people stereotyped as "exotic" than to Black people. He was not passing as Indian but as "exotic," which he believed was a safer option than to be viewed as Black.

African-Americans found the use of turbans to be equally useful for them. According to Misra, Reverend Jesse Routté donned a turban and robes when he went to Alabama, where he fooled everyone into receiving him as a foreign dignitary. In the case of Korla Pandit, he wore a turban and played the Hammond organ on television, which catapulted him to be regarded "as a precursor to Liberace."[19] While playing the organ each week, he surrounded himself with smoke and "dancing courtesans and elephants," which combined to make him appear more exotic than he really was.[20] He claimed to be the son of Indians hailing from New Delhi, but he was actually an African-American from Missouri. Like Gooneratne before him, Pandit became "Indian" to avoid Jim Crow discrimination.

For Harry S. Murphy Junior, he did not need special attire to hide his identity. A "military official checked the 'W' box for white when Murphy enlisted in the Navy."[21] He began passing inadvertently, which continued when he was a Black student at University of Mississippi from 1945 to 1946. Murphy "had a white complexion and wavy brown hair," ran track for the school, dated White women and dined in segregated restaurants.[22] Since this mistake went undetected, he used the error to integrate Ole Miss almost two decades before James Meredith officially did so in 1962. The only comment Murphy reportedly made about the resistance to Meredith's integration was that "they're fighting a battle they don't know they lost years ago."[23] Though he passed as White because an official misread him, he returned to Blackness

---

[18] Quoted in Misra, "How Turbans Helped Some Blacks Go Incognito."
[19] Misra.
[20] Misra.
[21] Hobbs, "The 'White' Student Who Integrated Old Miss."
[22] Hobbs.
[23] Hobbs.

after a year when he transferred to Morehouse College. In 1991, he committed suicide in New York City at age 63. Murphy's trajectory parallels some of the people described in this book. Like Broyard, legal paperwork helped to set him on the path to passing; like Coleman Silk and Angela Murray, he passed in school; like Birdie Lee, he returned to Blackness after passing; like Solaria Cox, he was motivated by the death drive and committed suicide. The line between real life and fictional iterations of passing is fluid. Moreover, passing is distinctly an urban phenomenon, which many of the racial passers in this book attest to. Murphy ended up in New York City years after he shifted identities at the University of Mississippi. Travelling to the metropolis is paramount for the passing hustle to continue; those who want to live secretly and without the fear of discovery must abscond to a big city in search of perpetual anonymity.

Though these real and fictional instances of passing occurred during the era of Jim Crow, this does not imply that passing is over. Alas, the passing hustle is now aided by the ubiquity of technology. In December 2013, for example, Yolanda Spivey articulated the role of race during her lengthy job search. After losing her job in the insurance industry, she began applying to over three hundred positions using the popular website for job-seekers Monster.com. Applicants are required to complete a diversity questionnaire to apply to positions on this site. Even though the site claims that the questionnaire "will not jeopardize your chances of gaining employment," Spivey proved otherwise. First, she checked the box indicating that she is a Black woman, before employing the "decline to identify" option. Still, her job search was futile.[24]

Only after creating another profile did she hear from potential employers. She used the name "Bianca White" on her resume and Monster profile and identified as a White woman on the diversity survey. While her true profile remained open, her White one received the most attention. As she summarizes, "At the end of my little experiment, (which lasted a week), Bianca White had received nine phone calls—I received none. Bianca had received a total of seven emails, while I'd only received two…a total of twenty-four employers looked at Bianca's resume while only ten looked at mine."[25] Similarly, José Zamora did not quantify the number of employers who contacted him

---

[24] Spivey, "Unemployed Black Woman."
[25] Spivey.

when he performed an experiment similar to Spivey's. Instead, he notes that "his inbox was full" one week after he changed his name from José to Joe Zamora.[26] He did not change anything on his resume, meaning his qualifications were the same as before. Once he dropped the s, his name became stereotypically White-sounding, thus guaranteeing that employers would interview him.

Spivey and Zamora did not fundamentally alter their identities but changed their names online to more mainstream, ethnically ambiguous ones. In doing so, they engaged in short-term passing that allowed them to be considered for employment. They were invested in more than attaining jobs; they were also interested in highlighting the ways in which racism functions today. Even though, as Matthews argues, "digital job applications would seem to be the ultimate exercise in colorblind hiring," she cites research proving that employers "consciously or subconsciously" look over applications with stereotypically Black or Latino-sounding names. Spivey and Zamora are the latest examples of this phenomenon, demonstrating that the color line remains a problem of the twenty-first century, thanks to continued racism and White privilege. It is this privilege that Damon Young disparages in his memoir in essays *What Doesn't Kill You Makes You Blacker* (2019), when he makes a backhanded reference to Dolezal by listing all of the privileges that are afforded to White people. According to him, the epitome of White privilege is "stealing opportunities and occupations away from Black people—and hav[ing] sociologists coin a new word to synopsize their plight and sympathize with their thievery."[27] The "their" in that statement is Dolezal, and he rails against the freedom with which she took opportunities from African-Americans and was able to have a new term created to accommodate her racial duplicity. Of course, "transracial" does not adequately capture the depths of Dolezal's inexplicable behavior, but it is a failed attempt to legitimize her long-term racial deception.

I refer to these examples to reiterate a few claims about passing. Chief among them is that passing has not ended but has shifted according to historical context. Although legal segregation is no longer a problem, which means light-skinned African-Americans do not need to pass for their safety to escape Jim Crow laws, the more pernicious systematic racism persists

---

[26] Matthews, "He Dropped One Letter in His Name."
[27] Young, *What Doesn't Kill You Makes You Blacker*, 143.

today. This forces people of color to find unique ways to create identities for themselves to circumvent discrimination. Today, wearing a turban to look "Indian" or otherwise trying to pass as something other than Black is not the only recourse for African-Americans; changing identities to "look White on paper" reflects the institutional racism that has replaced the explicit racism that defined much of the twentieth century.[28] In Spivey's and Zamora's cases, they passed temporarily in response to discriminatory hiring practices based on biases about names. Moreover, passing in any form—whether it is short-term or long-term—reveals much more about society than it does individuals. Racial passers pass because society has compelled them to do it; more to the point, jumping the color line is an implicit admission that the color line still exists.

These cases of passing were exposed during what was purportedly the "postrace" era. *The New York Times* marked the perceived end of racism with its cover story on the day after Barack Obama's historic election: "Obama: Racial Barrier Falls in Decisive Victory" read its front page on November 5th, 2008. According to the article, Obama's ascendency to the White House marked the end of racism in America, yet he is technically the first *biracial* president. Citing his ascendency to the White House as "proof" of racism's end, while downplaying his White ancestry, inadvertently reinforces the one-drop rule. The appraisals of the first Black president implies that his White-ness does not matter because he is half Kenyan. The irony of course, is that utilizing "postrace" as a contemporary term vis-à-vis Obama's Blackness, is itself racist because it stems from antiquated notions of Black classifications based solely on bloodlines. Furthermore, Perkins-Valdez believes the term "postracial suggests that race no longer matters, when in fact the failure of the term is its refusal to allow race to continuously evolve in the context of its history."[29] The problem with using "postracial" is that it historicizes race in

---

[28] In Signithia Fordham's often-cited ethnography, *Black Out: Dilemmas of Race, Identity, and Success at Capital High*, she examines the students at an urban high school to determine the factors of academic success for African-American pupils, while uncovering the stakes of attaining it. For her, passing is less about wanting to be visibly White, but is required in the form of displaying "the credentials that were traditionally associated with White Americans"—meaning that "looking White on paper" has been a contemporary way some Black Americans have passed to achieve upward mobility (39).

[29] Perkins-Valdez, quoted in Skyhorse and Page, *We Wear the Mask*, 124.

the past, as though racism is something that America has now overcome. If the presidency of Obama offered the premature illusion of postrace, the presidency of his successor reaffirms the continued implications of race and racism in American society.

Related to "postrace" is the term "color-blindness," defined as a society in which race or complexion is insignificant, when nobody is to be judged by such arbitrary categories. In a color-blind society, even though discrimination based on gender, sexuality, class, and disability might still persist, discrimination based solely on complexion would cease to exist. It is an ideal version of humanity, one which Martin Luther King, Jr. hoped for, yet it is one that is light years away in the United States. Color-blindness and postrace are tethered to each other; if we live in an era when racism fails to exist, then discrimination would also cease to be a problem since the focus away from color would prevent discrimination based on color. The desire not to see color is now tantamount to not seeing racial discrimination, which is a highly offensive and short-sighted endeavor. In yet another irony, "postrace" and "color-blindness" gained newfound prominence during Obama's presidency, at a time when the Black Lives Matter movement also took off. As I conclude this book in 2023, Black Lives Matter continues to bring our attention to the sustained and systematic mistreatment of African-Americans. The murders of Ahmaud Arbery, Breonna Taylor, and George Floyd, who were all killed in spring 2020, are just a few of the many examples of unarmed African-Americans murdered by police that prompted widespread protests in the summer of 2020. In short, while "postrace" and "color-blindness" anticipate an idyllic country where race is no longer a defining feature, Black Lives Matter evidences the complete opposite: race and racism will not disappear anytime soon. The Black Lives Matter movement, which is now international in scope, is the twenty-first-century Civil Rights movement.

W. E. B. Du Bois believed that racism was the defining problem of the twentieth century, yet it remains the primary way Americans are classified and discriminated against today. Black Lives Matter makes it unequivocally clear that the problem of the twenty-first century is the problem of the color line. This is due in part to the sustained belief in biological aspects of race, which is deeply imbedded in the American psyche even though science has long discredited the biology of race in favor of viewing it as a social construct. Racial passing is the foremost way in which we understand the social constructions of race. While race still has real-world implications, the ability to pass as something other than one's birth race is proof positive that it is socially constructed; boundaries dividing us are far more arbitrary and permeable than we have been socialized to believe. Du Bois verbalized his thoughts over a century ago, at a time when he and Freud developed theories to understand human development. They went about this exploration in different ways, with Freud emerging as the founder of psychoanalysis—a clinical field tethered to his own double consciousness as a Jew in an anti-Semitic context and a married man hiding his same-sex tendencies. Both Du Bois and Freud alluded to passing in their theories, since race and transgressing color lines were as relevant in the first decades of the twentieth century as they are in the first decades of the twenty-first.

Carl Jung articulated these connections well. As a disciple of Freud's, he wrote this letter to him in 1930:

> Naturally it works both ways. Just as every Jew has a Christ complex, so every Negro has a white complex and every American [White] a Negro complex. As a rule the coloured man would give anything to change his skin, and the white man hates to admit that he has been touched by the Black."[30]

In this passage, Jung offers an underhanded comment on Jews having a Christ complex, equating it with the desire that Blacks have to be White, and that Whites have to be Black. Jung, like Freud, "surmised that every subject maintains an intersubjective dependence on his perceived Other."[31] Yet he was more direct than Freud by placing "the thorny matter of race within a psychoanalytic frame" in the time period of the 1930s.[32] Jung is not only criticizing Freud for his Christ complex, but also arguing that everyone wants to pass and create another identity, just as Freud alluded to fifteen years previously in *The Unconscious* (1915). If every Black person has a "white complex," it helps to explain the persistence of racial passing: light-skinned African-Americans might seek Whiteness because it is an internal feeling they have after living in a raced society. Similarly, some White Americans have a subconscious desire to be Black, thus explaining why passing "works both ways." Undergirding Jung's argument is the premise that all humans maintain a psychoanalytic desire to be another race. According to this logic, Rachel

---

[30] Jung, *Collected Works*, vol. 10, 508.
[31] Ahad, *Freud Upside Down*, 1.
[32] Ahad, 1.

Dolezal, Jessica Krug, and CV Vitolo-Haddad are not just passing as Black but are expressing a deep internal disposition that psychoanalysis has cogently uncovered.

Reading Jung's diction from our modern standpoint helps us to see parallels to Freud, Du Bois, and Fanon, who made similar hypotheses about passing as a response to the racist contexts in which they lived. The psychoanalysts and authors of passing narratives in this book all expand the definition and scope of passing by proving that there is no one way to jump the color line. Passing strictly as White is not the sole option; it requires a series of complex negotiations based on context and anticipated outcome. Given the unique racial history of America, the various motivations to pass are clear, yet the modern terminology used to describe it is still lacking. The terms "transracial," "color-blindness," and "postracial" fail to encapsulate all the nuances of race in the United States, as does my own tongue-in-cheek neologism "passing hustle." While race continues to divide our country, those who can transgress rigid racial boundaries will continue to do so. It is notoriously difficult to discuss race in an American context, given that we continue to use inadequate rhetoric. What is more effective, however, is psychoanalysis, which offers critical tools and terminology to understand such racial differences, since it began as a way for Freud to explore his own racial anxiety and is rooted in childhood and the unconscious. While postrace is a complete fiction, there will be several more ways to redefine passing in the post-Obama era. If, according to Jung, African-Americans "would give anything to change [their] skin," we can see elements of this inclination through the multitudinous ways in which psychoanalysis has animated racial passing narratives over the past century.

WORKS CITED

Abel, Elizabeth, Barbara Christian, and Helene Moglen, eds. *Female Subjects in Black and White: Race, Psychoanalysis, Feminism*. Oakland: University of California Press, 1997.

Aciman, André. "Reflections of an Uncertain Jew." *The Threepenny Review* 81 (Spring 2000). https://www.threepennyreview.com/reflections-of-an-uncertain-jew/#:~:text=I%20was%20proud%20of%20being,am%20a%20provisional%2C%20uncertain%20Jew. Accessed August 30, 2023.

Ahad, Badia. *Freud Upside Down*. Champaign: The University of Illinois Press, 2010.

Althusser, Louis. "Ideology and Ideological State Apparatuses (Notes Towards an Investigation)." In *Lenin and Philosophy and Other Essays*, 79–87. New York: Monthly Review Press, 1971.

Altman, Neil. *The Analyst in the Inner City: Race, Class, and Culture Through A Psychoanalytic Lens*. New York: Routledge, 2009.

Andrade, Heather. "Revising Critical Judgments of 'The Autobiography of an Ex-Coloured Man'," *African-American Review* 40, no. 2 (Summer 2006): 257–70.

Andrews, William L. *To Tell a Free Story: The First Century of Afro-American Autobiography, 1760–1865*. Urbana: University of Illinois Press, 1986.

———. *The Literary Career of Charles W. Chesnutt*. Baton Rouge: Louisiana State University Press, 1980.

Angelo, Bonnie. "The Pain of Being Black: An Interview with Toni Morrison." In *Conversations with Toni Morrison*, edited by Danielle Guthrie-Taylor, 258. Jackson: University Press of Mississippi, 1994.

Baker, Houston, Jr. *Workings of the Spirit: The Poetics of Afro-American Women's Writing*. Chicago: University of Chicago Press, 1993.

Bakerman, Jane S. "Vera Caspary's Chicago, Symbol and Setting." *MidAmerica* 11 (1984): 81–89.

———. "Vera Caspary's Fascinating Females: Laura, Evvie, and Bedelia." *Clues* 3 (1980): 45–52.

Balibar, Etienne and Immanuel Wallerstein. *Race, Nation, Class: Ambiguous Identities*, 2nd ed. New York: Verso Press, 2011.

Baldwin, James. *Another Country*. New York: Vintage, 1962.

Baraka, Amiri. *Dutchman*. New York: Harper Perennial, 1964.

Barker, Deborah. *Aesthetics and Gender in American Literature*. Lewisburg, PA: Bucknell University Press, 2000.

Bassey, Magnus O. "The Place of Group Consciousness in Black Autobiographical Narratives." *Journal of African-American Studies* 11 (August 2007): 214–24.

Belluscio, Steven J. *To Be Suddenly White: Literary Realism and Racial Passing*. Columbia: University of Missouri Press, 2006.

Bennett, Juda. "Black by Popular Demand: Contemporary Autobiography and the Passing Theme." *a/b Auto/Biography Studies* 17, no. 2 (Winter 2002): 262–75.

Bergner, Gwen. *Taboo Subjects: Race, Sex, and Psychoanalysis*. Minneapolis: University of Minnesota Press, 2005.

Boisseron, Bénédicte. *Creole Renegades: Rhetoric of Betrayal and Guilt in the Caribbean Diaspora*. Gainesville: University Press of Florida, 2014.

Boyarin, Daniel. "What Does a Jew Want?; Or, The Political Meaning of the Phallus." *Discourse* 19, no. 2 (1997): 21–52.

Braxton, JoAnn. *Black Women Writing Autobiography*. Philadelphia: Temple University Press, 1989.

Brittian, Aerika S. "Understanding African American Adolescents' Identity Development: A Relational Developmental Systems Perspective." *Journal of Black Psychology* 38, no. 2 (2012): 172–200.

Brody, Jennifer DeVere. "Clare Kendry's 'True' Colors: Race and Class Conflict in Nella Larsen's *Passing*." In *Passing: A Norton Critical Edition*, edited by Carla Kaplan, 393–409. New York, W. W. Norton & Co., 2007.

Brooks, Kristina. "Alice Dunbar-Nelson's Local Colors of Ethnicity, Class, and Place." *MELUS* 23, no. 2 (1998): 3–26.

Brossard, Chandler. *Who Walk in Darkness*. New York: New Directions, 1952.

Broyard, Anatole. "American Sexual Imperialism." *Neurotica* 7 (Autumn 1950): 36–40.

———. "Books of the Times." *New York Times*. June 30, 1983. https://www.nytimes.com/1983/06/30/books/books-of-the-times-004759.html.

———. "Ha! Ha!" (1953). In *Discovery: An American* Review, edited by Vance Bourjaily, 5–12. New York: Cardinal Editions by Pocket Books, 1955.

———. *Intoxicated by My Illness And Other Writings on Life and Death*. Edited by Alexandra Broyard. New York: Clarkson Potter, 1992.

———. *Kafka Was the Rage: A Greenwich Village Memoir*. New York: Carol Southern Books, 1993.

———. "Portrait of an Inauthentic Negro." *Commentary* 10 (July 1950): 56–64.

———. "Sunday Dinner in Brooklyn" [1954]. In *The Beat Generation and the Angry Young Men*, edited by Gene Feldman and Max Gartenberg, 21–33. New York: Citadel, 1958.

———. "What the Cystoscope Said" (1954). In *Intoxicated by My Illness And Other Writings on Life and Death.*, edited by Alexandra Broyard, 89–133. New York: Clarkson Potter, 1992.

Broyard, Bliss. *One Drop: My Father's Hidden Life—A Story of Race and Family Secrets*. New York: Back Bay Books, 2007.

Broyard, Sandy. *Standby*. New York: Knopf, 2005.

Bruce, Dickson D., "W. E. B. Du Bois and the Idea of Double Consciousness." *American Literature* 64, no. 2 (1992): 299–309.

Bruner, Jerome. "Life as Narrative." *Social Research* 54, no. 1 (1987): 11–32.

Bryan, Violet Harrington. *The Myth of New Orleans in Literature: Dialogues of Race and Gender*. Knoxville: University of Tennessee Press, 1993.

———. "Race and Gender in the Early Works of Alice Dunbar-Nelson." In *Louisiana Women Writers*, edited by Dorothy H. Brown and Barbara C. Ewell, 120–38. Baton Rouge: Louisiana State University Press, 1992.

Butler, Judith. "Passing, Queering: Nella Larsen's Psychoanalytic Challenge." In *Passing: A Norton Critical Edition*, edited by Carla Kaplan, 417–35. New York, W. W. Norton & Co., 2007.

Butterfield, Stephen. *Black Autobiography in America*. Amherst: University of Massachusetts Press, 1974.

Caldwell, Gail. "Philip Roth's Latest Hero is a Man Undone by Freedom and Identity." *Boston Globe*. May 7, 2000.

Campanella, Richard. *Lincoln in New Orleans: The 1828–1931 Flatboat Voyages and Their Place in History*. Lafayette: University of Louisiana Press, 2010.

Camus, Albert. *The Myth of Sisyphus and Other Essays*. Translated by Justin O'Brien. New York: Vintage Books, 1991. Translation originally published by Alfred A. Knopf, 1955. Originally published in France as *Le Mythe de Sisyphe*. Paris: Librairie Gallimard, 1942.

Carson-Newman University. "Literary Terms and Definitions: H." April 24, 2018. http://web.cn.edu/kwheeler/lit_terms_h.html.

Carter, Greg. "Anatole Broyard's *Kafka Was the Rage: A Greenwich Village Memoir*." *Journal of American Ethnic History* 32, no. 1 (Fall 2012): 95–100.

Caspary, Vera. *The Secrets of Grown Ups*. New York: McGraw-Hill, 1979.

———. *The White Girl*. New York: Sears, 1929.

Cheng, Anne. *The Melancholy of Race: Psychoanalysis, Assimilation, and Hidden Grief*. New York: Oxford University Press, 2001.

———. *Second Skin: Josephine Baker & the Modern Surface*. New York: Oxford University Press, 2011.

Chesnutt, Charles. "The House Behind the Cedars." In *Charles Chesnutt: Stories, Novels & Essays*, 267–461. New York: Library of America, 2002.

Christian, Barbara. "The Race for Theory." In *The Black Feminist Reader*, edited by Joy James and T. Denean Sharpley-Whiting, 11–23. Oxford: Wiley-Blackwell, 2000.

Coviello, Peter. "Intimacy and Affliction: Du Bois, Race, and Psychoanalysis." *Modern Language Quarterly* 64, no. 1, (March 2003): 1–32.

Craft, William, and Ellen Craft. *Running a Thousand Miles for Freedom*. New York: Arno Press, 1969.

Crawford, Margo. *Dilution Anxiety and the Black Phallus*. Columbus: Ohio State University Press, 2008.

Dalal, Farhad. *Race, Colour and the Processes of Racialization: New Perspectives from Group Analysis, Psychoanalysis and Sociology*. Sussex: Routledge, 2002.

Danticat, Edwidge. *The Art of Death: Writing the Final Story*. Minneapolis: Graywolf Press, 2017.

Davis, Thadious. *Nella Larsen: Novelist of the Harlem Renaissance.* Baton Rouge: Louisiana State University Press, 1994.

———. "Nella Larsen's Harlem Aesthetic." In *Passing: A Norton Critical Edition*, edited by Carla Kaplan, 379–87. New York, W. W. Norton & Co., 2007.

Dawkins, Marcia Alesan. *Clearly Invisible: Racial Passing and the Color of Cultural Identity.* Waco: Baylor University Press, 2012.

Dean, Michelle. "The Secrets of Vera Caspary, The Woman who Wrote 'Laura'." *The New Yorker.* September 21, 2015.

Derricotte, Toi. *The Black Notebooks: An Interior Journey.* New York: W. W. Norton & Co., 1997.

DiAngelo, Robin. *White Fragility: Why It's So Hard for White People to Talk About Racism.* Boston: Beacon Press, 2018.

Diggs, Marylynne. "Surveying the Intersection: Pathology, Secrecy and the Discourses of Racial and Sexual Identity." In *Critical Essays: Gay and Lesbian Writers of Color*, edited by Emmanuel Nelson, 1–19. New York: Haworth, 1993.

Diner, Hasia. *In the Almost Promised Land: American Jews and Blacks, 1915–1935.* Baltimore: Johns Hopkins University Press, 1995.

Domínguez, Virginia R. *White by Definition: Social Classification in Creole Louisiana.* New Brunswick: Rutgers University Press, 1989.

Donaldson, Ian. "Biographical Uncertainty." *Essays in Criticism* 54, no. 4 (October 2004): 305–22.

Douglas, Ann. *Terrible Honesty: Mongrel Manhattan in the 1920s.* New York: Farrar, Straus, and Giroux, 1995.

Douglass, Frederick. *Narrative of the Life of Frederick Douglass.* New York: Barnes and Noble Classics, 2003.

Du Bois, W. E. B. *The Autobiography of W. E. B. Du Bois.* New York: International Publishers, 1968.

———. "The Present Condition of German Politics (1893)." *Central European History* 31, no. 3, (1998): 171–87.

———. *The Souls of Black Folk.* In *Three Negro Classics*, edited by John Hope Franklin, 207–389. New York: Avon Books, 1965.

Dudley, David. *My Father's Shadow: Intergenerational Conflict in African-American Men's Autobiography.* Philadelphia: University of Pennsylvania Press, 1991.

Dunbar, Paul Laurence. "We Wear the Mask," (1895). In *Majors and Minors; Poems*, 18. Miami: Mnemosyne Pub. Co., 1969.

Dunbar-Nelson, Alice. "A Creole Anomaly." *Leslie's Weekly.* July 15, 1897, 43.

———. "People of Color in Louisiana, Part I." *The Journal of Negro History* 1, no. 1 (1916): 361–76.

———. *The Works of Alice Dunbar-Nelson.* Edited by Gloria T. Hull. 3 vols. New York: Oxford University Press, 1988.

Dyson, Michael Eric. "How Black America Saw Obama." *New York Times.* January 14, 2017.

Elam, Michele. *The Souls of Mixed Folk: Race, Politics and Aesthetics in the New Millennium*. Stanford: Stanford University Press, 2011.
Emerick, Ronald. "Archetypal Silk: Wily Trickster, Tragic Mulatto, a Schlemiel in Philip Roth's *The Human Stain*." *Studies in American Jewish Literature* 26 (2007): 73–80.
Emrys, A. B. *Wilkie Collins, Vera Caspary and the Evolution of the Casebook Novel*. Jefferson, NC: McFarland & Company Press, 2011.
Erikson, Erik H. *Identity: Youth and Crisis*. New York: W. W. Norton & Co., 1968.
———. "The Concept of Identity in Race Relations: Notes and Queries." *Daedalus* 95, no. 1 (1966): 145–71.
———. *The Life Cycle Completed*. New York: W. W. Norton & Co., 1982.
Fanon, Frantz. *Black Skin, White Masks* [1952]. New York: Grove Press, 2008.
Fauset, Jessie R. *Plum Bun*. London: Pandora Press, 1985.
Fiedler, Leslie. *Waiting for the End*. New York: Stein & Day Publishers, 1970.
Fitzgerald, F. Scott. *The Great Gatsby* [1925]. New York: Penguin Classics, 2010.
Fordham, Signithia. *Black Out: Dilemmas of Race, Identity, and Success at Capital High*. Chicago: University of Chicago Press, 1996.
Franco, Dean J. "Being Black, Being Jewish, and Knowing the Difference." *Studies in American Jewish Literature* 23 (2004): 88–103.
Franklin, V. P. *Living Our Stories, Telling Our Truths: Autobiography and the Making of the African-American Intellectual Tradition*. New York: Oxford University Press, 1996.
Freud, Sigmund. *Beyond the Pleasure Principle*. Originally published in Vienna: International Psycho-Analytical, 1922. Translated by C. J. M. Hubback. New York: Bartleby.com, 2010.
———. "The Interpretation of Dreams, Third Edition" (1931). In *The Basic Writings of Sigmund* Freud, edited by A. A. Brill, 139–517. New York: The Modern Library, 1995.
———. "The Unconscious" (1915). In *The Standard Edition of The Complete Psychological Works of Sigmund Freud*, vol. 14, edited by James Strachey, 159–215. London: The Hogarth Press, 1957.
———. "Three Contributions to the Theory of Sex" (1905). In *The Basic Writings of Sigmund Freud*, edited by A. A. Brill, 521–600. New York: The Modern Library, 1995.
Gaddis, William. *The Recognitions*. New York: Harcourt, 1952.
Gallego, Mar. *Passing Novels in the Harlem Renaissance*. London: Transaction, 2003.
Gallo, Rubén. *Freud's Mexico: Into the Wilds of Psychoanalysis*. Cambridge, MA: The MIT Press, 2010.
Gates, Henry Louis, Jr. *Thirteen Ways of Looking at a Black Man*. New York: Random House, 1997.
———. "White Like Me." *The New Yorker*. June 17, 1996.

Gayarré, Charles. "The Creoles of History and the Creoles of Romance: A Lecture Delivered in the Hall of the Tulane University, New Orleans by Honorable Charles Gayarre on the 25th of April, 1885." New Orleans, C. E. Hopkins Publisher, 1885.

Gebhard, Caroline. "Masculinity, Criminality, and Race: Alice Dunbar-Nelson's Creole Boy Stories." *Legacy: A Journal of American Women Writers* 33, no. 2 (2016) 336–60.

Gibson, Charles F. "Concerning Color." *The Psychoanalytic Review* 18, no. 4 (January 1931): 413–25.

Gilman, Sander L. *Freud, Race, and Gender*. Baltimore: Johns Hopkins University Press, 1993.

Gilman, Sander L., and James M. Thomas. *Are Racists Crazy?: How Prejudice, Racism, and Antisemitism Became Markers of Insanity*. New York: New York University Press, 2016.

Gilroy, Paul. *The Black Atlantic: Modernity and Double Consciousness*. New York: Oxford University Press, 1994.

Goffman, Ethan. *Imagining Each Other: Blacks and Jews in Contemporary American Literature*. New York: State University of New York Press, 2000.

Gooblar, David. "'Oh Freud, Do I Know!': Philip Roth, Freud, and Narrative Therapy." *Philip Roth Studies* 1, no. 1 (2005): 67–81.

Green, Tara. *Reimagining the Middle Passage: Black Resistance in Literature, Television, and Song*. Columbus: Ohio State University Press, 2018.

Griffith, Jennifer L. *Traumatic Possessions: The Body and Memory in African-American Women's Writing and Performance*. Charlottesville: University of Virginia Press, 2010.

Groos, Karl. *The Play of Animals*. Translated by Elizabeth L. Baldwin. New York: Appleton, 1898.

Gubar, Susan. *Racechanges: White Skin, Black Face in American Culture*. New York: Oxford University Press, 2000.

Haizlip, Shirlee Taylor. *The Sweeter the Juice: A Family Memoir on Black and White*. New York: Touchstone Press, 1995

Hall, Stuart. "Race, Articulation and Societies Structured in Dominance" (1980). In *Essential Essays. Volume 1*, edited by David Morley, 172–221. Durham: Duke University Press, 2018.

Hall, Wade. *Passing For Black: The Life and Careers of Mae Street Kidd*. Lexington: University Press of Kentucky, 1997.

Harper, Frances Ellen Watkins. *Iola Leroy, or, Shadows Uplifted*. New York: Oxford University Press, 1988.

Harrison-Kahan, Lori. "Passing for White, Passing for Jewish: Mixed Race Identity in Danzy Senna and Rebecca Walker." *MELUS* 30, no. 1 (2005): 19–48.

Hobbs, Allyson Vanessa. *A Chosen Exile: A History of Racial Passing in American Life*. Cambridge, MA: Harvard University Press, 2014.

Hobbs, Allyson. "The 'White' Student Who Integrated Old Miss." *CNN*. February 5, 2014.

Holland, Sharon Patricia. *Raising the Dead: Readings of Death and (Black) Subjectivity*. Durham: Duke University Press, 2000.

Holloway, Karla F. C. *Passed On: African-American Mourning Stories*. Durham: Duke University Press, 2002.

Hook, Derek. "Fanon and the Psychoanalysis of Racism." In *Critical Psychology*, 114–37. Lansdowne, South Africa: Juta Academic Publishing, 2004.

hooks, bell. *remembered rapture: the Writer at Work*. New York: Henry Holt, 1999.

Hull, Gloria. "Shaping Contradictions: Alice Dunbar-Nelson and the Black Creole Experience." *New Orleans Review* 15, no. 1 (1988): 34–37.

Hutchinson, George. "Introduction." In *American Cocktail*, by Anita Reynolds. edited by George Hutchinson, 15–52. Cambridge, MA: Harvard University Press, 2014.

Hutson, Jean Blackwell. "Letter About Nella Larsen to Louise Fox." In *Passing: A Norton Critical* Edition, edited by Carla Kaplan, 151–52. New York, W. W. Norton & Co., 2007.

Jacobs, Harriet. *Incidents in the Life of a Slave Girl*. Cambridge, MA: Harvard University Press, 2000.

JanMohamed, Abdul R. *The Death-Bound-Subject: Richard Wright's Archaeology of Death*. Durham: Duke University Press, 2005.

Japtok, Martin. *Growing Up Ethnic: Nationalism And The Bildungsroman In African American And Jewish American Fiction*. Iowa City: University of Iowa Press, 2005.

Jeffries, Stuart. "But What Does it Mean?" *The Guardian*. February 21, 2003.

Johnson, James Weldon. *The Autobiography of an Ex-Colored Man*. In *Three Negro Classics*, edited by John Hope Franklin, 391–511. New York: Avon Books, 1965.

———. *The Book of American Negro Poetry:* Chosen and Edited, with an Essay on the Negro's Creative Genius. New York: Harcourt, Brace, and Co., 1922.

Jones, Ernest. *The Life and Work of Sigmund Freud* [1953]. Edited and abridged by Lionel Trilling and Steven Marcus. New York: Basic Books. 1961.

Jones, Suzanne. "Tragic No More? The Reappearance of the Racially Mixed Character." In *American Fiction of the 1990s: Reflections of History and Culture*, edited by Jay Prosser, 89–103. London: Routledge, 2008.

Joseph, Ralina. *Transcending Blackness*. Durham: Duke University Press, 2013.

Jung, Carl G. *Collected Works of C. G. Jung*. Vol. 10, *Civilization in Transition*. Edited by Gerhard Adler and R. F. C. Hull. Princeton: Princeton University Press, 2014.

Kakutani, Michiko. "Confronting the Failures of a Professor Who Passes." *New York Times Books of the Times*. May 2, 2000.

Kampf, Fay B. *The Psychology and Psychotherapy of Otto Rank: An Historical and Comparative Introduction*. Westport, CT: Greenwood Press, 1977.

Kaplan, Brett Ashley. "Anatole Broyard's Human Stain: Performing Postracial Consciousness." *Philip Roth Studies* 1, no. 2 (Fall 2005): 125–44.

Kaplan, Carla. Introduction to *Passing: A Norton Critical Edition*, edited by Carla Kaplan, ix–xxvii. New York, W. W. Norton & Co., 2007.

Karpman, Ben. "Imitation of Life." *The Psychoanalytic Review* 23 (January 1936): 149–72.

Kaul, Chandrika. "From Empire to Independence: The British Raj in India 1858–1947." *BBC*. March 3, 2011. http://www.bbc.co.uk/history/british/modern/independence1947_01.shtml.

Kennedy, Randall. *Interracial Intimacies: Sex, Marriage, Identity, and Adoption*. New York: Pantheon, 2003.

Khanna, Nikki, and Cathryn Johnson. "Passing as Black: Racial Identity Work among Biracial Americans." *Social Psychology Quarterly* 73, no. 4 (2010): 380–97.

Khanna, Ranjana. *Dark Continents: Psychoanalysis & Colonialism*. Durham: Duke University Press, 2003.

Kroeger, Brooke. *Passing: When People Can't Be Who They Are*. New York, Public Affairs Press, 2003.

Lacan, Jacques. "Position of the Unconscious" (1960). In *Ecrits: The First Complete Edition in English*, translated by Bruce Fink, 703–21. New York: W. W. Norton & Co., 2006.

———. "The Function and Field of Speech and Language in Psychoanalysis" (1953). *In Ecrits: The First Complete Edition in English*, translated by Bruce Fink, 197–268. New York: W. W. Norton & Co., 2006.

———. "The Instance of the Letter in the Unconscious." In *Ecrits: The First Complete Edition in English*, translated by Bruce Fink, 412–44. New York: W. W. Norton & Co., 2006.

———. "The Mirror Stage as Formative of the *I* Function as Revealed in Psychoanalytic Experience." In *Ecrits: The First Complete Edition in English*, translated by Bruce Fink, 75–81. New York: W. W. Norton & Co., 2006.

Lane, Christopher. *The Psychoanalysis of Race*. New York: Columbia University Press, 1998.

Larsen, Nella. "Letter to Carl Van Vechten, May 14, 1932." In *Passing: A Norton Critical Edition*, edited by Carla Kaplan, 170. New York, W. W. Norton & Co., 2007.

———. "Letter to Dorothy Peterson, July 21, 1927." In *Passing: A Norton Critical Edition*, edited by Carla Kaplan, 164–65. New York, W. W. Norton & Co., 2007.

———. *Passing* [1929]. *A Norton Critical Edition*. Edited by Carla Kaplan. New York: W. W. Norton & Co., 2007.

Leonard, John. "A Child of the Age." *New York Review of Books*. June 2, 2000.

Lieberman, E. James. *Acts of Will: The Life and Work of Otto Rank*. New York: Free Press, 1985.

Logan, Frenise. "The British East India Company and African Slavery in Benkulen, Sumatra, 1687–1792." *The Journal of Negro History* 41, no. 4 (October 1956): 339–48.

Madigan, Mark J. "Miscegenation and 'The Dicta of Race and Class': The Rhinelander Case and Nella Larsen's *Passing*." *Modern Fiction Studies* 36, no. 4 (1990): 523–29.

Marrant, John. "Narrative of the Lord's Wonderful Dealings" (1785). In *Pioneers of the Black Atlantic: Five Slave Narratives From the Enlightenment* (1772–1815), edited by Henry Louis Gates, Jr. and William L. Andrews, 60–80. Washington, D. C.: Civitas, 1998.

Matory, J. Lorand. *The Fetish Revisited: Marx, Freud, and the Gods Black People Make*. Durham: Duke University Press, 2018.

Matthews, Cate. "He Dropped One Letter in His Name While Applying For Jobs, And the Responses Rolled In." *Huffington Post*. September 2, 2014.

McDowell, Deborah. From "Black Female Sexuality in *Passing*." In *Passing: A Norton Critical Edition*, edited by Carla Kaplan, 363–79. New York, W. W. Norton & Co., 2007.

McGrath, Charles. "Zuckerman's Alter Brain: An Interview with Philip Roth." *New York Times Book Review*. May 7, 2000.

Melnick, Jeffrey. *A Right to Sing the Blues: African-Americans, Jews, and American Popular Song*. Cambridge, MA: Harvard University Press, 2001.

Michaels, Walter Benn. "Plots Against America: Neoliberalism and Antiracism." *American Literary History* 18, no. 2 (2006): 288–302.

Michie, Helena. From *Sororophobia: Differences among Women in Literature and Culture*. In *Passing: A Norton Critical Edition*, edited by Carla Kaplan, 409–17. New York, W. W. Norton & Co., 2007.

Misra, Tanvi. "How Turbans Helped Some Blacks Go Incognito in the Jim Crow Era." July 19, 2014. National Public Radio. *Code Switch*. Podcast. https://www.npr.org/sections/codeswitch/2014/07/17/332380449/how-turbans-helped-some-blacks-go-incognito-in-the-jim-crow-era.

Mitchell, Stephen A., and Margaret J. Black. *Freud and Beyond: A History of Modern Psychoanalytic Thought*. New York: Basic Books, 1995.

Moore, Lorrie. "The Wrath of Athena." *New York Times Books of the Times*. May 7, 2000.

Morrison, Toni. *The Origin of Others*. Cambridge, MA: Harvard University Press, 2017.

Moynihan, Sinead. *Passing Into the Present: Contemporary American Fiction of Racial and Gender Passing*. Manchester: Manchester University Press, 2010.

Mullen, Harryette. "Optic White: Blackness and the Production of Whiteness." *Diacritics* 24, no. 2/3 (1994): 71–89.

National Archives of the United Kingdom. "Slavery and the British transatlantic slave trade." https://www.nationalarchives.gov.uk/help-with-your-research/research-guides/british-transatlantic-slave-trade-records/.

Nin, Anais. *The Diary of Anais Nin*. Volume 2, *1934–1939*. Edited by Gunther Stuhlmann. New York: Harcourt, 1971.

Nin, Anais. *The Diary of Anais Nin*. Volume 4, *1944–1947*. Edited by Gunther Stuhlmann. New York: Harcourt, 1971.

Obama, Barack. *Dreams From My Father: A Story of Race and Inheritance*. New York: Three Rivers Press, 1995.

Page, Clarence. "America's Peculiar 'Passing' Fancy." *Chicago Tribune*. November 9, 2003.

Patterson, Orlando. *Slavery and Social Death*. Cambridge, MA: Harvard University Press, 1985.

Peck, Raoul, dir. *I Am Not Your Negro*. 2016; United States: Magnolia Pictures.

Perkins, Maureen. "Resisting the Autobiographical Imperative: Anatole Broyard and Mixed Race." *a/b Auto/Biography Studies* 26, no. 2 (Winter 2011): 265–80.

Perkins-Valdez, Dolen. "On Historical Passing and Erasure." *We Wear the Mask: 15 True Stories of Passing in America*. Eds. Skyhorse and Page (122–128).

Petry, Ann. *The Street*. New York: Mariner, 1946.

Piaget, Jean. *Play, Dreams and Imitation in Childhood*. New York: W. W. Norton & Co., 1962.

Piper, Adrian. "Passing for White, Passing for Black." In *Passing And the Fictions of Identity*, edited by Elaine K. Ginsberg, 234–69. Durham: Duke University Press, 1996.

Posnock, Ross. "Purity and Danger: On Philip Roth." *Raritan: A Quarterly Review* 21, no. 2 (2001): 85–101.

Prudhomme, Charles. "The Problem of Suicide in the American Negro." *The Psychoanalytic Review* 25 (January 1938): 372–91.

Ramon, Donavan L. "'The Times, Alas, The Times!' Nella Larsen's *Passing* and the American Tradition." *South Atlantic Review* 84, no. 2-3 (Summer/Fall 2019): 15–23.

Rank, Otto. *The Trauma of Birth* [1929]. New York: Harper and Row, 1973.

Rankine, Claudia. "The Condition of Black Life is One of Mourning." *New York Times Magazine*. June 22, 2015.

Reynolds, Anita. *American Cocktail*. Edited by George Hutchinson. Cambridge, MA: Harvard University Press, 2014.

Rigo, Darlene. "The Psychoanalysis of Race." *Theory and Psychology* 11, no. 4 (2001): 582–84.

Roth, Philip. "An Open Letter to Wikipedia." *The New Yorker*. September 6, 2012.

———. *The Human Stain*. New York: Vintage, 2000.

Royal, Derek Parker. "Plotting the Frames of Subjectivity: Identity, Death, and Narrative in Philip Roth's *The Human Stain*." *Contemporary Literature* 47, no. 1 (2006): 114–40.

Rummell, Kathryn. "Rewriting the Passing Novel: Danzy Senna's *Caucasia*." *The Griot* 26, no. 2 (Fall 2007): 1–14.

Ryan, Melissa. "Rena's Two Bodies: Gender and Whiteness in Charles Chesnutt's *The House Behind the Cedars*," *Studies in the Novel* 43, no. 1 (Spring 2011): 38–54.

Safer, Elaine B. "Tragedy and Farce in Roth's *The Human Stain*." *Critique* 43 (2002): 211–27.

Sandweiss, Martha. *Passing Strange*. New York: Penguin Books, 2009.

Saslow, Eli. *Rising Out of Hatred: The Awakening of a Former White Nationalist*. New York: Doubleday, 2018.

Scheurer, Maren. "'What It Adds Up To, Honey, Is *Homo Ludens*!' Play, Psychoanalysis, and Roth's Poetics." *Philip Roth Studies* 11, no. 1 (2015): 35–52.

Scott, Darieck. *Extravagant Abjection: Blackness, Power and Sexuality in the African-American Literary Imagination*. New York: New York University Press, 2010.

Senna, Danzy. *Caucasia*. New York: Riverhead Books, 1999.

Seshadri-Crooks, Kelpana. *Desiring Whiteness: A Lacanian Analysis of Race*. London: Routledge, 2000.

Sharfstein, Daniel J. *The Invisible Line: Three American Families and the Secret Journey from Black to White*. New York: Penguin Press, 2011.

Sheehy, John. "The Mirror and the Veil: The Passing Novel and the Quest for American Racial Identity." *African-American Review* 33, no. 3 (1999): 401–15.

Sherrard-Johnson, Cherene. *Portraits of the New Negro Woman: Visual and Literary Culture in the Harlem Renaissance*. New Brunswick: Rutgers University Press, 2007.

Skyhorse, Brando and Lisa Page, eds. *We Wear the Mask: 15 True Stories of Passing in America*. Boston: Beacon Press, 2017.

Smith, Sidonie. *Where I'm Bound*. Westport, CT: Greenwood Press, 1974.

Smith, Sidonie, and Julia Watson. "The Trouble with Autobiography: Cautionary Notes for Narrative Theorists." In *A Companion to Narrative Theory*, edited by James Phelan and Peter J. Rabinowitz, 356–71. London: Blackwell, 2005.

Sollors, Werner. *Neither Black Nor White Yet Both*. Oxford: Oxford University Press, 1997.

Spielrein, Sabina. "Destruction as the Cause of Coming Into Being." *Journal of Analytical Psychology* 39, no. 2 (1994): 155–86.

Spillers, Hortense J. "'All the Things You Could Be by Now, If Sigmund Freud's Wife Was Your Mother': Psychoanalysis and Race." *Boundary 2* 23, no. 3 (1996): 75–141.

Spivak, Gayatri Chakravorty. "Three Women's Texts and Circumfession." In *Postcolonialism & Autobiography*, edited by Alfred Hornung and Ernstpeter Ruhe, 7–24. Amsterdam: Rodopi, 1998.

Spivey, Yolanda. "Unemployed Black Woman Pretends to be White, Job Offers Suddenly Skyrocket." December 12, 2013. https://katepavelle.wordpress.com/2014/09/05/unemployed-black-woman-pretends-to-be-white-job-offers-suddenly-skyrocket/.

Starkey, Marion L. "Jessie Fauset." *The Southern Workman* 61, no. 5 (May 1932): 217–20.

St. Félix, Doreen. "'The Rachel Divide' Review: A Disturbing Portrait of Dolezal's Racial Fraudulence." *The New Yorker*. April 26, 2018.

Stepto, Robert. *A Home Elsewhere: Reading African-American Classics in the Age of Obama*. Cambridge, MA: Harvard University Press, 2010.

Stoler, Ann. *Race and the Education of Desire: Foucault's History of Sexuality and the Colonial Order of Things*. Durham: Duke University Press, 1995.

Stouck, Jordan. "Identities in Crisis: Alice Dunbar-Nelson's New Orleans Fiction." *Canadian Review of American Studies* 34, no. 3 (2004): 269–89.

Stoute, Beverley. "Race and Racism in Psychoanalytic Thought: The Ghosts in Our Nursery." *The American Psychoanalyst* 51, no. 1 (2017): 13–41.

Sue, Derald Wing. *Microaggressions in Everyday Life: Race, Gender, and Sexual Orientation*. Hoboken: Wiley, 2010.

Syed, Moin, and Jillian Fish, "Revisiting Erik Erikson's Legacy on Culture, Race, and Ethnicity," *Identity: An International Journal of Theory and Research* 18, no. 4 (2018): 274–83.

Sylvander, Carolyn W. *Jessie Redmon Fauset: Black American Writer*. Troy, NY: Whitston, Publishing Company, 1981.

Tate, Claudia. "Nella Larsen's *Passing*: A Problem of Interpretation." In *Passing: A Norton Critical Edition*, edited by Carla Kaplan, 342–50. New York, W. W. Norton & Co., 2007.

———. *Psychoanalysis and Black Novels: Desire and the Protocols of Race*. New York: Oxford University Press, 1998.

Tatum, Beverly. *Why Are All the Black Kids Sitting Together in the Cafeteria?* New York: Basic Books, 2003.

Tierney, William G. "Interpreting Academic Identities: Reality and Fiction on Campus." *Journal of Higher Education* (Jan/Feb 2002): 160–72.

Trent-Scales, Judy. *Notes of a White Black Woman: Race, Color, Community*. University Park: Pennsylvania State University Press, 1995.

Tritt, Michael. "'The Force, the Fire, and the Artistic Touch' of Alice Dunbar-Nelson's *The Stones of the Village*." *Journal of the Short Story in English* 54 (2010): 1–11.

University of Delaware. "Introduction." *Alice Dunbar-Nelson Reads*. Accessed April 2, 2020. https://sites.udel.edu/alicereads/introduction.

Viego, Antonio. *Dead Subjects: Toward a Politics of Loss in Latino Studies*. Durham: Duke University Press, 2007.

X, Malcolm, and Alex Haley. *The Autobiography of Malcolm X*. New York: Ballantine Books, 1992.

Wall, Cheryl A. *Women of the Harlem Renaissance*. Bloomington: Indiana University Press, 1995.

Walton, Jean. *Fair Sex, Savage Dreams: Race, Psychoanalysis, Sexual Difference*. Durham: Duke University Press, 2001.

Washington, Booker T. *Up From Slavery*. In *Three Negro Classics*, edited by John Hope Franklin, 23–205. New York: Avon Books, 1965.

Washington, Mary Helen. "Nella Larsen: Mystery Woman of the Harlem Renaissance." In *Passing: A Norton Critical Edition*, edited by Carla Kaplan, 350–56. New York, W. W. Norton & Co., 2007.

Watson, Reginald. "The Tragic Mulatto Image in Charles Chesnutt's *The House Behind the Cedars* and Nella Larsen's *Passing*." *CLA Journal* 46, no. 1 (2002): 48–71.

Webb, Frank J. *Fiction, Essays, Poetry*. Edited and Introduced by Werner Sollors. New Milford: The Toby Press, 2004.

Williams, Gregory Howard. *Life on the Color Line: The True Story of a White Boy Who Discovered He Was Black*. New York: Dutton Press, 1996.

Wilson, Harriet E., and Henry Louis Gates. *Our Nig: or, Sketches from the Life of a Free Black, in a Two-Story White House, North: Showing That Slavery's Shadows Fall Even There*, 2nd ed. New York: Vintage Books, 1983.

Wilson, Matthew. "Reading *The Human Stain* Through Charles W. Chesnutt: The Genre of the Passing Novel." *Philip Roth Studies* 2, no. 2 (2006): 138–50.

Worden, Daniel. "Birth in the Briar Patch: Charles W. Chesnutt and the Problem of Racial Identity," *Southern Literary Journal* 41, no. 2 (Spring 2009): 1–20.

Wright, Richard. "Psychiatry Comes to Harlem." *Free World*. September, 1946.

Youman, Mary Mabel. "Nella Larsen's *Passing*: A Study in Irony." In *Passing: A Norton Critical Edition*, edited by Carla Kaplan, 337–42. New York, W. W. Norton & Co., 2007.

Young, Damon. *What Doesn't Kill You Makes You Blacker: A Memoir in Essays*. New York: Harper Collins, 2019.

INDEX

Aciman, André, 12
active death, 79–80, 83, 96, 131, 209, 213
Adler, Alfred, 136, 142
Africa: customs agent's colonial attitude toward, 154–55; "inner Africa," Freud viewing id as, 14; Morocco, Anita Reynolds in, 152–55
African-Americans: displacement and irrational fear of Black men, 5n14; educational issues, 25; Erikson on identity development in, 28–29; humility topos, use of, 160n80; Jewishness in Austro-Germany compared to Blackness in United States, 7–8; Johnson's *Autobiography of an Ex-Colored Man* on, 46–48; life writing and, 140–41; mourning and fear as permanent condition for, 73–74; passing and self-segregation from, 86–88, 91–92, 106, 107–8, 109, 178–81, 191; political assassination, concerns about, 73–74; psychoanalysis, relationship with, 1–3, 74–75, 137; reasons for passing by, 219; Roth's *Human Stain*, "spooks" remark in, 192, 201–3, 212, 216–17; self-hate, Black experience of, 29, 48, 63, 181; suicide rates for, 1n1; turbans worn to facilitate passing by, 226–27; untimely death, experience of, 73, 79–80n27
Ahad, Badia, 2, 12, 18, 19–20, 33n40, 67–68, 75, 136, 137, 142, 161n87, 182n166
Althusser, Louis, 24–25
American Cocktail: A Colored Girl in the World (Reynolds), 17, 144–63, 226; alternative titles for, 162; childhood and career in America, 144–49; colonialism, confronting, 154–57; passing/hiding racial background, 147–52, 186; publication of, 137n12, 138; racial identities in, 147–48, 150, 154, 156–59, 161, 162; recording and transcription of, 144; return to US and confrontation with racism, 157–59; Senna's *Caucasia* and, 150n52; significance of title, 145, 150, 158, 162–63; social interactions in Europe and race, 152–55; travel and relocation in, 69, 144, 148–49, 152–55; writing, struggles with, 151–52, 159–63, 186
American Indians: Mexicans passing as, 23; Anita Reynolds and, 150; in Senna's *Caucasia*, 150n52
American Psychoanalytic Association, 10
"American Sexual Imperialism" (Anatole Broyard), 178n150
Andrade, Heather, 43
Andrews, William, 39n57
Another Country (Baldwin), 205n54
anti-Semitism. *See* Jews and anti-Semitism
Arbery, Ahmaud, 231
Aroused by Books (Anatole Broyard), 177
"The Artificial Nigger" (O'Connor), 71
The Atlantic Monthly, 97
autobiography. *See* life writing
The Autobiography of an Ex-Colored Man (Johnson), 16, 41–49; anonymous initial publication of, 41, 98; books, importance of, 49, 58, 85n43; Broyard's *One Drop* compared, 166, 168; Caspary's *White Girl* compared, 112; Chesnutt's *The House Behind the Cedars* compared, 33, 35, 42, 43, 44, 45, 48, 49; childhood race-learning and passing in, 30, 31–32, 41–49, 226; Dunbar-Nelson's "Stones" compared, 85n43; Erikson's theories and, 45, 47, 49, 67; Fauset's *Plum Bun* compared, 50; geography and time period, effects of, 67, 68; mirrors, significance of, 42, 45, 49; Roth's *Human Stain* compared, 194, 198; Senna's *Caucasia* compared, 60,

63n133; travel and relocation in, 68–69
Baker, Houston, 50
Baker, Josephine, 149
Bakerman, Jane S., 114n145
Baldwin, James, 29, 72, 205n54
Balibar, Etienne, 24n10
Bambara, Toni Cade, 178
Baraka, Amiri, 205n54
Barker, Deborah, 50
Barnes, Djuna, 151
Barnett, Ida B. Wells, 151
Baron, Jacques, 161
Barthes, Roland, 143n30
Bassey, Magnus, 140n22
Bayliss, Esther, in *Plum Bun,* 54
Belluscio, Steven J., 40n59
Bennett, Juda, 221
Bergner, Gwen, 2, 18, 19, 26, 27
Beyond the Pleasure Principle (Freud), 76–77, 123, 134
biography. *See* life writing
bisexuality, congenital, Fliess's theory of, 13, 76
Black, Derek, 71–72
Black Autobiography in America (Butterfield), 140n22
Black feminism, 2
Black Lives Matter movement, 73, 224, 231
Black Out (Fordham), 230n28
Black Power, 2
Black Skin, White Masks (Fanon), 16, 26–27, 61, 153, 181, 199, 205n54
Blackface minstrelsy, 222
Blackness
childhood race-learning and passing, 16, 26, 32, 68–69, 70–72; in Chesnutt's *House Behind the Cedars,* 33–41; in Fauset's *Plum Bun,* 52–56, 67; in Johnson's *Autobiography of an Ex-Colored Man,* 41–45, 47–49; in Senna's *Caucasia,* 57–58, 60–62, 64–65, 67
Creole ancestry and, 82
death and passing, 17, 79n26, 80, 133; in Caspary's *White Girl,* 98, 100–112, 131; in Dunbar-Nelson's "Stones," 83, 87–88, 91–96, 131; in Larsen's *Passing,* 120, 122, 129–31
gender differences in learning about, 49–50
illegitimacy, Blackness, and slavery, 183
Jews associated with, 7, 8, 10, 11, 12, 13–14n42
life writing and passing, 17, 138, 141, 142, 186, 188; Anatole Broyard and, 164, 167–69, 175, 177–81, 183, 185; Anita Reynolds and, 146, 151–53, 157, 161
Harry S. Murphy, Jr.'s return to, 228
of Barack Obama, 74
passing as means of understanding, 1 (*See also* psychoanalytical perspective on passing)
psychoanalysis, use of language of Blackness in, 12–15, 18
Roth's *Human Stain* and, 192, 194–95, 201–2, 204, 206–8, 211–15, 218
travel/relocation and discovery of, 68–70
White to Black passing and markers of, 225
blood and blood imagery: in American imagination, 89, 230; in Caspary's *White Girl,* 102–3, 105; in Dunbar-Nelson's "Stones," 89, 105; one-drop rule, 12, 36, 37, 89; in Roth's *Human Stain,* 197
Boisseron, Bénédicte, 12, 78, 90, 118, 164–65, 177, 211
The Book of American Negro Poetry (1922), James Weldon Johnson's preface to, 47
books, importance of, and passing, 32, 36, 38–39, 49, 58, 68, 70, 85n43, 152, 169–70, 192–93
Boston, school desegregation in (1970s and 1980s), 67
Boyarin, Daniel, 8
Bradley, William Aspenwall, 144, 151, 152, 161
British East India Company, 154
Brittian, Aerika, 29

Brody, Jennifer DeVere, 117–18, 125n201
Brossard, Chandler, 182–84, 218
Brown, Michael, 73, 79n26
Brown, William Wells, 74n4, 222
Brown v. Board of Education (1954), 25
Broyard, Anatole, life of. *See One Drop*
Broyard, Anatole, writings of: "American Sexual Imperialism," 178n150; *Aroused by Books,* 177; "Ha Ha," 142; *Intoxicated by My Illness and Other Writings on Life and Death,* 184–85; *Kafka Was the Rage* (posthumously published autobiography), 170, 185; "Keep Cool, Man," 173; *Men, Women, and Other Anticlimaxes,* 177; "Portrait of the Inauthentic Negro," 172–73; "Sunday Dinner in Brooklyn," 173, 174; "What the Cystoscope Said," 173, 174, 184
Broyard, Bliss (daughter). *See One Drop*
Broyard, Edna (mother), 163, 165, 174, 176, 187
Broyard, Paul (Nat; father), 163, 165–66, 173–74, 180, 184
Broyard, Sandy (second wife), 167n108, 170–71, 176–77, 179, 184, 188–89
Broyard, Shirley (sister), 163, 165, 166
Broyard, Todd (son), 189, 191
Bruce, Dickson, Jr., 9
Bruner, Jerome, 140
Bryan, Violet Harrington, 83n35
Bryant, Louise, 152
Bunyan, John, 36, 44
Butler, Judith, 118, 120n177, 125n201, 128
Butterfield, Stephen, 140n22
Campanella, Richard, 90n65
Camus, Albert, 130
Carter, Greg, 185
Caspary, Vera: *Laura* (detective novel), 98; psychoanalysis, interest in, 75; race and passing in work of, 20; *The Secrets of Grownups* (autobiography), 98. *See also White Girl*

Caucasia (Senna), 16, 57–65; books, importance of, 58, 68; childhood race-learning and passing in, 16, 30, 32, 57–65, 226; Erikson's theories and, 51, 59, 61, 66; Fauset's *Plum Bun* compared, 51, 57, 60, 62–63; gender differences in race-learning and, 49–50; geography and time period, effects of, 67–68; Johnson's *The Autobiography of an Ex-Colored Man* compared, 60, 63n133; Larsen's *Passing* compared, 63n133, 119n175; mirrors, significance of, 59, 61; play in, 57, 60, 61, 62–63, 65, 68; reasons for passing, understanding of, 219n98; Anita Reynolds's *American Cocktail* and, 150n52; Roth's *Human Stain* compared, 199; travel and relocation in, 68–69
Cervantes, Miguel, 36
Chateaubriant, Guy de, 157
Chaucer, Geoffrey, 160n80
Cheng, Anne, 31n35
Chesnutt, Charles: life and career, 41; *The Literary Career of Charles W. Chesnutt* (Andrews), 39n57. *See also The House Behind the Cedars*
Chicago: in Caspary's *White Girl,* 98, 100, 101, 103, 104, 107, 114n145; in Larsen's *Passing,* 69, 116, 125, 131, 132; Anita Reynolds born in, 137
Chicago Tribune, 191
Child, Lydia Maria, 74n4
childhood race-learning and passing, 16, 22–72; books, importance of, 32, 36, 38–39, 49, 58, 68, 70, 85n43; Anatole Broyard and, 28, 165–66, 168; in Chesnutt's *The House Behind the Cedars,* 30, 33–41, 226; classroom trauma, role of, 10, 23–26, 30–33, 65–67, 70–72; duality, divided identity, and double consciousness, 31–33; in Dunbar-Nelson's "Stones," 226; Erikson's theories and, 26–28, 31, 32, 66–67;

Fanon and, 26–28, 31, 32, 65; in Fauset's *Plum Bun,* 16, 30, 32, 50–57, 226; Freud and Du Bois, classroom trauma experienced by, 10, 70; gender differences in, 32, 40, 49–50, 51, 53, 66, 67, 70; geography and time period, effects of, 67–68; in Johnson's *Autobiography of an Ex-Colored Man,* 30, 31–32, 33, 35, 41–49, 226; mirrors, significance of, 32, 35–38, 39n57, 42, 45, 49, 59, 61, 68, 70; psychoanalysis, importance of childhood for, 225–26; Anita Reynolds and, 144–45; in Roth's *Human Stain,* 192–98, 202–3; in Senna's *Caucasia,* 16, 30, 32, 57–65, 226; travel and relocation, role of, 68–70; White education in racism, 71–72. *See also* Blackness; play

A Chosen Exile (Hobbs), 19n51

Christian, Barbara, 2

Civil Rights movement, 15n46, 28–29, 158, 180, 231

Civil War, 25, 46, 90n65, 222

classroom racial trauma, 10, 23–26, 30–33, 65–67, 70–72. *See also* childhood, rooting of passing in

Clotel (Brown), 74n4, 79n26, 222

colonialism: Erikson on, 30; Fanon on trauma of racism and, 27, 226; independence movements of 1950s and 1960s, African and Caribbean, 15n46; Anita Reynolds and, 154–57

color-blindness, 231, 233

Comedy: American Style (Fauset), 55

Commentary (periodical), 172, 173, 178

communism, 156

"The Concept of Identity in Race Relations: Notes and Queries" (Erikson), 28–29

"Concerning Color" (Gibson), 1n1

"The Condition of Black Life is One of Mourning" (Rankine), 73

"Configurations in Play" (Erikson), 28

Cooper, James Fenimore, 222

Coviello, Peter, 8–9

Cox, Solaria. *See White Girl*

"A Creole Anomaly" (Dunbar-Nelson), 81–82

Creoles, 81–82, 89n62, 138, 163–65

The Crisis (Du Bois's periodical), 50

Cullen, Countee, 149

cultural appropriation, White to Black passing as, 223

Currer, in Brown's *Clotel,* 74n4, 79n26

Dalal, Farhad, 4, 100

Danticat, Edwidge, 132

Davis, Angela, 178

Davis, Thadious, 132

Dawkins, Marcia Alesan, 207n61, 214–15n86, 215, 221

Dean, Michael, 114n147

death and passing, 16–17, 73–134, 226; active death of twentieth-century versus nineteenth-century passers, 79–80, 83, 96, 131, 209, 213; African-American interest in psychoanalysis, 74–75; Anatole Broyard and, 176, 184–85, 188–89; in Caspary's *White Girl,* 17, 74, 77, 80, 98–114, 226 (*See also White Girl*); in Dunbar-Nelson's "Stones," 17, 74, 77, 80, 81–97, 226 (*See also* "Stones of the Village"); Freud's creation of psychoanalysis and, 132–34; Freud's racial/sexual identity issues and, 75–76, 80–81; gender differences in, 74, 78, 101, 106; hastening of one's own death by passing, 74, 77, 79; identity, killing off, 74; in Larsen's *Passing,* 17, 74, 77, 80, 115–32, 226 (*See also Passing*); mourning and fear, as Black state of mind, 73–74; Anita Reynolds and, 185–86; in Roth's *Human Stain,* 192, 203–16, 226; scholarship on, 79–80n27; sexuality and, 17, 74, 78, 101–5, 113, 226; taboo sexualities, 78, 80, 90–91, 95, 102, 109, 113, 116, 118–19, 128, 131; tragic mulatto image and, 74, 79–80, 97; untimely death, African-American experience of, 73, 79–80n27. *See also* Blackness; family,

INDEX

symbolic killing of; mouth/lip imagery and death in passing narratives; suicide

death drive, Freud's theory of, 17, 76–81, 130–31, 133, 226, 228; Caspary's *White Girl* and, 98, 100, 104, 113; Dunbar-Nelson's "Stones" and, 83, 94; Larsen's *Passing* and, 114, 123–24, 125, 128, 129; life writing and, 141; Roth's *Human Stain* and, 210, 212, 214, 215; sexuality and, 77, 123

The Death-Bound Subject (JanMohamed), 80n27

Deception (Roth), 218n95

"Destruction as the Cause of Coming Into Being" (Speilrein), 123

d'Haulleville, Eric, 161

DiAngelo, Robin, 223

The Diary of Anaïs Nin (Nin), 182

Diggs, Marylynne, 83n35

displacement, fear of Black men as, 5n14

Dolezal, Rachel, 223–24, 225, 226, 229, 232

Donaldson, Ian, 139, 185

double consciousness, 6–13, 32, 44, 200, 232

Douglas, Ann, 51

Douglass, Frederick, 25, 44, 47, 71

Drew, Charles, 105

Du Bois, W. E. B.: on African-American education, 25; classroom racial trauma of, 10, 23, 70; *The Crisis*, 50; double consciousness, theorization of, 6–11, 13, 44, 200, 232; Erikson citing, 29; Fauset and, 50; humility topos, use of, 160n80; on Jews and anti-Semitism, 7–8; Johnson's *Autobiography of an Ex-Colored Man* and, 44, 47; masking, psychological, 11; mixed-race heritage, anxiety about people of, 11; on racism as defining problem of twentieth century, 231, 232; Anita Reynolds and, 146–47, 159; *The Souls of Black Folk*, 7, 25n12, 32, 70n150, 160n80

Du Bois, Yolande, 149

Dumas, Alexandre, 44

Dunbar, Paul Laurence, 61

Dunbar-Nelson, Alice: career of, 81; "A Creole Anomaly," 81–82; Creole characters, depiction of, 41–42, 89n62; Gayarre and, 89n62; literary criticism of, 81, 83, 96–97; psychoanalysis, interest in, 75. *See also* "Stones of the Village"

Dutchman (Baraka), 205n54

Dyson, Michael Eric, 73

education and racial trauma, 10, 23–26, 30–33, 65–67, 70–72. *See also* childhood race-learning and passing

Elam, Michele, 19n51, 207n62

Ellis, Trey, 23–24, 33

Ellison, Ralph, 29

Emerick, Ronald, 207n61, 214–15n86

Emerson, Ralph Waldo, 9

employment searches, modifying Black or Latino-sounding names in, 228–30

Emrys, A. B., 98, 113–14

England: British East India Company, 154; racial prejudice in, 155; Anita Reynolds in, 153–56; Russia, detention of English engineers in, 155–56

Epic of Gilgamesh, 68

Erikson, Erik: Chesnutt's *The House Behind the Cedars* and, 37–39, 67; classroom trauma, childhood race-learning, and Theory of Psychosocial Development, 26–28, 31, 32, 45, 66–67; Fauset's *Plum Bun* and, 51, 66; Johnson's *Autobiography of an Ex-Colored Man* and, 45, 47, 49, 67; on play, 28, 50, 56–57, 61, 63; "Revisiting Erik Erikson's Legacy on Culture, Race, and Ethnicity" (Syed and Fish), 29–30; Senna's *Caucasia* and, 51, 59, 61, 66; as source, 4, 16

Erikson, Erik, writings of: "The Concept of Identity in Race Relations: Notes and Queries," 28–29; "Configurations in Play," 28; *Identity: Youth and Crisis*, 28; *The Life Cycle Completed*, 28, 45n75, 66; Stages of

253

Psychosocial Development, 16, 28, 30, 31, 37–40, 45
eugenics, 13–14n42, 197
Evers, Medgar, 73
family, symbolic killing of, 74, 77, 226; Anatole Broyard and, 173, 176; in Caspary's *White Girl*, 98–100, 103, 107; in Dunbar-Nelson's "Stones," 82, 83–89, 93–94, 96, 111; Freud on, 77, 100; in Larsen's *Passing*, 115, 124–25; in Roth's *Human Stain*, 205–8, 211–12, 215
family and parents: of Anatole Broyard, 163, 165–66, 173–76, 187, 188–89; Cole (sister), in Senna's *Caucasia*, 51, 57–58, 60–62, 64–65; Deck (father), in Senna's *Caucasia*, 51, 57–58, 61, 62, 64–65, 67, 68; in Fauset's *Plum Bun*, 51–57; in Johnson's *Autobiography of an Ex-Colored Man*, 42–43; Molly Walden (mother), in Chesnutt's *The House Behind the Cedars*, 33, 34, 36, 37; Rank on mother relationship, 5n14, 17, 136–37, 141, 142, 146, 186–87; of Anita Reynolds, 145–46, 152, 159–60, 161, 162, 187; in Roth's *Human Stain*, 192–98; Sandra (mother), in Senna's *Caucasia*, 51, 57–60, 62–63, 65, 67
Fanon, Frantz: *Black Skin, White Masks*, 16, 26–27, 61, 153, 181, 199, 205n54; Chesnutt's *The House Behind the Cedars* and, 36; childhood, importance of, 225–26; classroom trauma and, 26–28, 31, 32, 65; on colonialism and racism, 27; Du Bois's *Souls of Black Folk* and, 32; Erikson and, 29, 30; Fauset's *Plum Bun* and, 51; on internalized racism, 180–81; on Jews and passing as Jewish, 199; Johnson's *Autobiography of an Ex-Colored Man* and, 44, 48, 49; life writing, problem of, 141; "Look! A Negro!" scene, 36, 153, 205n54; on play, 65; Roth's *Human Stain* and, 199, 205n54, 207, 218; Senna's *Caucasia* and, 51; as source, 4, 16, 19
Fauset, Jessie: birthplace in Lawnside, NJ, 207n60; *Comedy: American Style*, 55; life story of, 50; scholarly critiques of, 50–51. *See also Plum Bun*
Ferenczi, Sándor, 136
Fiedler, Leslie, 225
Fielding, Henry, 36
Fish, Jillian, 29–30
Fitzgerald, F. Scott, 144, 162–63, 171–72
Flash (periodical), 162
Fliess, Wilhelm, 13, 75–76, 78, 133, 135
Flight (White), 97
Floyd, George, 231
Ford, Ford Madox, 151
Fordham, Signithia, 230n28
Franco, Dean J., 199n29
Freud, Anna, 28
Freud, Sigmund: acculturated Jew, self-image as, 8, 11–12; antiquities, use of, 20; Anatole Broyard and, 14, 134, 142, 181; childhood, importance of, 225–26; disciples as psychoanalytical sons of, 135–37, 142; Du Bois and double consciousness, 6–13, 232; family, on symbolic killing of, 77, 100; Fanon's revision of, 27; ideas, desire to be remembered for, 13–14, 135; "inner Africa," id viewed as, 14; masking, psychological, 11; mixed-race heritage, anxiety about people of, 11, 12, 14; on mouths and lips, 77–78, 102; racial and sexual identity concerns of, 4–6, 8, 9–10, 11–14, 75–76, 80–81, 132–35, 192, 218, 232; Rank and, 5n14, 135–37, 142; Anita Reynolds's familiarity with, 142; Rome, desire to go to, 9–11; on suicide, 133. *See also* death drive, Freud's theory of
Freud, Sigmund, writings of: *Beyond the Pleasure Principle*, 76–77, 123, 134; *The Interpretation of Dreams*, 9–10,

11, 14, 33; *Three Contributions to the Theory of Sex,* 17, 75, 78, 102, 116, 134; "The Unconscious," 11, 14, 232

Freudian slip, "spooks" remark in Roth's *Human Stain* as, 202–3, 212

Freud's Mexico (Gallo), 1, 20

The Function and Field of Speech and Language in Psychoanalysis (Lacan), 14

Gaddis, William, 182

Gallego, Mar, 50, 53

Gallo, Rubén, 1, 20–21

The Garies and Their Friends (Webb), 79n26, 222

Garifuna, vii–viii

Gates, Henry Louis, 175, 177, 179, 184

Gayarre, Charles, 89n62

gaze: imagery of, 36, 60, 103; White gaze, Black experience of, 36, 152–53, 182n166, 198

Gebhard, Caroline, 82, 87, 97

gender: death in passing narratives and, 74, 78, 101, 106; race-learning and, 32, 40, 49–50, 51, 53, 66, 67, 70

Gibson, Charles, 1, 87, 129

Gilroy, Paul, 140n22

Gooblar, David, 218

good breast/bad breast theory, 206, 226

Gooneratne, Chandra Dharma Sena, 227

Gould, Norma, 147–48

Grabért, Vincent. *See* "Stones of the Village"

The Great Gatsby (Fitzgerald), 163, 171–72

Green, Tara, 73

Griffiths, Jennifer L., 31n35

Groos, Karl, 56

Gubar, Susan, 78, 178, 224, 225

"Ha Ha" (Anatole Broyard), 142

Haitian Revolution, 15n46

Hall, Stuart, 24n10

Hall, Wade, 139n140n18

Hannibal of Carthage, 10

Harlem Renaissance, 41, 50, 69, 75, 97, 114, 137, 182n166

Harper, Frances, 79n26, 82n34, 139n15

Harrison-Kahan, Lori, 199n29

Hegel, Georg Wilhelm Friedrich, 15n46

Hemingway, Ernest, 144

Hispanics: American Indians, Mexicans passing as, 23; Anatole Broyard's marriage to Puerto Rican woman passing as white, 167; employment searches, modifying Black or Latino-sounding names in, 228–30; *Freud's Mexico* (Gallo), 1, 20; Puerto Rican, passing as, 23, 59, 63, 65; Anita Reynolds passing as Mexican, 147–48; "Spanish masquerade" in *Uncle Tom's Cabin,* 222

Hobbs, Allyson, 19n51

Holland, Sharon, 79n27

Holloway, Karla, 79–80n27

Homer, 68, 204

homosexual cathexis, 13

homosexuality: Freud's issues with, 13, 75–76, 80–81, 133, 135, 232; Larsen's *Passing* and, 116–20; Anita Reynolds and German man on way to Morocco, 152–53

Hook, Derek, 70

hooks, bell, 143

Hopkins, Pauline, 19–20, 75

The House Behind the Cedars (Chesnutt): books, importance of, 36, 38–39, 58, 85n43; Broyard's *One Drop* compared, 166; childhood race-learning and passing in, 30, 33–41, 226; Dunbar-Nelson's "Stones" compared, 82n34, 85n43; Erikson's theories and, 37–39, 67; geography and time period, effects of, 67, 68; Johnson's *Autobiography of an Ex-Colored Man* compared, 33, 35, 42, 43, 44, 45, 48, 49; mirrors, significance of, 35–38, 39n57; Roth's *Human Stain* compared, 36–37, 194, 211; travel and relocation in, 69

Hughes, Langston, 148

Hull, Gloria T., 96–97

The Human Stain (Roth), 17–18, 191–219; "active death" in, 209, 213;

ambiguous death of Silk in, 208–16; boxing and running in, 195, 196–97, 203, 214; Anatole Broyard and, 187–89, 191–92, 200, 216, 217, 218, 219; Caspary's *White Girl* compared, 211, 215; Chesnutt's *House Behind the Cedars* compared, 36–37, 194, 211; childhood trauma and race-learning in, 192–98, 202–3; death and passing in, 192, 203–16, 226; death drive, Freud's theory of, 210, 212, 214, 215; Dunbar-Nelson's "Stones" compared, 215; family, symbolic killing of, 205–8, 211–12, 215; Jewish, Silk choosing to pass as, 191, 192, 198–200, 210–15; Johnson's *Autobiography of an Ex-Colored Man* compared, 194, 198; Larsen's *Passing* compared, 119n175, 215; life writing, struggle with, 188, 191, 192; passing narratives, influence of, 192, 217–18; plotline of, 191–92; referenced in Sandweiss's *Passing Strange,* 139n15; romantic relationships, marriage, and affairs in, 200–201, 203–4, 208–11, 212, 215; Roth's account of influences and inspirations for, 216–19; Senna's *Caucasia* compared, 199; "spooks" remark in, 192, 201–3, 212, 216–17; taboo sexualities in, 210–11, 218; Melvin Tumin and, 216–17, 218

humility topos, 159–60
Hurst, Fannie, 1n1, 97
"Hustle" and "Passing," intersection of (in Central Point, VA), 222–23
Hutchinson, George, 142, 143, 147, 150, 153, 158
Hutson, Jean Blackwell, 132
I Am Not Your Negro (Baldwin), 72
Identity: Youth and Crisis (Erikson), 28
Iliad (Homer), 204
imagos, psychoanalytic concept of, 202
Imitation of Life (Hurst), 1n1, 97
Incidents in the Life of a Slave Girl (Jacobs), 160n80, 222

"inner Africa," Freud viewing id as, 14
"The Instance of the Letter in the Unconscious" (Lacan), 14–15, 141, 152
International Society for the Protection of Mothers and Sexual Reform, 13n42
The Interpretation of Dreams (Freud), 9–10, 11, 14, 33
Intoxicated by My Illness and Other Writings on Life and Death (Anatole Broyard), 184–85
The Invisible Line (Sharfstein), 19n51
Iola Leroy (Harper), 79n26, 82n34
Jacobs, Harriet, 71, 160n80, 222
James, William, 9, 19–20
JanMohamed, Abdul, 80n27
Japtok, Martin, 53
Jefferson, Thomas, 2, 74n4
Jews and anti-Semitism: acculturated Jew, Freud's self-image as, 8, 11–12; American racial binary, Jewishness complicating, 199n29; Blackness, Jews associated with, 7, 8, 10, 11, 12, 13–14n42; Du Bois on, 7–8; Freud's racial and sexual identity concerns, 4–6, 8, 9–10, 11–14, 75–76, 80–81, 132–35, 192, 218, 232; in Larsen's *Passing,* 119; "Portrait of an Inauthentic Jew" (Sartre), 172; Rome, Freud's desire to go to, 9–10; in Roth's *Human Stain,* 191, 192, 198–200, 210–15; Senna's *Caucasia,* passing as Jewish in, 60, 62–65, 67, 68. *See also Human Stain*
Jim Crow: childhood race-learning and, 25, 67, 69; death and, 80n27, 131, 132; Freud and, 13; life stories and, 145, 147, 165, 174; passing attributed to, 31; recent examples of passing to avoid discrimination of, 226, 227, 228, 229; in Roth's *Human Stain,* 205, 207, 215
Johnson, Cathryn, 224
Johnson, James Weldon: *The Book of American Negro Poetry,* preface to, 47; college education of, 46n77; Larsen and Reynolds, friendships

with, 143, 146; Piper's autobiographical essay referencing, 139n15; Anita Reynolds compared, 151. *See also Autobiography of an Ex-Colored Man*
Jones, Ernest, 135, 136
Jones, Gayl, 178
Joseph, Ralina, 51
Joyce, James, 144
Jung, Carl, 19, 135, 142, 232–33
Kafka Was the Rage (Anatole Broyard), 170, 185
Kakutani, Michiko, 191
Kaplan, Brett, 171–72, 187
Kaplan, Carla, 114n147
Karpman, Ben, 1n1
"Keep Cool, Man" (Anatole Broyard), 173
Kendry, Clare. *See Passing*
Kennedy, Randall, 32
Khanna, Nikki, 224
Kidd, Mae Street, 140n18
King, Clarence, 19n51, 139n15
King, Martin Luther, Jr., 23, 73, 180, 231
Klein, Melanie, 19, 206, 218, 226
Knopf, Alfred A., 41, 129
Kroeger, Brooke, 222
Krug, Jessica, 224, 232
Lacan, Jacques, 4, 14–15, 19, 35, 51, 80n27, 141, 152, 202
Lane, Christopher, 18
language and linguistic passing: Black or Latino-sounding names, modifying, 228–30; Anatole Broyard and, 179; in Senna's *Caucasia*, 61–62
language of race, 18, 221–33; color-blindness, 231, 233; passing, etymology and use of, 221–23; postracialism, 30, 71, 221, 230–31, 233; transracialism, 223–24, 225, 229, 233; for White to Black racial passing, 223–25
Larsen, Nella: nonfictional life stories compared to fiction of, 6; passing by, 131–32; Piper's autobiographical essay referencing, 139n15;

psychoanalysis, interest in, 75; *Quicksand,* 132; Anita Reynolds and, 143; writing herself into her fiction, 132–33, 134. *See also Passing*
Last of the Mohicans (Cooper), 222
Latinos/as. *See* Hispanics
Laura (Caspary), 98
Lawnside, New Jersey, 207
Lee, Birdie, and family. *See Caucasia*
The Life Cycle Completed (Erikson), 28, 45n75, 66
life writing: absence at heart of, 141, 143; African-American literature and, 140–41; literary criticism and, 138–41; mixed-race subjects of, 139–40n18
life writing and passing, 17, 135–89, 226
absence at heart of, discovering, 141–43
critical difficulties in addressing, 138–40
Freud's death drive and, 141
Rank's psychoanalytic theories and, 136–37, 141, 142, 161–62, 174, 186–87, 226
writing struggles of racial passers: Anatole Broyard, 163–64, 170, 172, 174–76, 177–78, 184, 185, 186; Anita Reynolds, 151–52, 159–63, 186; in Roth's *Human Stain,* 188, 191, 192
See also Blackness; Broyard, Anatole; Reynolds, Anita
lips. *See* mouth/lip imagery and death in passing narratives
The Literary Career of Charles W. Chesnutt (Andrews), 39n57
Logan, Frenise, 154n61
Loos, Anita, 151
Loving v. Virginia (1967), 113
lynching: in Johnson's *Autobiography of an Ex-Colored Man,* 48–49, 168; racial trauma leading to passing, interpreted as, 16, 31, 65; Anita Reynolds on, 147, 149, 151, 158; social anxieties about Black men and, 5n14
Macmillan's (publishing house), 97
Mailer, Norman, 174
Malcolm X, 70, 73

mambo, Anatole Broyard on, 178n150
Marrant, John, 160n80
Marx, Karl, 142
Marxism, 24n10
Matelle, Anita. *See* Reynolds, Anita
Mather, Cotton, 62
Matory, J. Lorand, 8, 13, 13n42, 75, 76, 133, 135
Matthews, Cate, 229
McDowell, Deborah, 117–18, 125n201
McKay, Claude, 148, 151
McNair Scholars Program, 224
Mellon Mays Fellowship, 224
Men, Women, and Other Anticlimaxes (Anatole Broyard), 177
Meredith, James, 227
#MeToo movement, 102
Mexico and Mexicans. *See* Hispanics
Michaels, Walter Benn, 200
Michie, Helena, 115n155, 118, 125n201
Millay, Edna St. Vincent, 144, 149
Miller, Michael Vincent, 180, 181
Mills, Florence, 149
Milton, John, 36
"The Mirror Stage as Formative of the I Function" (Lacan), 35
mirrors: imagos or mirror image, psychoanalytic concept of, 202; in Johnson's *Autobiography of an Ex-Colored Man*, 42, 45, 49
miscegenation, 78, 88–91, 119, 121–23
Misra, Tanvi, 226–27
mixed-race persons: Creoles, 81–82, 89n62, 138, 163–65; Du Bois's anxiety about, 11; Elam's *The Souls of Mixed Folk*, 19n51; Freud's anxiety about people of, 11, 12, 14; in Harper's *Iola Leroy*, 79n26, 82n34; life writing by, 139–40n18; Barack Obama, racial identification of, 74, 230; passing as Black, 224 (*See also Caucasia*); Anita Reynolds on, 159; tragic mulatto, 17, 74, 79–80, 97, 214–15
Monster.com, 228
Moore, Lorrie, 191

Morocco, Anita Reynolds in, 152–55
Morrison, Toni, 26, 71, 72, 178
mouth/lip imagery and death in passing narratives, 77–78; Caspary's *White Girl*, 101–2, 103, 110; Dunbar-Nelson's "Stones," 82, 95; Larsen's *Passing*, 116–17, 120–22, 126
Moynihan, Sinead, 19n51, 201, 221
Mullen, Henrietta, 31–32
Murphy, Harry S., Jr., 227–28
Murray, Angela, and family. *See Plum Bun*
"The Myth of Sisyphus" (Camus), 130
NAACP, 147
names, Black or Latino-sounding, modifying, 228–30
Narrative of the Lord's Wonderful Dealings (Marrant), 160n80
Native Americans. *See* American Indians
Natural Theology (Paley), 44
Neither Black Nor White (Sollors), 79n26
Neurotica (periodical), 178n150
New Criticism, 139
New Orleans, 81, 83n35, 84, 90n65, 93, 138, 163, 165, 182
New York City: Baraka's *Dutchman* set in subway, 205n54; Anatole Broyard in Brooklyn and, 138, 164–67, 169, 170, 173–74, 180–81, 187; in Caspary's *White Girl*, 100, 104–5, 107; in Fauset's *Plum Bun*, 55, 56, 68, 69; in Johnson's *Autobiography of an Ex-Colored Man*, 48, 68; in Larsen's *Passing*, 131; Harry S. Murphy, Jr. in, 228; opportunities for passing in, 69–70; Anita Reynolds in, 138, 143, 148–49; in Roth's *Human Stain*, 187, 198
New York Times, 73, 132, 134, 138, 157, 163, 178, 179, 183, 191, 230
New York Times Book Review, 216
New Yorker, 114n147, 175, 177, 184, 216, 218
Nin, Anias, 182
Nkrumah, Kwame, 58
Norma Gould School of Dancing, 147

noses, Freud's and Fliess's examination of, 75, 78
Obama, Barack, 71, 73–74, 230–31
O'Connor, Flannery, 71
Odyssey (Homer), 68
Oedipus Complex, 5n14, 136
Of One Blood: The Hidden Self (Hopkins), 19–20
One Drop (Bliss Broyard) and life of Anatole Broyard, 6, 17, 138, 163–84, 226; African-Americans, relationships with/attitudes toward, 178–81; background, family, education, and army career, 138, 163–69; Black writers, criticism of, 178–79; bookstore in New York City, 85n43, 169–70; Chesnutt's *The House Behind the Cedars* compared, 166; childhood experience and race-learning, 28, 165–66; children's knowledge of father's racial identity, 188–89; death and, 176, 184–85, 188–89; Dunbar-Nelson's "Stones" compared, 166, 180; fictional origins, creation of, 169, 170–72; Fitzgerald's *Great Gatsby* and, 171–72; Freud and, 14, 134, 142, 181; Johnson's *The Autobiography of an Ex-Colored Man* compared, 166, 168; life writing, struggles with, 163–64, 170, 172, 174–76, 177–78, 184, 185, 186; literary portrayals of Anatole by other authors, 181–84, 187–89, 191, 218; marriages, 167, 169, 176–77; as *New York Times* book critic, 134, 138, 163, 170, 176, 178–79, 183–84; passing, first instance of, 164, 166–67, 186; passing, justification for, 171–72; psychoanalysis, Anatole's interest in, 142; public knowledge of Anatole's racial background, 175, 184, 192; published writings of, 172–74, 177, 184–85; racial status, determining, 164–65, 166–67, 176–77; Anita Reynolds compared, 163, 170, 171, 172, 181, 184–87; Roth's *Human Stain* and, 187–89, 191–92, 200, 216, 217, 218, 219; sexuality and, 175, 177–78, 185; *Standby* (Sandy Broyard) and, 176–77; transplantation from New Orleans to Brooklyn, 164, 165
one-drop rule, 12, 36, 37, 89
O'Neill, Eugene, 149
Our Nig (Wilson), 79n26, 160n80
The Oxford Book of Death, 142
Page, Clarence, 191
Page, Lisa, 23
Pandit, Korla, 227
parents and families. *See specific entries at* family
Paris, France: Jessie Fauset studying in, 50; in Fauset's *Plum Bun,* 68; in Johnson's *Autobiography of an Ex-Colored Man,* 68; Anita Reynolds in, 144, 149–52
Passed On (Holloway), 79–80n27
passing: American literature, importance in, 222 (*See also specific texts*); biracial people passing as Black, 224 (*See also Caucasia*); etymology and use of, 221–23; hustle, as type of, 223; racism, as response to, 219, 232–33; recent nonfictional examples of, 226–30; as societal issue, 230; trauma theory and, 31–32; White to Black, 19n51, 139n15, 223–25, 229, 232–33. *See also* psychoanalytical perspective on passing
Passing (Larsen), 115–32; ambiguous death of Clare Kendry, 124–31; author's encounter with, vii, viii; Caspary's *White Girl* compared, 114, 122, 124, 129, 130–31; color imagery in, 115–16, 126, 127, 129; death and passing in, 17, 74, 77, 80, 115–32, 226; different endings of, 129–30; Dunbar-Nelson's "Stones" compared, 122, 124, 129, 130–31; family, symbolic killing of, 115, 124–25; Freud's death drive and, 114, 123–24, 125, 128, 129; literary criticism of, 114n147, 115, 117–18,

125; miscegenation in, 119, 121–23; mouth and lip imagery in, 116–17, 120–22, 126; publication of, 97; Roth's *Human Stain* compared, 119n175, 215; Senna's *Caucasia* compared, 63n133, 119n175; sexuality in, 116–20; slavery and slavery tropes, 131; taboo sexualities in, 116, 118–19, 128, 131; travel and relocation in, 69

"Passing" and "Hustle," intersection of (in Central Point, VA), 222–23

"Passing for White, Passing for Black" (Piper), 139n15

Passing into the Present (Moynihan), 19n51

Passing Strange (Sandweiss), 19n51, 139n15

Passing: When People Can't Be Who They Are (Kroeger), 222

Patrimony (Roth), 218n95

Patterson, Orlando, 111

Pavageau, Mr., in Dunbar-Nelson's "Stones," 92–93, 103

Perkins, Maureen, 175, 185

Perkins-Valdez, Dolen, 230

Perry, Ann, 205n54

Perry, Bliss, 97

Peterson, Dorothy, 97, 132, 143

The Phenomenology of Spirit (Hegel), 15n46

Philadelphia, 55, 59, 67, 68, 204

Piaget, Jean, 56

Pilgrim's Progress (Bunyan), 36, 44

Piper, Adrian, 70–71, 139n15

play: in Fauset's *Plum Bun*, 52, 55–57; as psychoanalytic tool, 28, 50, 56–57, 61, 63, 65–66; in Senna's *Caucasia*, 57, 60, 61, 62–63, 65, 68

The Play of Animals (Groos), 56

Playboy, 177

Plessy v. Ferguson (1896), 25

The Plot Against America (Roth), 200

Plum Bun (Fauset), 16, 50–57; childhood race-learning and passing in, 16, 30, 32, 50–57, 226; Erikson's theories and, 51, 66; gender differences in race-learning and, 50; geography and time period, effects of, 67; play in, 52, 55–57; publication of, 97; reasons for passing, understanding of, 219n98; Senna's *Caucasia* compared, 51, 57, 60, 62–63; title, significances of, 56; travel and relocation in, 68, 69

political assassination, African-American concerns about, 73–74

Portnoy's Complaint (Roth), 218n95

"Portrait of an Inauthentic Jew" (Sartre), 172

"Portrait of the Inauthentic Negro" (Anatole Broyard), 172–73

Position of the Unconscious (Lacan), 15n46

Posnock, Ross, 199

postcolonial life writers, 140

postracialism, 30, 71, 221, 230–31, 233

The Prague Orgy (Roth), 218n95

Prudhomme, Charles, 1n1

The Psychoanalytic Review, 1

psychoanalytical perspective on passing, vii–viii, 1–21, 225–26, 232–33; African-American relationship with psychoanalysis, 1–3, 74–75, 137; disciples of Freud, use of language of Blackness by, 14–15; double consciousness, theorizations of, 6–13; Freud's racial and sexual identity concerns, 4–6, 8, 9–10, 11–14, 75–76, 80–81, 132–35, 192, 218, 232; recent scholarship on passing, 19–20, 23; sources and primary texts, 4, 6, 19; value of, 3–6, 15–16, 18–21; White to Black passing, 19n51, 139n15, 223–25, 229, 232–33. *See also* childhood race-learning and passing; death and passing; language of race; life writing and passing; *specific texts*

Puerto Ricans. *See* Hispanics

"The Quadroons" (Child), 74n4

Quicksand (Larsen), 132, 187

race: social construction of, 72, 231–32. *See also* African-Americans; Blackness; language of race
Race, Nation, Class (Balibar and Wallerstein), 24n10
"Race, Articulation and Societies Structured in Dominance" (Hall), 24n10
racechange, 224, 225
Racechanges (Gubar), 78
race-learning. *See* childhood race-learning and passing
"The Rachel Divide" (documentary), 226
racial passing. *See* passing
racism: death, leading to, 205; as defining problem of twenty-first century, 231–33; Fanon on trauma of colonialism and, 27, 226; passing as response to, 219, 232–33; White education into, 71–72. *See also* Jim Crow
Raising the Dead (Holland), 79n27
Randolph, A. Philip, 146
Rank, Otto, 4, 5n14, 17, 135–37, 141, 142, 146, 161–62, 174, 182n166, 186–87, 226
Rankine, Claudia, 73
The Recognition (Gaddis), 182
Redfield, Irene. *See Passing*
Reimagining the Middle Passage (Green), 73
"Revisiting Erik Erikson's Legacy on Culture, Race, and Ethnicity" (Syed and Fish), 29–30
Reynolds, Anita, 6, 17, 143–63, 226; background, family, and career, 137–38, 145–46; Anatole Broyard compared, 163, 170, 171, 172, 181, 184–87; Guy de Chateaubriant, relationship with, 157; death and discovery of papers at Howard University, 143; enjoyment of life by, 185–86; final marriage to Guy Reynolds, 137n12; first marriage to Charles (English military captain), 153–57; Freud compared, 14, 134; humility topos, use of, 159–60;

psychoanalysis, interest in, 142; Kristians Tonny, relationship with, 150. *See also American Cocktail*
Rice, Tamir, 73
Rising Out of Hatred (Saslow), 71–72
Robeson, Eslanda, 155
Robeson, Paul, 148, 155
Rome, Freud's desire to go to, 9–11
Roth, Philip: Anatole Broyard and, 187–89; on dating African-American woman passing as White, 216, 217; nonfictional life stories compared to fiction of, 6; psychoanalysis and, 218; on reasons for passing, 219; as White author, 20
Roth, Philip, writings of: *Deception*, 218n95; *Patrimony*, 218n95; *The Plot Against America*, 200; *Portnoy's Complaint*, 218n95; *The Prague Orgy*, 218n95; *Sabbath's Theater*, 218n95. *See also Human Stain*
Routté, Jesse, 227
Royal, Derek Parker, 215
Rummel, Kathryn, 63n133
Running a Thousand Miles for Freedom (Craft and Craft), 63n133
Russia, detention of English engineers in, 155–56
Russian Revolution, 146–47
Ryan, Melissa, 39n57
Sabbath's Theater (Roth), 218n95
Sanchez, Ada, 167
Sandweiss, Martha, 19n51
Sartre, Jean Paul, 172
Saslow, Eli, 71–72
Scheurer, Maren, 218
schoolroom racial trauma, 10, 23–26, 30–33, 65–67, 70–72. *See also* childhood race-learning and passing
Scott, Walter, 36
The Secrets of Grownups (Caspary), 98
self-hatred, 29, 48, 63, 181
Senna, Danzy. *See Caucasia*
separate but equal doctrine, 25, 131
sexual harassment in Caspary's *White Girl*, 98, 101–3

sexuality and passing: bisexuality, congenital, Fliess's theory of, 13, 76; Anatole Broyard and, 175, 177–78, 185; Caspary's *White Girl,* romantic relationship in, 106–13; death, passing, and sexuality, 17, 74, 78, 101–5, 113; death drive, Freud's theory of, 77, 123; Freud's sexual identity concerns, 13, 75–76, 80–81, 133, 135, 232; in Larsen's *Passing,* 116–20; miscegenation, 78, 88–91, 119, 121–22; mouth, Freud's focus on, 78, 102; Anita Reynolds and German man on way to Morocco, 152–53; Roth's *Human Stain* and, 200–201, 203–4, 208–11, 212, 215. *See also* homosexuality; taboo sexualities

Shakespeare, William, 36

Sharfstein, Daniel, 19n51

Sheehy, John, 35, 42

Sherrard-Johnson, Cherene, 50

sight: Fanon's "Look! A Negro!" scene, 36, 153, 205n54; gaze imagery, 36, 60, 103; in Larsen's *Passing,* 116; in Senna's *Caucasia,* 58, 63; White gaze, Black experience of, 36, 152–53, 182n166, 198

Silk, Coleman. *See Human Stain*

Skyhorse, Brando, 23, 33

slavery and slavery tropes: British East India Company and, 154n61; in Caspary's *White Girl,* 99, 110–11, 131; in Dunbar-Nelson's "Stones," 90–91, 111, 131; education/reading and literacy laws, 25, 38, 71; Erikson on African-American identity and, 29, 30; illegitimacy, Blackness, and slavery, 183; Johnson's *Autobiography of an Ex-Colored Man* and, 46; in Larsen's *Passing,* 131; Middle Passage and mass deaths of Black people, 73; passing and, 219, 221; psychoanalysis making use of, 14–15; racism, as education in, 71, 72; in Reynolds's *American Cocktail,* 146; Roth's *Human Stain* and, 206–7; self-hate, Black experience of, 48;

suicide and, 79n26; tragic mulatto image as abolitionist tool, 74n4

"Slavery's Pleasant Homes" (Child), 74n4

social construction of race, 72, 231–32

socialism, 7, 162

Socrates, 160n80

Sollors, Werner, 79n26, 221

The Souls of Black Folk (Du Bois), 7, 25n12, 32, 70n150, 160n80

The Souls of Mixed Folk (Elam), 19n51

Speilrein, Sabina, 123

Spillers, Hortense, 2

Spivak, Gayatri Chakravorty, 140

Spivey, Yolanda, 228–29, 230

St. Denis, Ruth, 147

St. Félix, Doreen, 226

Stages of Psychosocial Development (Erikson), 16, 28, 30, 31, 37–40, 45

Standby (Sandy Broyard), 176–77

Staples, Brent, 179

Stepto, Robert, 26, 71

"The Stones of the Village" (Dunbar-Nelson), 6, 81–97; African-Americans, Victor's self-segregation from, 86–88, 91–92, 106; blood imagery in, 89, 105; Anatole Broyard compared, 166, 180; Caspary's *White Girl* compared, 98, 99, 100, 101, 103, 105, 106, 111, 130–31; Chesnutt's *House Behind the Cedars* compared, 82n34; childhood race-learning and passing in, 226; Creoles and, 81–82; dating and publication history, 74n5, 97; death and passing in, 17, 74, 77, 80, 81–97, 226; death of Victor in, 82–83, 86, 87, 93–97; family, symbolic death of, 82, 83–89, 93–94, 96, 111; Freud's death drive and, 83, 94; Harper's *Iola Leroy* compared, 82n34; Johnson's *Autobiography of an Ex-Colored Man* compared, 85n43; Larsen's *Passing* compared, 122, 124, 129, 130–31; miscegenation in, 88–91; Roth's *Human Stain* compared, 215; silence and images of lips in, 82, 86–

87, 95; slavery and slavery tropes in, 90–91, 111, 131; socioeconomic class and race in, 90; taboo sexualities in, 90–91, 95
Stouck, Jordan, 83n35
Stoute, Beverly, 10
Stowe, Harriet Beecher, 222
Straight, Archibald, in Chesnutt's *The House Behind the Cedars,* 36–40, 49
The Street (Perry), 205n54
subject formation: Althusser's theory of, 24–25; Erikson on, 28; Fanon on, 27; school and, 25–26
Sue, Derald Wing, 194
suicide: as confession, 130; Freud on, 133; Larsen's *Passing,* ambiguous death of Clare in, 125, 127–28, 130; by Harry S. Murphy, Jr., 228; in passing narratives, 77, 79, 104, 106, 107, 111–14; rates for African-Americans, 1n1; Roth's *Human Stain,* ambiguous death of Silk in, 208–16; in slave narratives, 79n26
"Sunday Dinner in Brooklyn" (Anatole Broyard), 173, 174
Swanson, Gloria, 149–50
Syed, Moin, 29–30
taboo sexualities: in Caspary's *White Girl,* 102, 109, 113; concept of, 13, 78; death and passing, 78, 80, 90–91, 95, 102, 109, 113, 116, 118–19, 128, 131; in Dunbar-Nelson's "Stones," 90–91, 95; in Larsen's *Passing,* 116, 118–19, 128, 131; Anita Reynolds's encounter with German man on way to Morocco, 153; in Roth's *Human Stain,* 210–11, 218
Tales of the Jazz Age (Fitzgerald), 162
Tar Baby (Morrison), 178
Tate, Claudia, 2–3, 4–5, 19
Taylor, Breonna, 231
Thanatos (death instinct). *See* death drive, Freud's theory of
Theory of Psychosocial Development (Erikson), 45, 66

Thirteen Ways of Looking at a Black Man (Gates), 175
Thompson, Anita. *See* Reynolds, Anita
Thompson, Beatrice (mother), 145–46, 159, 162, 187
Thompson, Samuel (father), 146
Three Contributions to the Theory of Sex (Freud), 17, 75, 78, 102, 116, 134
Till, Emmett, 73
Tonny, Kristians, 150
Toussaint L'Ouverture, François-Dominique, 44
tragic mulatto, 17, 74, 79–80, 97, 214–15
trains and train rides, 36, 152–53, 164, 204–5, 211, 215
"The Transcendentalist" (Emerson), 9
transracialism, 223–24, 225, 229, 233
The Trauma of Birth (Rank), 5n14, 17, 136–37, 141, 142
trauma theory and passing, 31–32
travel and relocation in passing narratives, 68–70, 104–5, 106, 144, 148–49, 152–55, 162, 228. *See also* trains and train rides; *specific cities*
Tritt, Michael, 88, 96
Tumin, Melvin, 216–17, 218
turbans worn to facilitate passing, 226–27, 230
Uncle Tom's Cabin (Stowe), 222
"The Unconscious" (Freud), 11, 14, 232
"Understanding African American Adolescents' Identity Development" (Brittian), 29
Up from Slavery (Washington), 160n80
Updike, John, 174
Van Vechten, Carl, 131–32
Victoria (queen of England), 154m61
Vitolo-Hadad, CV, 224, 232
Le voyage aux Iles Galapagos (d'Haulleville), 161
Waiting for the End (Fiedler), 225
Wake Up, We're Almost There (Brossard), 183–84
Walden, Molly, in Chesnutt's *The House Behind the Cedars,* 33, 34, 36, 37
Walker, Madame C. J., 147

Wall, Cheryl, 50, 55, 125n201
Wallerstein, Immanuel, 24n10
Warwick, John and Rena. *See House Behind the Cedars*
Washington, Booker T., 25, 47, 146, 160n80
Washington, Mary Helen, 125n201
Watson, Reginald, 74n4
We Wear the Mask (Skyhorse and Page, eds.), 23–24
"We Wear the Mask" (Dunbar), 61
Webb, Frank J., 79n26, 222
What Doesn't Kill You Makes You Blacker (Young), 229
"What the Cystoscope Said" (Anatole Broyard), 173, 174, 184
Wheeler, Arthur, 152
White, Gladys, 97, 143
White, Walter, 97, 143, 151
White Fragility (DiAngelo), 223
The White Girl (Caspary), 6, 98–114; African-Americans, Solaria's self-segregation from, 106, 107–8, 109; blood imagery in, 102–3, 105; death and passing in, 17, 74, 77, 80, 98–114, 226; Dunbar-Nelson's "Stones" compared, 98, 99, 100, 101, 103, 105, 106, 111, 130–31; family, symbolic death of, 98–100, 103, 107; Freud's death drive and, 98, 100, 104, 113; Johnson's *Autobiography of an Ex-Colored Man* compared, 112; Larsen's *Passing* compared, 114, 122, 124, 129, 130–31; lips in, 101–2, 103, 110; literary criticism of, 98, 113–14; publication of, 97; romantic relationship in, 106–13; Roth's *Human Stain* compared, 211, 215; sexual harassment in, 98, 101–4; slavery and slavery tropes, 99, 110–11, 131; suicide, Solaria's contemplation of, 104, 106, 107; suicide, Solaria's death by, 111–14; taboo sexualities in, 102, 109, 113; travel and relocation in, 69, 104–5, 106; as White-authored novel, 98, 114n145
"White Like Me" (Gates), 184
White privilege, 229
White to Black passing, 19n51, 139n15, 223–25, 229, 232–33
Who Walk in Darkness (Brossard), 182–83
Williams, William Carlos, 144, 151
Wilson, Harriet, 79n26, 160n80
Wilson, Matthew, 199, 214–15n86
Wiltz, Teresa, 23, 33
Wright, Richard, 1–2, 80n27
Youman, Mary Mabel, 115, 125n201
Young, Damon, 229
Zamora, José, 228–29, 230
Zuckerman, Nathan. *See Human Stain*
Zweig, Arnold, 76